Breaking the
Free Will Illusion
for the Betterment of Humankind

'Trick Slattery

Published by Working Matter
Author and Illustrator: 'Trick Slattery
TrickSlattery.com

ISBN-13: 978-0-9938669-0-6
ISBN-10: 0-9938669-0-5

First Edition
Paperback

Contents

Contents

A note to the consciousness of the far future, if you exist:
The free will concept expressed in this book may be so foreign to
you that it may seem absurd to have written an entire book arguing
against it. Needless to say, at the time this book was written, such a
belief in free will was rampant and causing great harms in the world.

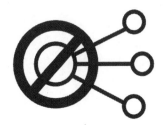

Introduction

'My intention is to shed light on the claims made; to dispel the myths; to give the case as to why free will cannot exist per an acceptable definition of what most people mean by it; and to explain the importance for humanity to begin to accept and utilize this fact of life.'

Ideas are often contrived. They tend to spread like wildfire if they provide comfort or fill a desired void in a person's knowledge. They stem from deep psychological needs, long term indoctrinations, poor critical thinking skills, or any combination of the three. Such ideas create a slew of dogmatic assertions about religion, spirituality, politics, the nature of reality, and more. Many of these ideas begin with one or more people developing an idea that propagates to others through an informational meme, either spoken or advertised through some other means.

There is one, however, that doesn't start as an idea or concept. It begins as something far more intuitive; as if it exists as a thought way before someone conceptualizes an idea of it. It worms its way into an individual's psyche at an early age. It doesn't require someone to teach it, which isn't to say it's never taught. Most of the time the ideas about it are a description of what people already deem as self-evident. It stems from something perceived. Something felt. Something that seems obvious to the person selecting chocolate ice cream over thirty other available flavors. Free will.

Why write a book about free will?
Because the fate of the universe depends on it.

1

Okay, I'm being overly dramatic. Perhaps not the *entire* universe. Really just a speck of the universe that hosts thinking creatures. But within that speck, the issue is at the heart of many ideologies people hold and mindsets they portray, even if they don't recognize it. For that speck, it's one of the most important topics, and true wisdom begins with an understanding of it (or rather an understanding of the *lack of it*).

If the feeling[1] of free will happens prior to conceptualizing an idea of it, you might ask: Where is the contrivance?

To answer that question it's important to note when the contrivance happens. The contrivance of free will comes *after* a belief in it and *after* that belief is challenged. To reiterate, free will is something that most people hold a belief in even before they think about the words "free will." Since this is the case, and since the belief in it is so strong and deeply embedded, when its existence is challenged, people contrive, and then contrive some more. And they do so without regard to logic or evidence.

Seemingly brilliant people--from philosophers, to scientists, to the most thoughtful laypersons--when prompted with the idea that their choices are not free like their intuition[2] tells them they are, not only strongly disagree, but after the case is made to them, they make contrivances around the case to curve that demand in their psyche. Some twist and bend logic into a pretzel. Some make cases that quantum physics allows for free will. Some define free will in a way that is neither free nor willed. Some argue that without free will there can be no morality or ethics, and therefore we should believe in free will even if it does not exist. Others dismiss the subject as pointless and unimportant altogether.

Each contrivance is far from the truth. And these untruths are not benign.

My intention is to shed light on the claims made; to dispel the myths; to give the case as to why free will cannot exist per an acceptable definition of what most people mean by it; and to explain the importance for humanity to begin to accept and utilize this fact of life. Ignoring it can no longer be an option. The time has come to call people out on scare tactics, slippery slope arguments, and dismissal of the facts.

The issue will be attacked from every angle I can fathom. By doing so, I'll give an arsenal of arguments against those that contrive the existence (or any reasonable[3] possibility) of free will.

Philosophers and scientists have addressed this topic throughout the ages. I'm looking to shed light on some of these older ideas. To make them fresh and palatable to the current day layperson. It's also my intention to offer new insight into the topic. To offer different perspectives into the nature of causality and acausality. I'm also offering a renewed outlook to the psychology people hold based on this fresh and exciting understanding.

The goal is to bring these ideas into mainstream; something that people will begin to incorporate into their personal and philosophical views and attitudes. To raise awareness. To give people an important perspective that will allow humanity to grow for the betterment of consciousness. To be a positive cog in the machine.[4]

Of course whether (or not) people listen to the reasoning of this book won't be freely chosen. Rather it will be determined by if they had the causal (or possibly acausal) events that have lead to them being critical thinkers that are open minded enough to absorb the information in an unbiased fashion. I'll get deeply into those types of events later on.

And of course I didn't write this book of my own free will. The need and desire to write this book to disseminate the information within to others was one that came about through long processes that stem from events I had no control over. Though my *ego* desires that I take full credit for my work, the fact of the matter is, I don't really deserve such. I'll argue later on in the book that with the realization that there is no free will, we need to move away from such ego driven results, to an understanding of the importance of productivity without it.

3

This isn't a typical philosophy book that's designed using big words only for those in certain academic circles. I'm not looking to scare people away from the content. I'm not looking to complicate, confuse, or create ambiguity. Where something can be simplified, I'll simplify it. Where things are not easily simplified, I'll provide details and explanations. This book is as much about passion as it is about philosophy, reasoned arguments, and psychology. This passion doesn't take away from any of the arguments. Parts of the book are meant to be a fun and lighthearted romp through a thoughtful and serious topic; other parts are in your face serious. Making the content fun also doesn't take away from any of the arguments. There is no need to make serious, thoughtful topics dry, boring, and humorless. Philosophy is for everyone; it needs to be.

To illustrate the points in the book, I've decided to use various methods. Analogies and thought experiments make the content relatable and easy to absorb. Imagery helps visualization of key concepts, allows breaks from text, and is just plain fun. Dialogue will help those more inclined to learn from back and forth feedback.

Also, if you own the book, you can download extra book content by going here:

http://breakingthefreewillillusion.com/book-extras/

This includes a workbook that can help you work through some of the ideas in this book. I plan on adding more content to this site in the future.

Before the philosophy is delved into, the first chapter will give you an idea of why the content of this book is of great importance to you. It's to give you an idea of what to look forward to and the pitfalls to avoid as you read. The rest of the book will delve into everything from the philosophy and why free will can't exist, to the psychology to let go of such a belief, and everything in between.

1

What's to Gain and What it Does and Doesn't Mean

'This topic permeates up to a large number of extremely important social, political, and philosophical topics. It also helps to define a person's psychology, perceptions, and outlook.'

You have much to gain by understanding that free will doesn't exist, much more than you can ever imagine. Especially if you currently believe you have free will. This is great news. It's, in fact, an exciting step toward enlightenment. The term *enlightenment* isn't used in some mystical or "spiritual" sense, but rather as a notion of understanding something extremely important that's beyond what many currently do understand or are willing to attempt to understand.

This understanding will allow you to see things in an entirely new light. If your psychology doesn't block it, the way you view yourself, others, the world, and even the universe, will change for the better. It's my assertion that this is an important path to progression that humankind must take, and by the end of the book you should see that such an assertion is a supported one.

In a sense, you'll obtain new eyes. Without these eyes to view the world with, humankind will be stuck in the past muck, falsely blaming themselves and other individuals, immersing themselves in hatred, placing themselves or others on faux pedestals, putting temporary band-aids on problems instead of fixing them at base level, making poor decisions based on untruths and archaic fairytales, and relating to the world around them with a harmful egocentric point of view.

A thorough understanding may help you minimize much of the past baggage that weighs heavily on your mind. It will allow you to see yourself and others for what you truly are. It will allow you to focus your efforts on what's important: the present and future. We all must deal with our own psychology. Everyone, at some point, wishes they could turn back the clock and fix something they've done. They blame themselves and they blame others for things done in the past. Such blame is an unnecessary weight riding on their shoulders. It's unnecessary because what has happened in the past could not have been helped or prevented by you or them. You could not have, of your own accord, chosen otherwise than what you did. They could not have, of their own accord, chosen otherwise than what they did.

Understanding this will also give you an important base for many of the beliefs you hold. Beliefs and ideas regarding ethics, politics, economics, philosophy of life, and a slew of other containers of thought connect to the false notion of free will. When free will appears to be self evident, or is even taught[5], an enormous number of important topics become built on it without ever noticing. Topics that aren't benign to the actions of people.

Much like the belief that people have invisible wings that allow them to fly, the belief in free will is a fiction with harmful consequences. Maybe not as obvious as someone pushing another off of a cliff thinking that they'll fly in a circle and come back. The belief in free will creates much harm in the world due to the psychology it manifests and the ideologies and feelings that spring forth from such mindsets. This psychology will be addressed later.

Once you begin to strengthen your understanding regarding the nature of events and realize they are a *base level understanding* for numerous higher level concepts, many of your beliefs and mindsets can begin to repair along side of this new understanding. This isn't something to fear. It's an exciting progression. Seeing how many people still don't have this realization, and how many hold on to their free will ideas as tightly as they can, will become the fearful thing for you, not vice versa.

If you're already aware that free will is a fiction, congratulations for having the causality to understand this important fact. You're in the minority. This book will help you reinforce that understanding, give you the tools to describe it to others, and fill in any gaps. If you're unaware of this fact, congratulations as well. You've taken the first causal step toward awareness, progress, and enlightenment.

Keep a logically open mind. Don't allow mistaken fears to prevent you from reading and understanding the content of this book. As long as you don't close your mind off based on an illusionary foundation, that spark can go off in your mind that says "aha, that's how things *really* are!"

A brief understanding of what a lack of free will means and what it doesn't mean will help you avoid some of the pitfalls as you read along. These ideas will be elaborated on as you progress through the book. Again, this section is just to keep in the back of your mind as you navigate through your reading.

What it Means

Why does it matter that you don't have free will? Should you act that same as if you thought you had it? Some would make the argument that you should or will act as if you and others have free will regardless if you or they actually have it. I argue against this sentiment.

This topic permeates up to a large number of extremely important social, political, and philosophical topics. It also helps to define a person's psychology, perceptions, and outlook. To dismiss the point as unimportant misses a key understanding to almost everything a person does. It's a life changing understanding.

To list only a few, the belief in free will breeds:

- Self blame
- Blame of others
- Egoism
- The illusion of deservingness over others
- Anger or hatred of others
- Divisiveness
- Allowances of inequality
- Poverty dismissal
- Retribution or vengeance desires
- Non-connectedness

These feelings and more come about naturally when you think you or someone else could have, of your or their own accord, done otherwise than what you or they did. It also grows out of this feeling of the "self" that we compartmentalize as

8

separate from the interconnections that make it up. The more you begin to understand the nature of it, the more you can begin to repair the damage that the idea of free will has done.

This understanding is a causal necessity for humanity to progress from a selfish state to one of unity, equality, and acceptance. It's important, as without it, ideas will continue to be built on a foundation of free will quicksand. Harmful ideas. This will become clear as you delve deeper into the content.

What it Doesn't Mean

Equally as important is what a lack of free will doesn't mean. Understanding the lack of free will doesn't, for example, give a person a license to do whatever they so desire. It doesn't give people an excuse to act on bad or socially unacceptable behavior. It shouldn't lead a borderline-criminal over the edge.

If it does, it's due to a complete misunderstanding regarding what a lack of free will means. It's not the person concluding we lack free will that's dangerous, but rather ignorance and confusion about what it means and implies that's dangerous. An ignorance and confusion that's created, not by the new understanding, but rather by a psychology built on a feeling and belief in free will. Keep in mind that ignorance and misunderstanding can cause many negative outcomes, regardless of what such ignorance or misunderstanding is based on.

Also, a defeatist attitude does not follow from a lack of free will. The lack of free will does not mean that our thoughts don't cause important outputs of events. They do. A "why bother" attitude isn't reasonably acquired from an understanding of a lack of free will. Free will or no free will, there are reasons to bother. Reasons that can and do come about causally.

If someone takes a lack of free will to the wrong conclusion, this book is here to correct them. Part of the reason I've placed this sort of "disclaimer" in the beginning of the book prior to showing why free will doesn't exist is to prevent people from such poor misinterpretations. If someone cherry picks the contents of this book, and then concludes something negative based on it, they've missed some of the more important parts.

This cannot be helped. Anyone can take the most benign or helpful book fathomable, cherry pick sentences or ideas from it, and put them together in a way that makes them seem harmful. I am asking you, the reader, to avoid doing this. Though there are many chapters that can be understood and referred to on their own, I do suggest one full read through one time first. Afterward, you can go back to those parts that you found most interesting, or most confusing.

Also, lacking the belief in free will does not affect ethics in the way many think. If someone thought that an action was unethical when they believed they had free will, there would probably be little reason to conclude, at least based on the lack of free will alone, that it would make the action any less unethical. More likely, some actions that are currently considered ethical (or *not unethical*) may begin to align with what might be considered unethical. For example, retributive[6] punishment of an individual may now become ethically problematic.

Or the ethical system itself may need to be reassessed. If the free will idea is important to one's system of ethics (for example: Kantian ethics), there is a big problem with the ethical framework itself. A reassessment of the ethical system needs to be made.

Whether a person is ultimately ethically responsible for what they've done isn't the same thing as whether or not an action is ethical. Morality, ethics, responsibility, blameworthiness, and deservingness will all be addressed in detail regarding what a lack of free will means for them. For now, just keep in mind that a distinction needs to be made between an action being ethical or unethical, and someone being responsible for acting ethically or unethically. This difference will be made clear later on.

As you read, keep in mind what's to gain, what it means, and what it doesn't. These will also be detailed out later, but before that: You need to be convinced of the impossibility of free will. You need to be shown that the beating heart of such philosophy is a logic and rationality that cannot be denied.

And with that, on to the philosophy...

THE PHILOSOPHY

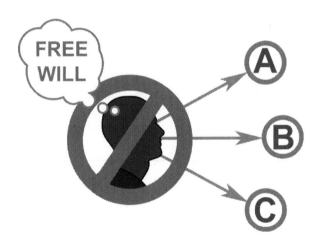

2
Defining Initial Terms

*'I know, I know, definitions are borrrring!
They are, however, a necessary evil.'*

This book contains terms that people may not be accustomed to or that, if not initially defined, may lead to misinterpretations or ambiguities. Some words such as "causal" and "acausal" will be used frequently, so it's important that an understanding of what is meant by those words precedes the information within the book. The term "Free Will" has its own chapter. The basic definitions below will be elaborated on throughout, and words not provided on this list will be defined as needed. I know, I know, definitions are borrrring! They are, however, a necessary evil.[7] Don't worry, I tried to make them as brief and succinct as possible. The below definitions are quick references for whenever you need to remember the basics of how words are being defined:

EVENT = An occurrence; something happening.

CAUSE = An event that creates or forces another event (effect).

EFFECT = An event that occurs due to another event (cause).

CAUSATION[8] = Necessary relationship between an event or events and another event or events, which the latter (effect) are a direct result of the former (cause).

CAUSAL = Following the principle of causation.

CAUSAL EVENT = An event that occurs due to a cause. In the case of a causal event, the event is an effect.

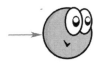

CAUSAL EVENT

ACAUSAL (Pronounced aye-causal even if you are not Canadian) = Not following the principles of causation. Non-causal is another word for this.

ACAUSAL EVENT = An event that occurs that does not have a cause. In the case of an acausal event, the event is not an effect.

ACAUSAL EVENT

DETERMINISM = The state in which every event has a cause.

INDETERMINISM = The state in which some acausal events can or do happen.

FREE WILL = The ability to choose between more than one viable option or action, in which the choice was "up to the chooser." The next chapter will elaborate on this.

NECESSARY = Required or "essential to." Keep in mind that the use of 'necessary'[9] has various meanings within philosophy, and it's important not to confuse the common definition I'm using with other academic usages.

NEURO-STRUCTURE = The structure of the brain at a specific point in time.

RESPONSIBILITY = The state of being accountable for an action, in a way that you can be blamed or deemed more deserving due to the action. * Keep in mind that this isn't the same usage of the word responsibility as holding a duty to do or not do something prior to an action.

TURKEY = A funny looking bird that has a wattle.

VIABLE = Feasible or possible. Capable of happening.

3

So what is "Free Will" anyway?

'The free will I am discussing in this book, and the free will that matters for the changing of minds that I propose needs to take place, is...'

This book needs to define the term that it argues against: free will. And no, it has nothing to do with freeing a killer whale named Willy from SeaWorld (cheesy '90s cliché alert).

I've summed it up into a one sentence definition that should be referred to throughout the book:

The ability to choose between more than one viable option or action, in which the choice was "up to the chooser."

It's this ability that I will argue against, and it's this ability that I think the majority of people intuitively believe they possess. To avoid misinterpretations of this definition, I've dedicated this entire chapter to break down the definition and dissect it. I'll also explain why I think this (or something equivalent) to be the common usage people think of when they hear the term "free will," and more importantly, why it's the definition that needs to be taken into account for various issues of concern.

Here's the breakdown:

16

"The ability" means that it's something a human can do. The power to make something happen. Jack might possess the ability to jump over a candlestick, but he doesn't have the ability to jump from the Earth to the Moon.

"Choose" or *"choice,"* in this definition, imply a selection. It consists of a mental process of judging alternatives, and the election of one of those. It will be shown that any acausal event (event without a cause) cannot be chosen. Such events would happen without judging alternatives.

"More than one" means multiple. Ice cream might have multiple flavor options a person can elect from, such as chocolate, vanilla, or spinach.

"Viable" means the multiple options are all possible. It will be argued that, if the universe is causally deterministic, it's only possible to select the specific option in which prior causality dictates, and all other options aren't "viable." The other options do, however, help determine the only viable one. They're part of the past causality.

It'll also be argued that the causality that dictates such selection ultimately stems to events outside of the person's control.

17

"Option or action" is the thing or the doing that the person chooses from. Spinach ice cream... Mmm...

"Up to the chooser" means that the chooser (the person[10] making the choice) can author their own actions. It means that at least part of the actions that the chooser creates isn't coerced by external forces or something beyond their control. It's of their (the chooser's) own accord. It will be shown that acausal events cannot be up to a chooser.

That's it. The definition in a nutshell. To repeat it: *The ability to choose between more than one viable option or action, in which the choice was "up to the chooser."*

This is the usage most people think of when they hear the words "free will." They, of course, don't think of this exact wording. No one walks around saying "I have the ability to choose between more than one viable option or action, in which that choice was up to me." They do, however, think or 'feel' they have the abilities portrayed in this definition.

For example, most people who think they have "free will" think they can choose either vanilla ice cream *or* chocolate ice cream. They think that, right before they decide, both of these options are *viable* options. Even after they had picked vanilla, they think that they *could have* chosen chocolate. Not only that, but they think that it's they that would be making the (different) choice to eat chocolate, and not some factor they have no control over.

There are many other ways people can define the term "free will." For example, they can define free will as: "the ability to make choices," even though that does not mean a person can freely decide what they choose. Or they may define free will as: "the ability to have chosen differently," which allows for different possibilities in an indeterministic universe (we will talk about this later) but disregards the person actually being able to will the different choice. I don't think these definitions are what the majority[11] of people *feel they have*.

More importantly, they are not the definitions of philo-sophical, ethical, political, and psychological importance. Even if we use one of these definitions instead of the one I propose, the concern would only revert to what having these types of "free will" and *only* these types of free will mean. The same questions would need to be answered in regards to important topics such as responsibility. Most of the times those that use these definitions of free will attempt to bypass such important questions by claiming: "free will, therefore X (responsibility, etc.)." They do so even though how they have defined free will offers no more X than the position that there's no free will as I have defined the term. They are used to push the points of the topic away instead of addressing them head on.

Authorities[12] on the subject can define free will any way they please. When they do so in a way that's not free (in the way it's meant for most regarding this topic), or not willed, or neither, they must understand they validate others' contrivances of free will. A free will that's felt or defined differently than what the authority suggests. Someone only has to hear that an "expert" believes in free will, and boom, they are validated in their own minds. I sometimes wonder if that's what some of these authorities want: To create enough ambiguity, noise, confusion, and smoke and mirrors to uphold the illusion. Maybe they feel they have reasons for this. This book will suggest that such reasoning is poor.

Regardless, the free will I'm discussing, and the free will that matters for the changing of minds that I propose needs to take place, is: The ability to choose between more than one viable option or action, in which the choice was "up to the chooser." Read it. Understand it. And then understand the implications of not having it. By the end of this book you will.

Dialogue

Orion and Liberius[13] sit down on a warm summer day while sipping drinks. Liberius heard through the grapevine that Orion doesn't believe in free will. As an attempt to show him where he's wrong, he starts a conversation, knowing that it will lead into a discussion about free will. Orion can't resist a good debate.

LIBERIUS: Ahh, life's good. I sit here on a relaxing Sunday afternoon sipping drinks with a friend. I had a few other options I could have done today, but I decided on this.

ORION: Ah yes. Sometimes one just needs a relaxing day. Buuuurp.

LIBERIUS: Nice burp. Ohh yeah! And like I said, I decided on this option instead of a number of different options I could have chosen.

(Liberius holds up his hands as if holding possible options in them, egging Orion on.)

ORION: When you say you could have chosen those other options, I wonder what you mean by that?

(Orion's left eyebrow raises.)

LIBERIUS: Free will, of course. I was given a number of options, and using my free will, I decided on this one.

(Liberius smirks slightly, knowing that he has drawn Orion in.)

ORION: Ahh, free will. Can you help me with what you mean by this term? You stated that you were given a number of options, and then you used your free will to decide on one of them. Could you have chosen another option, and if so, could you have done so of your own accord?

LIBERIUS: Yes, I could have chosen any one of those options presented to me, and the decision would have been up to me. Obviously if I couldn't have chosen the other options, I would have been forced to the one. Such a choice wouldn't be free. And if I couldn't have done so of my own accord, the decision wouldn't be mine.

ORION: That's what I thought you meant. Care to delve into the topic of free will a little more? I'd be interested in the discussion.

LIBERIUS: Suure, I enjoy the subject and would be glad to help.

Liberius grins, knowing he has reeled Orion in. After all, of course he has free will, it's quite obvious to him. *We aren't robots! We aren't gears, or machines! Thinking we don't have free will is silly. More than that, it's just plain disturbing. At the very least I can get Orion thinking about his absurd stance and hopefully, one day, he will change his mind.*

4

Key Understandings
(For the Philosophy)

Certain themes will be repeated throughout this book. A main theme is that of causality. Another is of acausality. Acausality means that an event occurs that does not have a cause. Both causality and acausality will be examined in depth. If you don't already understand why they are incompatible with free will, it's important that you read the chapters that pertain to them carefully. They explain key factors in understanding why free will is impossible. Other evidence will be supplied which supports a lack of free will as well. With only the understanding of causal and acausal events, it's a closed case: there's no free will. The free will idea is incoherent with the two possible ways events can come about. With all of the other evidence piled on, the lack of free will is the rationally undeniable position to take.

Though hardly an extensive list, below are a few key points that will be addressed as you read along that might be helpful to keep in the back of your mind. Don't worry about trying to understand them fully at this point. Just glance through them once. You can always refer back to them later:

In a universe (or beyond) where every event has a cause *(determinism)*, it will be shown that:

- When an event causes another event to happen, that second event could not have happened differently.

- All caused events are forced happenings, and we cannot change a chain of causal events.

- If our thoughts are caused, they are forced and could not have happened another way. They are not free.

- The choices we make can be said to be causally willed by our thoughts. Since we cannot change the causal path of our thoughts, the choices we make can only have one specific path.

- If our thoughts are caused, they are willed, but not freely willed. The will is forced by causal events. Causality that extends *prior* to the willer (linear time) or to a time in which the willer does not exist (other time conceptions).

- Causal events are incompatible with free will.

In a universe (or beyond) where acausal events happen, along with causal events, *(indeterminism)*, it will be shown that:

- Acausal events are not forced events. They could happen at any time or location, or never happen at all (or in philosophical terms they would have no temporal or spatial determinacy).

- Since nothing forces an acausal event, any such events cannot be willed.

- If a thought comes about acausally, that thought's not willed. This is a dangerous situation for a thinker to be in.

- If a thought comes about through a combination of acausal events and causal ones, it's partially willed and partially not. This too is dangerous as the decision can be changed based on non-willed, acausal events. Causal events are never free, but can be willed (or part of the process we call "willing"). Acausal events are never willed.

- Acausal events are incompatible with free will.

It will also be shown that:

- All thoughts that happen are events.

- All events must either be causal or acausal. There's no escaping this dichotomy.

- This dichotomy must (logically) pertain to every event, even within non-naturalistic worldviews.

- Causal events can be reliably and reasonably inferred as existing through evidence of them.

- Acausal events are problematic and not reasonably inferred. This should be taken into consideration before postulating their existence. In cases where causal events are problematic as well, it's best if one holds to an agnostic[14] position toward the event being acausal.

Keep some of these points in the back of your head as you read, especially the ones you disagree with, if any. This will allow you to focus on those points when you arrive to the justifications for them.

For those who are unfamiliar with the way some of these terms are used, it may be difficult to understand such points the first time you read them. If some of these points are unclear, don't feel you need to go back and re-read them before you move on. They will usually be clarified in another section.

5
Events

'Every single event--whether it occurs in our universe, a different universe, or some more mystical realm--either has a cause or it doesn't.'

Events are strange if you think about them. They happen. They occur. They seem to flow through time, or create what we perceive as time as they happen. Some say all events started at the big bang, when a primordial hot spot began to expand and space/time sprang into existence. Some say that the universe began from other universes in an infinite or circular pattern. Some have non-material or supernatural explanations for events beginning. The fact is we don't know if events have an initial starting point (an initial acausal event), or if they are infinite[15]. Whatever theory someone has for how events initially came to be (or not), one thing's fairly sure: If we accept (axiomatically) that the universe is approximately how we perceive it--if we accept the universe as reality, events occur within that universe. Rivers flow, planets orbit, rain falls, babies are born, dogs bark, particles decay, light travels, people belch, wood rots, stars explode, balls roll, fire spreads, turkeys gobble, and people think complex thoughts.

Why should any of these events happen at all? Why something instead of nothing? Why do we even exist? If you're asking these questions, you must already be around to ask them. The event that is "you" (in quotes) has already happened.

26

This is called the *weak anthropic principle*.[16] The events that have led up to you existing at a certain perceived time and location are a necessary condition for you to be thinking about the events that led up to you existing.

It's fun to ponder such "why" questions, as long as we don't let them distract us from understanding the *possible* "hows" for events and what those possibilities mean for our thoughts and actions. Ultimately, this book is about events, or rather, the possible ways in which events can come about. Those possible "hows." We may not have all of the answers for "why" (or rather such "why" questions may not have answer)[17], but we can know what the possibilities are for "how" events can happen, and we can know what those possibilities mean for free will.

Every single event--whether it occurs in our universe, a different universe, or some more mystical realm--either has a cause or it doesn't. There's no room for any other state for any given event. More clearly, an event is either a causal event, or an acausal event. This is a necessary dichotomy. If an event doesn't have a cause, it must be acausal; if an event isn't acausal, it must have a cause. To suggest otherwise is a logical absurdity.

To demonstrate these two types of events, let's consider a specific event. We'll call the event "door opening." The instant the door begins to open is when the event occurs (whether we can measure that exact instant or not is beside the point).

There are two options if the door really opened. Either "something"[18] caused the door to begin opening (e.g. the energy applied to the door from hands pushing, wind blowing, turkey pecking, a spring in the hinge springing, or a ghost doing ghostly stuff), or it began opening without something causing it to open. If something caused the door to open, we can call that something the cause, and the door opening the effect. If something did not cause the door to open, but it opened anyway, we can say the event occurred without a cause (actually we may have to say the acausal event caused the door to open, but we will get into that later). At this point, whether or not option two is feasible isn't important. The door can represent something happening on the quantum scale if you are more comfortable with that. The important part is that the event itself must either have a cause or not, regardless of the "thing" it happens to.

The door analogy is used only to illustrate the dichotomy. It's to show that these are the only two options feasible for any given event. There isn't any third option sitting along side of an event being caused or an event being uncaused. One opposes the other.

Event X **is** the effect of a cause (is causal)

is in opposition to

Event X **is not** the effect of a cause (is acausal)

Like the door opening, thinking, choosing, and doing are all events. They aren't magical exceptions.

Active Events vs. Inactive Events

Most of the examples given in this book will be of active events, meaning something appears to be happening. An obvious change of states or motion of some sort. But action (the appearance of something) is not necessarily what makes up an event. Active events[19] just happen to be more obvious because we can relate to them. Take a rock sitting on the ground, for example. One would hardly think just sitting there, not moving at all, as an "event," especially one that's being "caused." What's not being taken into account is the gravity, the mass of the rock, the shape of the rock, the texture of the rock, the flatness of the ground, and any other factor that would cause the rock to stay put. In other words, an inactive event can be causally happening, due to a number of other active or inactive events. Of course, we know that everything at the quantum level is in constant flux, we are simply addressing an object at the Newtonian level for our rock example.

Hypothetically, think of an unmoving rock with no gravity; no pushing or pulling energy; even the universe ceases to expand in this scenario. You might think that the rock stays in place without a cause. Actually, that very state that the universe is in, with no energetic factors, causes that rock to stay put. Of course we could say that an inactive event could possibly be inactive due to no cause, but this would dismiss the state that would cause such inactivity. In other words, the rock moving would be an active event that goes against the state that was causing the rock to stay put.

Confused yet? Don't be. The difference between active and inactive events isn't that important and just brought to light to assist with understanding what an entire causal chain of events might entail. Regardless, all events, whether active or inactive, either have a cause, or they don't. Understanding this dichotomy is much more important.

Most of the examples and focus in this book will be active events. This is because it's easier to illustrate and picture the relation between a cause and the event that is its effect with active events. It's also easier to picture an acausal event, and understand the implication of such, for active events. And lastly, and probably most importantly, the action of thinking, willing, choosing, or doing anything at all are all active events, and they are the concern when addressing the notion of "free will."

Caused or uncaused, that is the question!

So far we've addressed one event coming from a cause, or one event acausally happening. How about one event both acausally happening as well as happening via a cause. "Huh?" you might ask. "We already went over this. An event can only have one or the other." This is true, however this confusion needs to be addressed.

Let's go back to the door. In the one scenario, the door's opened by a cause. In the other, it just opens, without cause. Let's suppose, for the door, that both of these happen at the same time. In other words, if the cause was not there, the door would still open, but it so happens that a cause is there to open the door as well. To visualize why the two are separate events, picture the door as a swinging door that can swing both inside and outside. Picture the causal event causing the door to swing outside and picture the acausal event of the door swinging inside. Now imagine each event not being able to override the other, and both happening at the same time. The door would not open in either direction.

The cause prevented the door from opening in one direction acausally, and the acausal event prevented the door opening in the other direction, even though force was applied to it for the cause. The events are different, but they happened to the same object. One event is the prevention of the door swinging open in one direction while the other event's the prevention of the door swinging open in the other direction. In other words, the acausal event just happening in one direction (again, disregard if that's actually possible for now) would counteract the causal event of energy transferring in the other direction. The door stays put due to two events. Two events, one causal and the other acausal, led to the event of the door not opening--remember inactive events?

The point: One event can happen through complex interactions of other events. Such complexities will be addressed later, and as you will see, those complexities do not help grant free will.

Events are the "what" and causality/acausality are the "hows" (how those events can come about). Time to get into the details of those "hows." Time to move on to causality…

6
Causality Basics and Problems

*Causation, though we may not see the actual
cause, is inferred beyond any reasonable doubt.*

There is a saying: "Correlation does not imply causation." This means that two variables which we see a correlation for does not necessarily imply that one causes the other.

If you were to open a refrigerator door to snag your favorite beverage, and someone right after at the other end of the room gets a chill, it could be that the cold air from the refrigerator caused the chill. It could also be a draft from somewhere else in the room, or a reaction to something unrelated to the refrigerator. Just because the one event followed the other doesn't mean that the one necessarily caused the other.

This makes it difficult to determine the exact cause for any given event. Even obvious events we don't really see the actual cause for. We may see a cue ball collide with a billiard ball and think that the cue ball caused the billiard ball to move. In a sense, it did. What we aren't really seeing is the transferring of energy from one ball to the other, and that energy being applied to specific parts of the ball. We aren't seeing the gravity forcing the ball down on the smooth surface as it rolls. We aren't seeing the friction that the atmosphere places on the ball. Yes, the cue ball causes the billiard ball to roll, but through causal interactions that we don't really observe.

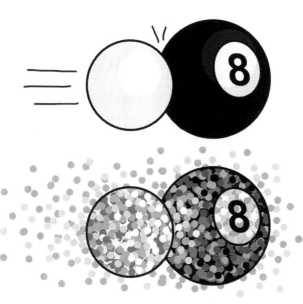

The causes appear to happen behind the scenes. What we observe is the correlation, and then we project that correlation on to future events (e.g. if I hit this cue ball into this 8 ball, the 8 ball will roll). The billiard ball moving after the cue ball "hits" it is the correlation we observe, not the cause we observe.

Since correlation doesn't necessarily imply causation, what evidence do we have for causation existing? Is inferring a cause problematic? This may seem to be a strange question to ask, but it's a valid one.

The evidence is in the form of those examples in which possible correlations and conditions can be repeatedly observed. This isn't evidence of what the actual cause *is*, but it's certainly evidence (in the inductive sense) that an actual cause *exists*. This is of key importance when talking about causality for the free will debate. We don't have to say that we know what the cause is. We don't even have to say that something has a cause. Repeatedly observed correlation does clue us in that there's *most likely* a cause. It's strong evidence for causality.

Let's use the example of striking a match to create fire on the end of it. What are some of the necessary correlations and conditions? Is it just a coincidence that when we strike a match on a rough surface under certain conditions a fire usually happens? Would the fire have happened anyway and we just happened to be striking the match at the same time it occurred?

We can test this. We take one thousand matches from the same box, strike one on the rough surface, and notice fire. Take a second one out, motion the strike without actually striking it on the rough surface, and no fire. If we keep doing this we notice a pattern. The ones that we strike light (for the most part) and the ones we do not strike do not light (for the most part). There may be occurrences of some not lighting when struck, and yes, maybe even one lighting when not struck. It's difficult to know all of the variables of the match or environment. If it's an excessively hot and dry day, maybe a match will light without striking it. For the most part, however, we can minimize these differences and conclude that yes, there's a necessary correlation between striking a match and a fire happening at the end of it. We might not know that the next match will light if we strike it, but we can infer that it probably will. The more matches we strike and don't strike, the more consistent the results. We don't have to see the exact cause at the chemical and friction level. Causation, though we may not see it, is inferred *beyond any reasonable doubt.*

We don't have to see an actual cause to know that a cause exists. We do, however, have to be careful in how we test for likely causes.

This doesn't mean everything has a cause, though everything may, but it does mean that--unlike acausality which we do not have much, if any, evidence for--we have strong evidence for causes.

We know that there is a causal element between gravity and a rock falling. We can test and verify the results of this. We don't need to know the exact connections at the micro level to understand that there's a connection. Much of science is based on causality, not because it leaps to the conclusion of it unreasonably, but because observed consistency points to it.

34

But even for those that take the stance that we cannot prove causes due to the problem of induction[20], if we were to say that a cause does not exist for an event, such event must come about acausally. If we are to say we cannot "know" if an event has a cause or not (due to the problem of induction), deductively we can understand that it either does or doesn't.

As you will see, neither of the two possibilities help the free will stance. You'll also quickly see the absurdity[21] of any implication that causality does not or *might* not exist in the universe.

7

A Cause Cannot Have
Multiple Possible Outcomes

'(A) cannot be both the cause of (B) and not the cause of (B). This would make (A) in opposition to itself. A self-contradiction.'

A cause cannot have multiple possible outcomes. This is a central point in understanding why free will and causality don't mix.

To understanding this, we'll start simple and then build on it. We will say that event (A) causes event (B) through time period (X) and that we're in a deterministic universe where all events are caused.

X=1 to 2

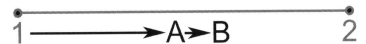

Note: Different time possibilities (and even no time) will be addressed later. For now, a linear approach will help illustrate the points. This will help you to understand other less common notions of time, but they all have the same types of problems regarding causality and free will.

Think of the time period for (X) as a player that you can rewind to the beginning and let

36

play again.

After rewinding and playing back the event, (A) would still have to cause (B) the exact same way as it did before.

X=1 to 2

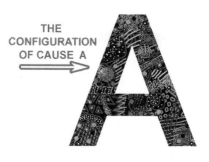

1 ————————➤A➤B   2

But why is this?

Simply put, the playback would be identical because all of the variables that caused the playback would be identical. The variables that make up (A) could not have changed on the second play through, because the causal events that caused (A) to happen in the first place would be identical as well (i.e. the causality that preceded (A) would be identical).

THE CONFIGURATION OF CAUSE A ⟹

If all causal elements are the same, the effect must be the same. A cause can't have more than one possible effect.

If it did, there would need to be an acausal element that dictated the different path in which the event could take. To illustrate this point, let's assume that cause (A) can have either effect (B) or effect (C):

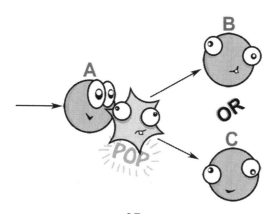

Without an acausal event, (A) could only take one path, for example to (B), no matter how many times we rewind time and hit play.

Another way to state this is: The cause that leads to (B) over (C) cannot be the same cause that leads to (C) over (B). Otherwise it would be the cause that leads to (C) over (B), not the cause that leads to (B) over (C). (A), which is that cause, can only be one or the other.

Since this is the case, it's impossible for an entirely causal system to have more than one possible path. Since no acausality exists in an entirely causal system, the outcome must always be the same on playback. It doesn't matter how many causal variables are injected in.

A cause cannot have more than one possible outcome for its effect.

Again, only an acausal event could change the trajectory of a causal chain. This point's so important that it bears stressing with multiple thought experiments to drive it home, at the risk of being redundant. If you already "get" this point, feel free to move on to the next chapter.

For our next example, we have an impervious ball heading straight toward an impervious, immovable two sided ramp:

For the ball to go down one side of the ramp or the other, in an entirely causal system, something must cause it to go down one ramp over the other. Maybe it's leaning a little more in one direction, or maybe the point of the ramp's a little skewed or slippery on one side, or maybe the ball's not perfectly weighted. There are a large number of possible causes that would make the ball go down one path over the other. In the scenario in which there's nothing that would cause the ball to go down one path over the other--if the ball is perfect, the direction is perfectly aligned and straight, the ramp is perfect, and there's no external forcing factor--the ball would either come to a dead stop on the tip of the ramp, or bounce straight back in the opposite direction (given the various qualities of the

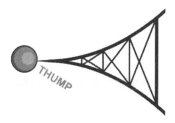

ball and ramp).

If it did not, if for example it took the left ramp instead of stopping at the tip or taking the right ramp, an acausal event must have happened. Whether it took one ramp over the other would be dictated by an entirely acausal event if it's not caused to go to a specific path. You cannot say the ball causally took the left ramp, without a causal factor for it taking the left ramp. And if there is a causal factor for it taking the left ramp, it'll always take the left ramp based on that causal factor. The causal factor that forces *left over right* isn't the same causal factor that would force *right over left*, or the same causal factor to come to a dead stop at the tip.

If a "causal" event has more than one possible effect, that "causal" event cannot really be causal (and hence it's not a causal event). The properties of a cause cannot hold opposing possibilities. In other words, (A) cannot be *both* the cause of (B) and not the cause of (B) (e.g. C instead). This would make (A) in opposition to itself. A self-contradiction. From this one simple understanding, we can understand the one important part about the nature of causes that is incompatible with free will. A causal chain can never change. It can never do otherwise than what's dictated by the beginning of such chain.

If it's a cause that determines the one effect over the other, and that cause is the effect of another cause, it always must be there (and hence the other option was never a causal possibility). If the cause isn't forced by a preceding cause, again, an acausal event is being injected in. There's no logical way around this.

To use another analogy: a coin is set on its edge perfectly balanced so that it does not topple over to heads or tails.

A minute later, it topples over to tails.

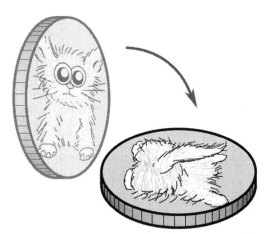

To suggest that if we were able to rewind time a minute back, that this time it could fall on heads, would mean that an acausal event happened at some point:

Either

- The acausal event happened the first time when the coin fell on tails, in which the acausal event overrode the causality that occurred on the second run through that pushed it to heads.

or

- The acausal event happened on the second run through which overrode the first run through of the causal event forcing it to fall on tails.

or

- Neither run through were causal events and both fallings happened acausally.

or

- An acausal event happened at some point in the past which changed the cause itself (the cause is not the same cause).

To suggest that both run throughs happened via entirely causal chains is absurd. If the causality is the table shaking, or the wind blowing, and those events came about through entirely causal means, the table shake or wind factors would always be the same. In which case the outcome of the coin will always be the same. For the wind to be different through the same run through of time (time being the same as well), an acausal event would be needed somewhere in the past to lead to that different wind. Simple, right?

Time to complicate things.

41

In the next scenario, we'll assume (A) causes both (B) and (C) events. Keep in mind that this is completely different than

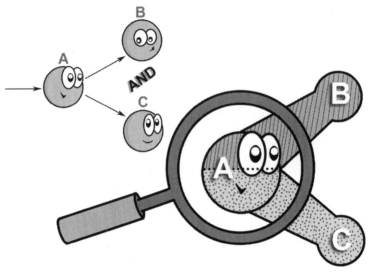

(A) being able to lead to either (B) or (C). Both (B) and (C) are the effect of (A).

In this instance, what we are really saying is that part of (A) is the cause of (B) and another part of (A) is the cause of (C). Regardless, we can just assume that (A) caused both (B) and (C) at the same time as it makes no difference either way. If part of (A) was the real cause of (B) and a different part of (A) was the real cause of (C), or if (A) in its entirety was the real cause of both (B) and (C), the forced events are (B) and (C). They cannot have happened any other way.

Now let's assume (B) causes (D) and (E) and both (D) and (E) cause (F):

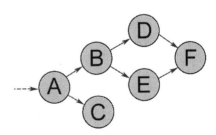

You can see how multiple simultaneous events can come about, and how multiple events can be a cause for one event. You can also see how this can create complex chains of events to happen.

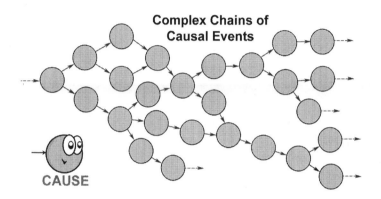

Complex Chains of Causal Events

CAUSE

No matter how complex we make this map, (A) is a specific configuration based on all of the causal elements that preceded it, and all of the events that come from (A) have no other path to take than what's dictated by (A). Only when and if an acausal event is thrown in the mix can those events be different when we hit the rewind time button and rerun it.

If the outcome of (A) is both (B) and (C), it could never have been only (B) or only (C). It never could have been (B) and (D). There's no logical way a cause can have the possibility of two different outcomes.

It may be easy to think such is possible when we cannot see the actual variables for similar tests done *at different times*. For example, aligning with our ramp type of scenario, if we were to roll a metal ball down a tube that splits off into two tubes (X and Y), sometimes when we do so it may roll down X, while other times it may run down Y.

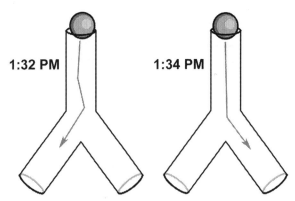

This is because we may drop the ball in differently each time, or something inside of the tube may change, or the ball's surface may change, or any number of variables could be a little different each time. Any small difference in the causality can lead to a different outcome. There's a good reason we analogize using a reversal of time, instead of doing similar experiments in different time periods. The way we'd drop the ball, and all of the factors involved when the ball goes down the tube, would be causally identical on a replay. If we rewind time and drop the ball, the ball would always go to X, or whatever initial tube it went down. It would never go down Y.

It's very important that this point's perfectly clear. You have no idea how many times I've run across a person suggesting that a cause can be a cause for more than one possible effect. It's a misunderstanding of causality that allows *some* people to contrive free will (e.g. them being able to have causally willed other than they did).

It would take an acausal event to get that metal ball to go down Y (on a rewind) if all of the causal variables are set. The same causal events cannot force the ball down both X and Y.

Hopefully by now it's abundantly clear that a cause can only have one possible effect in which that cause can ever take, no matter how many times we rewind time to before the event. The thought experiments and scenarios used are simplified for easy understandability, but they are not an over simplification.

In other words, they relate entirely to the most complex system you can fathom, at any level.

The complex system as it relates to free will is the brain or mind. Either all of the events that happen within the brain or the "mind" are causal, in which case the effects they have has only one possibility; or some acausal events can happen, in which case the outcome can be different (though as you will see, not in a desirable way, nor a freely willed way).

If the point is clear to you that a causal event can only have one possibility for its effect, please feel free to move on to the next chapter. If it's still not perfectly clear, allow me to present you with one last analogy.

Picture an object perfectly balanced on the top of a point.

Now imagine all of the possible directions that object can fall if something offsets or disrupts it. If an insect were to land on the object a little to the left of it, that may be enough to make the object fall off of the point. It would fall off of the point in the exact direction dictated by the causality of the energy imposed by the insect.

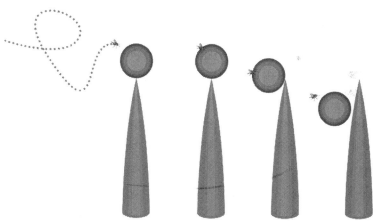

Now we rewind time to the exact moment the insect lands, and it always lands in the exact same way. Without any causal factors changing, the object would always fall in the same direction as the first run through. To suggest that the causality of the insect, when it lands in the exact same way, can allow for multiple possible effects of the direction of the object is absurd.

Suppose we could zoom in to the part of the insect that

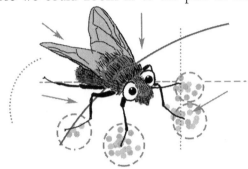

touches the object, understand the particles involved, the gravity involved, and all of the other factors.

Let's suggest that all of those factors--meaning not one missing, added, or different in any way--could have multiple possible effects. For example, the object falling could fall at point (B) OR point (C), with point (C) being a little to the right of where (B) was. The question must be asked, what's the causal factor for the object to fall to (B)? And what's the causal factor for the object to fall to (C)? If both have the same causal factor, this is logically problematic. Why (B) instead of (C), or (C) instead of (B)? If you say there's no reason for one over the other, you are automatically conceding an acausal event.

The event of the object going to point (B), if caused to go to point (B), has a cause for it going to point (B). You cannot say the cause for the object going to event (C) caused it to go to event (B) instead of (C), or vice versa. Either the event of going to (B) has a cause for it going to (B), or it doesn't. If it doesn't, but goes to (B) anyway, that would again be an acausal event.

If someone suggests that the event could have gone to (B) or (C) when we rewind time, they are bringing causeless events into the equation. Those acausal events are subject to the logical problems as well as the incompatibility addressed in later chapters on acausal events.

To conclude:

- If there isn't a cause leading to event (B) over event (C), or leading to event (C) over event (B), then going to one event over the other must happen acausally.

- If there is a cause leading to event (B) over event (C) and no acausal event, the cause cannot lead to event (C) over event (B).

- (A) cannot be both the cause that leads to event (B) and not the cause that leads to event (B) (e.g. being the cause that leads to C instead). This would make the state of (A) in opposition to itself (self-contradictory).[22]

This is the case for any concept of causality, if the concept of causality is to be coherent. For the free will debate, this is all we are required to know about the nature of causes. We are not required to know what they are exactly, when or how they happen, and so on. All we need to know is, if they do happen, they're logically restricted to only allow for one possibility per cause. And if they don't happen yet an event still arises, the event is acausal (not caused).

Dialogue

ORION: So Liberius, per how you're defining free will, you have the ability to choose more than one viable option, and that choice is up to you. In other words, if we were to go back in time to the point right before we started this discussion, you could have chosen not to have the discussion. And when I say "you" could have chosen not to, I mean that "you" wouldn't have been coerced by things beyond you to do so.

LIBERIUS: Yep. You got it.

ORION: This discussion will need to take us into the nature of causes. Can we, just for this part of the discussion, assume that all events come about causally?

LIBERIUS: Hmmm, sure, for now that's fine.

ORION: Greeeeat! In this entirely causal universe, could you have chosen not to have this discussion?

LIBERIUS: Of course.

ORION: So just to be clear, causal events led up to the mental state of you choosing to have this discussion, but those same causal events could have led up to a completely different state to not choose to have this discussion?

LIBERIUS: Yes, or different causal events.

ORION: You seem to be suggesting that a cause can lead to different possible events.

LIBERIUS: I see no reason why it couldn't. Do you think a cause can lead to different possible events?

ORION: Nope.

LIBERIUS: I think you are limiting your idea of causality.

ORION: That could be the case. So let's examine that, shall we? Let's suggest I'm wrong and that a cause can have more than one effect. How would such a cause determine which effect to go to?

LIBERIUS: I don't understand the question. The cause would either have one effect, or another effect. Maybe even more than two possibilities.

ORION: But what causes it to move to one effect over the other?

LIBERIUS: Nothing. The cause either goes to one effect or another effect.

ORION: By saying "nothing," you are automatically suggesting an acausal event. You are basically saying that there's no cause to determine which effect an event goes to.

LIBERIUS: No, I am saying that the cause takes it to the effect.

ORION: But does the cause take it to a *specific* effect. If not, what's the cause that takes it to the specific effect.

LIBERIUS: There is none.

ORION: If there is none, then it's an acausal event for it to go to one effect over another. In other words, if there's no forcing factor leading to a specific effect, an acausal event must lead it there. There's no escaping this dichotomy.

LIBERIUS: There's a forcing factor. The cause.

ORION: Does the cause force it to go to one effect over another? So if we have possible effect 1 and possible effect 2, and the effect ends up being 1, did the cause force the effect 1 to happen instead of effect 2?

(Liberius looks up in the air in thought.)

LIBERIUS: Yes.

ORION: Then it could never have gone to effect 2. Only effect 1 was viable based on the cause.

LIBERIUS: I don't see why the very same cause couldn't force it to effect 2 instead.

ORION: Again, what would force it to effect 2 instead of effect 1? If the cause is identical, what determines 2 over 1, or 1 over 2? You cannot say that an event is the cause that forces effect 2 and not effect 1, and the same event is the cause that forces effect 1 and not effect 2. To do so you've created a self contradictory cause. Something must determine one over the other. If it's a cause that determines one over the other, that cause must always determine that same one over the other. If nothing causes one over the other, yet it goes to one over the other, you are talking about an event without a cause. An acausal event.

(Liberius, noticing the flaw in his argument, becomes flustered.)

LIBERIUS: OK, I'll concede the point, however...

8

Simultaneous Causes and Effects

'Whenever someone is allowed to use two different meanings of a word that are so closely related, it makes it easy to throw such words in the mix.'

Aristotle distinguished between what he termed accidental causality (cause preceding effect) and essential causality (one event seen in two ways). For essential causality, Aristotle uses the example of a builder building a house. This single event can be analyzed into the builder building (cause) and the house being built (effect).

The idea of essential causality has been used as a way for people to contrive free will, among other things. Such contrivances usually stem from a misunderstanding, or poorly thought out conclusions of essential causality.

Let's go back to the example of a builder building and the house being built. We can picture these two things. It appears that as the builder builds, the house is being built. These don't happen one after another, but at the same time. Certainly we can't say that the builder is building without the house being built. Hence the term essential, the house being built (by the builder) is essential to the builder building (the house), and vice versa.

First, I would like to call out what this view of essential causality really entails. It entails the generalized grouping of a pile of accidental causes. It then takes that generalization and compares two inherent parts of it that happen simultaneously. So for example, it may categorize a man picking up a hammer and a nail, then swinging the hammer to hit the nail, and the nail going into a board, as "builder building." And the nail going into a board hanging on the wall of a partially built house as "house being built." All of these individual events are causes and effects, with the causes prior to the effects, and we could, of course, break them down more into the real cause and effects that we don't really see.

The essential cause of the "builder building" and the "house being built" merely zooms out of space and time to grab a section of happenings and group them all into one event. It then focuses on two parts of the zoomed out block that are essential to each other, which happen within the same block of time.

The "builder building" might happen in the block of time from time X to time Z, and the "house being built" would happen within that same timeframe. So from the perspective of viewing a block of action within a specific block of space and time, and categorizing such block as a single event, certainly we cannot separate out the categorizations.

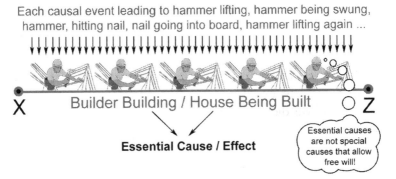

Accidental Causes and Effects
Each causal event leading to hammer lifting, hammer being swung, hammer, hitting nail, nail going into board, hammer lifting again …

X — Builder Building / House Being Built — O Z

Essential Cause / Effect

Essential causes are not special causes that allow free will!

So how do some people use essential causality to contrive free will? First, it allows them to disregard the type of causality most mean, even though this other usage is not the important usage for the free will debate. If they can say that the effect is simultaneous with the cause, they can conflate this with the type of causality the determinist or incompatibilist may be talking about. Whenever someone is allowed to use two different meanings of a word that are so closely related, it makes it easy to throw such words in the mix. Especially when the person at the other end might not be familiar with the words "essential" and "accidental" as applied to causality.

Another way it's contrived is by suggesting that decisions can be "essentially caused" in the sense that a decision being made and the person deciding are essential to each other. It's a way for them to frame that into what seems at first like an act of volition that is it's very own internal cause. But this is a mistake. Even if we accept the idea of essential causality, that does not mean that something didn't cause the builder building house/house being built in the first place. It does not allow us to frame the essential cause into something outside of what caused it.

In my opinion, I don't think that an essential cause should even be labeled a "cause." Give it some other name to avoid confusion and conflation. If simultaneous, the only reason we can say that "the builder building" is the cause and the "house being built" is the effect is if we move into the actual causes and effects that show the progression: the accidental causes. Otherwise, if both were the cause and effect of each other, we'd have to say "the house being built" is a cause of "the builder building." Of course that's counterintuitive. Why? Because we know the progression of those "accidental" causes. We know that the builder lifting up a hammer precedes the nail going in. If we didn't, how could we possibly consider one a cause of the other, or consider that such a simultaneous event contains both a cause and effect within it? Rather it's simply all the same event (builder building house/house being built) summed up within a given block of time.

Yet there are some people with a wee bit o' knowledge of these philosophical terms who will use them to their advantage as soon as someone talks about causality as it applies to free will. Don't let them. It's not pertinent and is just used to deflect the subject matter. Not only is essential causality not compatible with free will, when someone uses it for such a topic, they're playing a shell game. They are trying to suggest to you that this type of causality plays a role in the usage of the term "cause" for the debate, when it doesn't.

As a side note, I'm also not a fan of the words "accidental" and "essential" to describe these different types of causes. Today, such words are way too ambiguous and easy to confuse with the common usage of such words. A common usage might, for example, imply that a cause (such as an essential cause) would have a purpose (not done on accident). Or that a cause that precedes its effect does so in some non-forced way (happens by accident). This isn't what's meant by these words. The effect of an accidental cause would be just as "essential" to it if we used the common usage of the word essential.

Confusing words just muck up the water. I cannot stress enough the importance of clarity. It's unfortunate that I have to use such words to even address them as something that shouldn't be used for the free will topic. If I didn't have more than one person try such a shell game with me, I would have left this brief chapter out entirely. I would never have thought it important enough to address. But due to my own causality, I decided it important to note these differences in the word "cause" to avoid any ambiguity and to prevent any detractors from going there.

9

The Incompatibility of
Causality with Free Will

*'In an entirely causal universe, what a person thinks is
dictated before that person even exists. The decisions
we make come about through complex gears.'*

People who believe free will to be compatible in an entirely
causal (deterministic) universe are called compatibilists.
This chapter is about why such a view is flawed. In particular,
when defining free will as I have, and when addressing the
important issues attached to the free will debate.

Free will has two words: free & will. Causality is not incompatible with the "will" portion of the word. In fact, causality is a requirement of something being "willed." This shall be
addressed in the "Incompatibility of acausality with free will"
section of the book. For causality, the focus is on how "freedom" can't be offered in a causal system, no matter how
complex the causal system becomes.

Chapter 7 stressed that a cause cannot have more than one
possible outcome for its effect. So what does this mean for free
will? It means that, if everything happens causally, every
thought a person thinks is the output of antecedent events
(events that lead to the outcome). It also means that each of
those antecedent events is an output of antecedent events. This
means that each event that happens is dictated by the preceding
circumstance. What you think at any given point is a structure

built on preceding events that could not have happened differently. If you think "Should I run, walk, or sit?" and then you decide to "run," you could not have chosen to walk or sit. "Run" was determined by all of the causal events of the past, and part of those causal events was thinking about three options (run/walk/sit). Thinking about those three options was causally dictated as well. All of the causes that caused you to think about it and then do it were causally dictated as well.

These causes stem back, and back, and back. Each cause could not have happened any other way. In an entirely causal universe, what a person thinks is dictated before that person *even exists*.[23] The decisions we make come about through complex gears.

**PERSON
EXISTING**

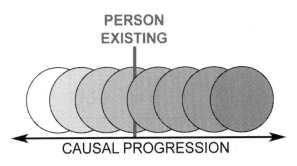

CAUSAL PROGRESSION

It's for this reason many people contrive acausal events as their free will savior. If acausal events exist, they don't have the problem of a fixed universe. What they fail to understand is that acausal events are even more of a detriment to thinking, let alone equally as incompatible to free will, than causal events. As you'll see, we'd be better off in an entirely causal universe, one where willing isn't "free."

To clarify free will's incompatibility with causal events, if various events have *caused* your decision, and if those very same events couldn't have *not caused* your decision, that decision was an output of those events. And if other events *caused* those events that caused your decision, and those other events couldn't have *not caused* those events that caused your decision, those events that caused your decision had to happen due to those other events. As you can see, we can regress the causal events that have led to your decision back to before you were even born, and potentially keep going back to the big bang, or perhaps events that have led to that depending on the theory proposed. The only thing that would stop such a regress would be an acausal event somewhere down the line. And that very event could never be a willed event that you would have any say in, and would simply be its own starting point of new causal interactions stemming from the acausal event.

Poorly defined freedom

Some compatibilists have a different idea of what's meant by the word "freedom." They may say that if a person's thoughts dictate the event (are the antecedent causes of the event), it's free, but if the person's thought does not control the event, it's not free.

For example, they may say that if a person is stuck in a rainstorm and there's no shelter available, they are not free to decide to stay dry. But if someone is under shelter during a rainstorm, they are free to step out from the shelter and get wet (or not) because they can make the conscious decision to do so.

This way of defining freedom bypasses the causes of the conscious decision being made, but it leads to some big problems.

Take the thought experiment of a microchip hooked up to a person's brain without them knowing. This chip is remotely controlled by a scientist who's able to control the chemicals in the brain, redirect the electrical impulses, and so on, in such a way that the scientist could control whether or not the person desires to and decides to step out in the rain. The decision happens after the scientist inputs variables into his computer that will causally lead to the decision in the person's mind.

The person would feel like they were in control of the decision to step out into the rain. The person would in fact desire to step out in the rain, even though the desire was ultimately controlled by the scientist. It was the person's brain state that dictated their decision, even though the brain state came about via an external process of a chip they had no control over.

The compatibilist who accepts this definition of freedom must also accept that the person with the microchip was just as free as a person without it. This is because instead of a microchip attached to the person controlling the output of their decisions, the causes or acausal events that extend outside of or prior to the person controls them. Even though the person makes a decision and feels they do it of their own accord, just as the person with the microchip in their brain feels they make decisions of their own accord, those decisions stem from something out of the person's control.

If the compatibilist decides to use such a definition of free will, it's important to note to them: the chances are such that most people wouldn't consider the person being controlled by the scientist as free. In other words, this is not the common free will usage. When the compatibilist defines free will in such a way, they cause confusion in the minds of those that think they have this other type of free will. The type in which they have the actual control over the path their own thoughts and actions take. The type that the compatibilist isn't talking about.

Of course I have not polled the entire populace of those believing in free will. Perhaps my intuition is incorrect on this. Perhaps most people would believe that the person with the microchip controlled by the scientist acted in accord to his or her free will. Perhaps most people would think they had free will regardless if every action was caused by what the scientist programmed ahead of time.

Perhaps my own experience of the illusion of free will has colored my perspective on what I think most people experience as free will. If I am right, however, and most people would think that the microchipped person was not acting due to free will, this is where I have the qualm with the compatibilist that holds to such a definition. Not so much that they hold that position, but rather with the confusion they cause to the people that do not. Maybe these compatibilists do it because they want others to hold on to this free will belief. Maybe they are worried about the consequences of the truth. If so, I think they are mistaken on that as well.

Compatibilists that hold this uncommon, unintuitive definition of free will also have a tendency to disregard the implications of their uncommon definition. The same implications addressed by me for what a lack of free will (defined in my way) means holds true. The point is not to quibble over definitions, but rather to understand what it means that we don't have the ability to choose between more than one viable option or action, in which that choice is up to us. Or to look at a past tense definition of free will: if we could not have, of our own accord, chosen otherwise than what we did.

If the compatibilist agrees to this, all of the important stuff follows. It matters not that they redefine the words "free will" as something consistent with reality. Such redefinition does not change the important points of this book. For example, those implying responsibility in the sense of blameworthiness or deservingness over others are still equally problematic.

Lower and Higher Order Causation

Some compatibilists suggest that higher order thoughts or desires produce a free will. They miss the point of how these "orders of thought" come about. For example, one might desire to eat a chocolate bar. This might be said to be a first order desire, based on an urge for such chocolaty goodness. But the person's second order thought might come in that says "I will not eat the chocolate bar even though I want to, due to the health concerns with eating it." They then will not eat the chocolate bar they initially desired. This would be considered a higher order desire by some compatibilists. These compatibilists suggest that, somehow, such second or higher order desires are "free will." That the first order desire is willed but not free, but the ability to go against that first order desire is freely willed.

This position misunderstands why the hard determinist or incompatibilist hold the position against free will they do. It compares desires that are stronger (e.g. addiction) or rudimentary (e.g. the taste of sugar – yummy) with those thoughts that are able to overcome these other desires. They fail to address the point that the thoughts that allowed them to overcome those desires *had to happen* due to the causal events that preceded them.

Indeed, it feels as if thoughts that are driven via addiction, basic needs or wants, etc. are less free than those that override them, but this is not the case. The second order, or third order, or highest order thought or desire had to come about via events beyond the person. It matters not how much layering and nesting we do; we cannot get around this fact. If one eats the chocolate based on the factor that they could not control themselves even though they know it's bad for them, that had to happen based on the preceding causality. If one chooses to not eat the chocolate even though they truly desire such yummy goodness, that had to happen based on the preceding causality. If time was rewound to before they avoided eating the chocolate, they could not change their mind and eat it the next time around. Unless, of course, an acausal event changes their mind, in which case that was beyond any control from them.

If we were to go back to the person with the microchip in their brain, and that person wanted chocolate, but the scientists programmed the chip so that the person recognized their health or weight concerns, that recognition that overrode the decision to eat chocolate for the immediate pleasure is not freely willed.

Neurologically, we might be able to compare the difference between orders of thoughts and desires and conclude many things about them in regards to the way a person thinks, or the parts of the brain involved for each. We cannot conclude, however, that there's any order that grants free will. It's just a way of avoiding the argument by playing to the feelings of freedom compared to the feelings of restriction for different events. These feelings have nothing to do with the *reality* of the situation; they have everything to do with the illusion. It's simply an illusion that overriding a first order desire with a second order desire is freer than not overriding the first order desire. Such overriding could be a *better* option depending on the scenario, but better does not equal freer, and freer isn't a requirement of better.

Word Contrivances

Some compatibilists like to play with words. One famous philosopher, for example, plays with the word "inevitable." He says that it's wrong to suggest that, in an entirely causal universe, everything's inevitable. He takes away the "in" from the word "inevitable," and shows how specific things are "evitable." Evitable, by definition, means the possibility to avoid or be averted. For example, avoiding a brick from hitting you in the face is "evitable." So yes, if you duck the brick, it was obviously possible to avoid the brick, and hence, evitable. But there's a problem in how he's using these words.

When someone like me makes the claim that if the universe is entirely causal, the future is inevitable, we mean so in the sense that it is preset to reach a certain state based on the causality that precedes it. It is, in a causal universe, inevitable that you will avoid the brick. So, though the brick was avoided, and hence was evitable because it could be avoided, the actual *state* of avoiding the brick was inevitable. You had to avoid the brick. The evitability was inevitable, or in other words, the avoided was unavoidable.[24] Even though this person uses the word evitable correctly, it does not contradict how the hard determinist or hard incompatibilist uses the word.

And supposing you decide to let the brick hit you. For example, you decide that you can collect disability if the brick hits you, so you let it smack into your face. The causality would have led up to that and the brick would have been unavoidable. In other words, it's not evitable as the brick must hit you. In that instance, it's the unavoided that would be inevitable.

This philosopher does, however, say that the future is inevitable. Regardless if a cause leads to it or not, the future is the future, and hence inevitable, he claims. But this isn't what's meant when a determinist says that the future is inevitable due to causality. It's much more than this. It means that a specific state of the universe is inevitable *prior* to it happening and that it's impossible to avoid reaching the state dictated by the causes. The causes cannot be different. It doesn't mean that *any* future is inevitable simply because the future must happen; it means that one *specific* future dictated by the past is inevitable. There are important distinctions between these two inevitabilities that this philosopher tries to blur.

This seems obvious to the person stating that a deterministic universe means an inevitable future. It appears that this is not so obvious to some. That's okay. To clear up the confusion:

If the universe is deterministic (entirely causal), there's only one specific state that the universe can take on in the future, which is set by causes before the state happens, and hence that state is unavoidable. It's inevitable.

Hopefully this helps with any confusion these murky words cause.

Agent Causation vs. Event Causation

Some of those that subscribe to a certain (Objectivist) philosophy disregard event driven causation altogether. Or at least they *think* they do. What they really do is select specific events and call them entities and actions. So they say that causes are a relationship between an entity (or agent) and its actions, not between one event and another. An explosion might be the action, and the bomb the entity. They disregard the bomb as an event that happens due to previous causality (the bomb maker, the materials available, etc), and the explosion as an event that happens due to the specific causal configuration of that bomb (a configuration that came about via causal factors external from the bomb).

Or in the case of human free will, they disregard the person as an event that happens. They say that a human acts in accord to that human's nature, and suggest such nature comes entirely from the human. They ignore someone trying to tell them that the human, including the nature of that human, is an event. It had to come about. A human does not always exist, he or she is born. An event that leads to the so called "nature" of that entity. Not to mention every other genetic and environmental event that leads to such nature. The nature of an agent is an event that comes from her genetics, and her interactions with the environment, and the agent herself is an event that comes from other events that takes place prior to the agent. And if the nature of an agent didn't come from other events, it would be the product of acausal events. You cannot bypass this dichotomy by disregarding that agents come about.

It's just more play on words to inject free will. A way to regard some events and not others. Such play on words does fool some. This is why I find it important to mention them, if only briefly.

Causation and the Definition of Free Will

Let's briefly go back to our definition of free will, shall we:

63

The ability to choose between more than one viable option or action, in which the choice was "up to the chooser."

So which parts of this definition are incompatible with causality? Well, in an entirely casual universe there simply cannot be more than one viable option or action. Only one is ever "viable," and that is the one dictated by the causal chains of events that stem from before a person is even born. But what if the universe isn't "entirely causal," you might say? That's up next, but let me give you a hint. It's not gonna help!

Dialogue

LIBERIUS: ...even if a cause can only have one possible effect, that doesn't mean free will couldn't come about in an entirely causal universe.

ORION: Am I correct in saying, in a universe where every event has a cause, that it would include the thoughts a person thinks?

LIBERIUS: Of course. A thought is an event, after all.

ORION: So if every event has a cause, wouldn't the cause of such an event be an event as well?

LIBERIUS: Yep.

ORION: So every cause itself is an event, which means every cause has a cause for it. Sort of like dominoes. One domino causes the next to fall, and the next causes the next to fall. No matter how complex we make the domino setup, one causing three to fall creating three different falling lines of dominoes, all events are caused by preceding events. Even the first domino has the finger that pushes it. And the finger that pushes it has a number of complex events leading back to the thought the person has to push the domino over. And that very thought has events that lead back ultimately to events

64

outside of the person, some possibly happening moments before the thought, and others happening even before the person's born.

LIBERIUS: Sounds about right.

ORION: Great, we agree. Now to address what this all means for free will. Suppose that I make a choice to draw a circle. Before I drew the circle, I had been wavering back and forth in my head to either draw a circle, a square, or a triangle, but I ultimately decided on a circle.

LIBERIUS: I would have drawn something less boring, perhaps an octagon. But fine. You've drawn a circle.

ORION: Great. So knowing what we know about causes, could I have drawn a triangle?

LIBERIUS: Causes could have led you to draw a triangle instead of a circle.

ORION: Could they have? The cause had led to the effect of my drawing a circle. So that specific cause could only go to circle, not triangle. Remember that a cause can only lead to a specific effect.

LIBERIUS: True, but the cause that led to the circle could have been different. It could have been a cause leading to a triangle.

ORION: That cause is also an effect of other causes, correct?

LIBERIUS: Correct.

ORION: Then just like the effect of me drawing the circle, the cause that led to me draw the circle is an effect of another cause. And that cause is an effect of another cause. And so on. This means that drawing the circle was dictated by causes that extend as far back as we can go into the past. In a completely causal universe, I couldn't have chosen to draw the triangle. In fact, me comparing a triangle and square with a circle and wavering between those options were all part of the causality that led me to drawing a circle.

LIBERIUS: Maybe free will was just your choice to draw a circle. You wanted to draw a circle over those other option, so you did.

ORION: Indeed, but why is that free?

LIBERIUS: Because you were free to choose the option you wanted, even though you could not have chosen those other options.

ORION: Was I free to choose my want or desire?

LIBERIUS: Possibly. Maybe you, of your own volition, previously willed yourself to desire circles.

ORION: Maybe, but such "volition" would not be free. What caused me to will such "desire" if not another event? It may be my desire for a circle that pushed me to it, but causes pushed me to such desire in the first place. Can you not see that if we keep back-tracking causes, it always leads to causes that are not internal to ourselves? Some of those are external causes that we perceive; others are causes before we even existed. The event of me desiring to draw a circle was forced from events outside of and even prior to me. We can use words like "will" and "volition," but the concern here is "free will" or "free volition." Our will or volition is constrained to one possibility, and we are not the authors initiating such constrains.

LIBERIUS: OK, but maybe one or more of those events that lead to a circle was not caused. This would lead to multiple possibilities.

ORION: Now you are getting into acausal events. We were only talking about an entirely causal universe. Now that you understand why causality is incompatible, we can start the discussion about acausality, and why it's just as incompatible. In fact, acausal events would be even more detrimental to a person's thought than causal events.

10

Acausality Basics and Logical Implications

'Since an acausal event can in no way be causally connected to an existing thing, it must be something that comes into existence from nothing else in existence. Once in existence, only then could it have an effect on things currently existing.'

An acausal event is one that occurs without a prior cause forcing the occurrence. What's the logical implication of such an event if it *could* happen?[25] What does it mean for something if it's not derived from something else? What does it mean regarding the time an acausal event occurs and the location it occurs at? What's with all these questions?

Hopefully I can answer some of them for you.

Time and Location of Acausal Events

Understanding the time an acausal event could happen and the location it could happen at is important to understand why such events would be so problematic for any reliable or consistent occurrence. Such events would not be bound by time or location. They would happen at any point in time and place in space.

Let's call the *location* of the event L and the *event* E. Let's also call the *object* that the event occurs in O and the *time* that it occurs T. As an example, we will say that the object is an atom,

68

the event's the start of the radioactive decay[26] of the atom (its nucleus), and the location is inside of the atom.

L = Inside of O
O = Atom
E = Start of Decay
T = Time of Start of Decay

Now let's examine the difference between E (event) happening via a cause as compared to it happening acausally. Inside of O we go.

We will begin with E happening causally and why L (location) and T (time) make more sense for it. In this scenario another event, either local or nonlocal (we will address non-locality later), influences the nucleus of the atom in a way that decay begins. The causal event forces E to a specific L and T. The L being inside of the atom, and the T being a specific time when such atom actually exists.

Now we move on to E happening acausally. What does that mean in regards to L and T? A specific L or T cannot be directed for an acausal event. There's nothing that can funnel such specifics.

To visualize this, think of the largest blank space you can fathom and then think of the tiniest dot existing somewhere in that blank space at some point in time. Now imagine rewinding time and hitting replay. Each time the dot would show up at a different location at a different time, or it would not show up at all. When it does show up, that's an acausal event. It would have no controlling factor regarding when it would happen in time or what location it would end up (it has no temporal or spatial determinacy). There would be no variable forcing the specifics for the acausal event.

In other words: Nothing can be a cause of E, if E is acausal, and that includes O (the object cannot be the cause for an event that happens to, or inside of, an object).

This means that an acausal event could happen between your nose and Uranus at any time, a hundred could happen in

69

your next door neighbor's eye at any time, a billion could happen in an insect at any time, or not one could ever happen.

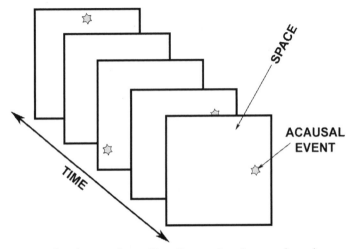

SPACE

TIME

ACAUSAL EVENT

There's no forcing or funneling factor for time or location until the acausal event's out and susceptible to the causality of other events. We might even be able to say that one acausal event could cancel out another acausal event if the events are opposing and happen in the very same time and location.

So let's go back to the (start of) decay of an atom. Since we can't predict the point when the nucleus of an atom will begin to decay, some suggest that there isn't a causal mechanism for the start. If this were so, what would the implication be for the atom? If we know the atom will decay at some point, but we do not know when that point will occur, that doesn't mean it's an acausal event. It could be, but the implication that a decaying atom happens acausally also means that we cannot predict the chance that it will begin decay within a certain time period, unless that time period's as general as "It will begin to decay at some point or never." As soon as we suggest that we can predict a probability that it will happen during time period X through Z, or even at all, we imply causality. We cannot gather that information for an acausal event.

More importantly, since nothing forces the acausal event to a specific time or location, O (the object) is not a forcing factor for the event. In our atom example, the size of the atom cannot be a factor, and neither can the state it's in. For the acausal event, it matters not that one atom's state is different than another. If the acausal event is the start of decay, the state of the atom itself (or it's nucleus) would not be a factor for when such event happens.

It may be that the acausal event is really something else other than the start of radioactive decay, and that something else *causes* the atom's decay. If that's the case, the state of the atom at a given time could matter in regards to whether it starts to decay. It may be that the state it's in prevents the acausal event from triggering the decay, or makes it easier to trigger. It must be noted that the acausal event in this scenario is not the atom starting to decay, but rather something entirely separate that triggers the decay.

This makes more sense. Since an acausal event can in no way be causally connected to an existing thing, it must be something that comes into existence from nothing else in existence. Once in existence, only then could it have an effect on things currently existing.

Usually when we imagine an acausal event happening, we think of the smaller quantum particles. We don't picture a rock appearing from nowhere and landing on your head. We must, however, picture an event happening for no rhyme or reason. Some have, however, attempted to conclude that acausality is possible on the larger scale as well. Take Norton's Dome for an example.

Norton's Dome

There have been attempts to show how acausal events are in theory possible at the larger scale. Norton's dome is a good example of this. It is a hypothetical dome that's perfectly symmetrical and frictionless. It was envisioned by John D. Norton. It has a specific curve and a ball is sitting on top, perfectly positioned so that it doesn't roll down. The mathematical formula shows how the ball could just start rolling down at any given point without a cause. Some have debated that the formula fails certain conditions or have other criticisms against the mathematics itself.

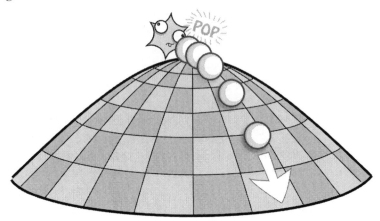

Personally, I don't care if the mathematics are correct or not. Instead, I'm going assume that the mathematics of Norton's Dome are correct, even though there may be flaws. In other words, I am not arguing against Norton's equations. I'm a philosopher, not a mathematician. Instead I am going to explain the implications if true. Confusions arise by examples such as Norton's dome, so we need to call out certain misunderstandings of what an acausal event is and isn't.

Let's assume this dome is possible, and even though it's impossible to physically recreate the perfect variables in it, let's assume that somehow we did, and at some point, without a cause, the ball started rolling down the dome.

What would this mean?

One thing it means is that the ball did not cause the ball to start rolling. It also means that the shape of the dome did not cause it to start rolling. It also means that the frictionless quality of the dome or ball did not cause it to start rolling. Why? Because the entire point is that the ball starts rolling without a cause, and these are all causes. It makes no sense to infer an acausal event using any variable. If something happens due to a variable, it happens causally.

So even though the very basis for Norton's dome is the variables of the setup and the mathematics that surround such variables, let's still assume that yes, this event that happens would be entirely acausal. What does it mean that the ball, the dome, and the setup are not causes for the ball rolling down the dome? It means that the acausal event happens *regardless* of those other things.

This implies that those things are not needed for the acausal event to happen. Whatever this acausal event is, it occurs regardless of the fact that these other factors are in place. The same acausal event that allowed the ball to roll down the dome would exist if the ball or dome was not there.

But, you may say, that just doesn't make sense. The ball rolling was the acausal event. It could not have occurred without the ball. This would appear to be a problem, and it's what comes about when attempting to derive an acausal event happening to an existing item in which that item cannot be a forcing factor for the event happening. The rolling ball must, instead, be an effect of the actual acausal event, because any qualities of *domeness* or *ballness* or *environment* cannot be a cause of an acausal event. The acausal event cannot be the ball rolling down the dome. The acausal event must happen regardless of the already existing ball and dome, and then *cause* the ball to roll down the dome.

Likewise, and here's the kicker, an acausal event would happen regardless of any qualities of a person, brain, mind, or thought. This will be addressed more in the chapter about the incompatibility of acausality with free will.

Conservation of energy

When addressing the physics of our universe, some would suggest that a truly acausal event would go against the first law of thermodynamics, which mandates the law of conservation of energy. The law of conservation of energy is a law in physics that states energy in a closed system remains constant over time. So if the universe is a closed system and contains X amount of energy, a million years from now the universe would contain X amount as well, since energy cannot be created nor destroyed, only changed in form.

Within the confines of physics, an event is one where energy is used. To have an effect on energy or matter, it takes energy. An acausal event that, once out and about, has the ability to cause other events must have energy to do so. If it does have energy, the question remains where such energy has come from. It would seem to need to create new energy instead of use existing energy that's already in the universe. After all, an acausal event can in no way be an effect. How can it possibly be derived from existing energy? It can't.

If this is the case, such events appear to go against the law of conservation of energy, if in fact new energy is brought in and old energy does not leave to balance out the system. If there's a way to work around this conundrum, it certainly isn't clear.

Word confusion: "Random"

Why, you might ask, did I not use the word "random" instead of acausal? The answer has to do with how people use the word "random." Most don't use it in the sense of a *truly* random event, but rather as an event that *appears* random. The rolling of a six sided die, for example, may appear random to a person that rolls it. It may seem that it landing on a 2 or a 6 is "random." And from our perspective, it is. This, however, leads to some confusion. The ambiguity of such a word is the very reason for not using the word in this debate.

The die, landing on a 6, may seem like a 1 in 6 probability (or 16.66667% chance of landing on a 6), but in actuality--if we don't inject in acausal events--it's a 1 in 1 probability (or 100% chance). The die landing on a 6 is entirely dictated by the die's initial position, how the die is thrown, the make-up of the die itself, the gravity, the surface it lands on, and so on. If we factor all of these in, we'd realize that there's no randomness to it. Only a perception of randomness.

Even computational random number generators are not truly random, and it's arguable if others random number generators such as those built around quantum mechanics (which we'll be delving deeper into) are. If they are, it's due to acausal events in the system. Hence an important distinction needs to be made between the word "random" as used by many, and the word acausal. There's nothing ambiguous about the word "acausal." It simply means the event does not have a cause. A die landing on a 6 showing was caused to do so, regardless if we can know what those causes were. Some may call that "random," but others would not.

Watch for people that use the word "random" in a debate or conversation. Make sure a clear understanding of what's meant by it is obtained, or rather, suggest the word acausal (or non-causal if you prefer) instead. Acausal is the word of importance for this topic and it's impossible to get it confused with complex causes in chaotic systems that we can't know all of the variables for.

Dialogue

ORION: How would an acausal event, meaning an event without a cause, come about?

LIBERIUS: I find that question strange. Since an acausal event would not have a cause, the question of "how" doesn't make much sense. To answer a how or why question, I think it assumes a causal element as the reason for the event. There can be no reason for an acausal event.

ORION: That's precisely why I ask and I will concede that point. So if we cannot ask how or why questions because there can be no possible answer to those, why don't we try for *what, where, and when* to see if we can answer any of those. Let's start with *what*. What is an acausal event?

LIBERIUS: It's an event, any event, which occurs without a cause.

ORION: Got it. So to give an example of this, imagine a perfectly spherical marble floating in a region of space that has no gravitational pull in any direction. The marble's perfectly still for thousands of years. This theoretical marble never changes in structure. In other words, the marble doesn't deteriorate atomically in any way. The region is also unchangeable, meaning there's still no gravitational pull, and nothing around that could cause an effect on the marble in any way from its current state. Now imagine the marble starting to move in a direction with nothing causing it to do so. Would the instant that the marble begins moving be that acausal event?

LIBERIUS: Indeed it would be.

ORION: Could this acausal event have happened ten feet away from the marble?

LIBERIUS: No, the marble is part of the event, so it's needed.

ORION: I am a little confused here. Perhaps I've lost my marbles.

(Liberius rolls his eyes.)

ORION: Hopefully you can clear up my confusion. First, an acausal event is an event without a cause, yet the acausal event can only occur to the marble. So are you saying acausal events only happen to things?

LIBERIUS: Not necessarily, but all events that do occur to things are either causal or not. In the example you provide, the marble moving is the event. For it to be a causal event, something might hit it, for example; or the marble moves without the cause of something hitting it or any other cause.

ORION: Let's compare the difference between the two, shall we? We'll say that the marble moving is causal, due to something hitting it. Let's say a small rock hits it. We know that the rock has come from some place, and it was moving in the proper direction to get to the marble. We know that the rock moving to that location occurs at a specific time as well. In other words, the rock has been (causally) funneled to hit the marble at a specific speed, location, and time; and a transfer of energy takes place to make the marble move at the specific location and time. So in essence, it's this transference of energy (the cause) that has been funneled to the marble by causal means. An acausal event can't have this funneling factor, as there is nothing, including the marble itself, to funnel it.

LIBERIUS: Obviously nothing can "funnel" an acausal event to happen at a specific time or location, because it's not caused.

ORION: Then why couldn't the acausal event have happened ten feet away from the marble?

LIBERIUS: Because there's no marble ten feet away from the marble. How can the event of the marble moving occur where there's no marble?

ORION: It cannot, I guess. But it seems to me you are saying that the marble itself causes the acausal event.

LIBERIUS: An acausal event cannot be caused, it just happens.

ORION: But it seems you are implying, at least in this example, that such can only happen to something, in this case the marble. Correct?

LIBERIUS: Correct.

ORION: Bear with me, as this boggles the mind. Since the marble obviously doesn't cause the acausal event to happen, does it make sense to say that the same event couldn't happen in a location and time in which the marble does not exist?

LIBERIUS: Sure, as long as the acausal event is happening to something else, say, a rock. Of course the acausal event would no longer be a marble moving, but in this case a rock.

ORION: This seems to suggest that the acausal event really isn't the marble moving, or the rock moving, but rather a happening that occurs which causes the marble or rock to move.

LIBERIUS: I'm not sure I understand.

ORION: To clarify, since an acausal event does not have a preceding cause to force it to happen at a specific time or location, it doesn't make sense to attribute it happening to something (such as the marble or rock), but rather it happens and since it might out of sheer luck happen inside of the marble, the marble would move as an effect of the *actual* acausal event. The marble moving itself wouldn't be the acausal event.

LIBERIUS: I see what you are saying. Since the marble or rock would have no effect on the time or location that the acausal event happens, technically, it could happen anywhere at any time, even without a marble or rock.

ORION: So you change your mind about acausal events needing to happen TO something.

LIBERIUS: I suppose I do, however, how is it an event if something doesn't happen?

ORION: I didn't say it doesn't happen. It just doesn't necessarily happen to something that already exists. What I am driving at here is the nature of an acausal event if it exists. The very nature of such an event would mean that it precedes what it happens to. In other words, it's problematic to say that a door swinging open is an acausal event. Rather, we must say an acausal event happens, and that acausal event (once existing) causes the door to open. We cannot really attribute the acausal event to the door itself. The acausal event just happened to occur at the same spot in time and location as the door, and the door opened as an effect of the acausal event that occurred before it.

LIBERIUS: But maybe the door opening is an acausal event as well. Maybe it just occurs.

ORION: I thought we just went over this. Let's say the door swinging open is an acausal event. Does the quality of doorness cause the acausal event to happen?

LIBERIUS: Of course not. Nothing causes an acausal event.

ORION: Now imagine that same space and time without the door. Imagine the door moved over ten feet. Will the door open based on that same acausal event?

LIBERIUS: It could.

ORION: So the acausal event would move along with the door? As if it's part of the door?

LIBERIUS: Well, you are suggesting that the acausal event would happen without the door. How can that be if the acausal event is the door opening and there's no door?

ORION: I'm saying that there's nothing about the door that would force the acausal event to happen, since obviously, an acausal event cannot be caused. In other words, the door cannot cause an acausal event. An acausal event can happen, which afterward has an effect on the door, but without a causal factor that same acausal event can happen ten feet away from the door.

LIBERIUS: That's absurd.

ORION: I hear ya, however, that's the nature of acausal events, if they exist. Without a cause, there's no determining factor for the time or location of such events. That includes the already existing something that the event may appear to happen to or reside in.

LIBERIUS: Okay, I can go with that.

ORION: Great, and one last thing. This also means that if the acausal event is able to interact with something in the physical universe, it must carry with it its own "energy." In other words, the event would bring new energy into the Universe.

LIBERIUS: Maybe it just uses the existing energy in the Universe.

ORION: That runs into the very same problem. Existing energy cannot cause an acausal event. The acausal event must happen regardless of the existing energy, and only once popped into existence, have an effect on such energy. And to do that, whatever popped into existence needs to have a way to interact with already existing energy. It needs to have energy itself.

LIBERIUS: That seems to go against the conservation of energy.

(Orion shrugs.)

11

The Incompatibility of
Acausality with Free Will

'Acausality not only doesn't grant free will, it would likely be a detriment to the creature that has acausal events happening in their brain or mind. Luckily, most brains or minds seem to follow causal means.'

Some believers in free will suggest that acausal events exist, and that such events allow for free will. After all, if acausal events happen, the future isn't set. An acausal event can pop in at any point and change the path the causality had originally dictated. (A) plus the acausal event can lead to (B) or (A) can lead to (C) instead (without the acausal event, or with a different acausal event). It does not have to lead to the one that the preceding causality leads to.

So you can make choices between more than one viable option, in which the choice was "up to you," right? Wrong. This concludes free will based off the assumption that causal determinism, which is incompatible with free will, isn't true, rather than its own merits of being able to allow free will. Time to go over those acausal merits.

Acausality has been previously defined as an event without a cause. Though it's perfectly reasonable to have some serious

NO
CAUSE...

doubts that an acausal event could actually happen, for this assessment we'll assume it can and does happen.

So why don't acausal events help with granting free will? To put the answer simply, it's because those events don't have a cause, and any event that is said to be willed must be caused by a "willer." Since those events just happen, and they do not arise from anything that's "you," those events can never be willed events. To help with this, let's put acausal events into the context of thought. We'll start out with a completely deterministic thought in which strings of causal events create the decision to say "hi" instead of "hello." The output is thinking and saying "hi," but the output is entirely determined by the causality that precedes it.

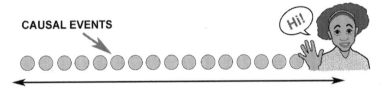

Let's throw some acausal events into the mix.

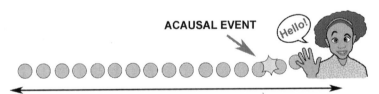

Here we have a mix of causal events as well as acausal events. The causal events right before the "hi" or "hello" can be said to come from the brain or the "mind." These can be said to be "willed" because the willer is the being that possesses the brain or mind in which the output comes about. So if all of the events that go from the mind to the vocal output of "hi" are caused, that output was willed by that mind. If some of the events that go from the mind to the vocal output are not caused, these events are acausal. Remember, acausal events cannot be caused *by* something. They may, in the end, push the vocal output to a different direction ("hello" for example), but no control was given for that push in that new and different direction, as those acausal events cannot come from the willer (the person trying to control the output). The person is a slave to those acausal events, just as they are a slave to any antecedent causes.

It can be imagined that the more acausal events that would happen in a mind in which they have an effect on, the more nonsense the person would think. Imagine a brain with only acausal events sparking neurons. You would have a brain that couldn't communicate a single word or idea. Indeed, the brain wouldn't even allow the person to be able to walk. Even involuntary actions like breathing could not happen if the brain was full of acausal events. Acausality not only doesn't grant free will, it would likely be a detriment to the creature that has acausal events happening to their brain or mind. Luckily, most brains or minds seem to follow causal means.

Imagine, if you will, a computer with a monitor and keyboard. As you type in letters, they show up on the display. The computer translates the letter you type with accuracy and you begin to write a story:

Once upon a time there was this person who thought that events without a cause could grant free will. He bended logic to the point that he was able to fool himself and others into believing that this was possible.

Now imagine, as you continue typing, acausal events kept popping into the computer, forcing random letters in.

At that poiknt a fl<urry of acausdal eBvents wenddddt into his brvain that changed the strupture of hisZ brain so mqch that he no lolger beli9eved that acausal eveSnts wo&uld grant bhim fr3e will.

You can see the problem here. The causal structure of the computer gave the computer consistency. As soon as we incorporate in acausal events, all consistency is thrown out the window. The computer no longer has a mechanism for controlling the output. In a person, the mind would no longer have a mechanism for controlling the output.

Of course, we can always fathom a possible setup in which an acausal event might be benign to a decision. If, for example, an acausal event would happen to lead to the same result as if it didn't exist. We could imagine, for example, a case where either button A or button B is available, and the button that happens to become available is dictated acausally; an acausal event pushes one particular button to be available over the other. If both of those buttons do the very same task when pressed, we can say that the particular acausal event that gave us either button A or button B was fairly benign to the task getting done by pressing the button. Likewise, if such types of "buttons" were available within our minds, they would be benign as well. That does not mean, however, that such acausal button availability can help grant free will, just that it is possible that an acausal event isn't *always* a detriment.

We could even fathom an instance where it could land on a helpful state. For example, if button A did something negative and button B did something positive, the acausal event that might make B available would be a positive acausal event. The problem here, however, is the acausal event that would give us A would be negative, and the "willer" would have no say in which button was available. If one of the buttons was indeed better than the other, it is always better that the willer has some say in the decision of which is available, in which case causality leading to the availability is usually better.

Not to mention the likelihood of acausal events (that have effects on our decisions) being benign are about as likely as them making up a readable sentence in a computer.

Those that suggest the brain or mind may have quantum indeterminacy (acausal events at the quantum scale) need to contend with this. Either the larger scale parts of the brain or mind are not affected by these acausal events, in which case causality of such larger scale overrides any acausal events, or the setup in which acausal events enter make them benign to the decision, or the events do affect those larger portions, in which case they would only serve to mix the brain or mind up. More importantly, such events, no matter which of these directions are postulated, would never be willed events.

Time and location matters for willing

In the previous chapter we discussed the nature of acausal events if they happen. We discussed that there is nothing that can push an acausal event to a specific time and location.

A thought and a person's action based on such thought occurs within a very specific timeframe and location that the person resides. Any acausal event that happens within a person could have happened in that very same location if no person was around. The only difference is it wouldn't, after it came into existence, have an effect on a person.

This shows that there's a huge disconnect between such events and the person or mind that they may happen to pop into. Such a disconnect cannot be rationally accounted for as being a part of or helping any willed process.

Acausal events are always a starting point.

Another way to think about acausal events is to think of them as starting points for new causal chains of events. An acausal event is *always* a starting point. It's never a connection to an existing line of events.

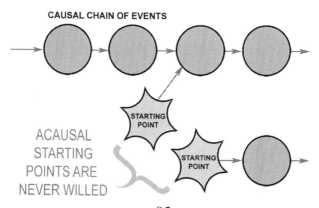

CAUSAL CHAIN OF EVENTS

STARTING POINT

STARTING POINT

ACAUSAL STARTING POINTS ARE NEVER WILLED

85

This is important when understanding why they are so completely incompatible with willing. If they are a starting point and you cannot have any control over that starting point, they are events that may lead to and connect with other events, however such leading to and connecting with other events had to happen based on that starting point in which you, the willer, had absolutely no control over.

Acausal events that have an effect on the brain, mind, or thoughts, are entirely incompatible with free will.

Acausation and the Definition of Free Will

Once again, let's revisit our definition of free will:

The ability to choose between more than one viable option or action, in which the choice was "up to the chooser."

So which parts of this definition are incompatible with acausality? It's not difficult. Any acausal event that happens simply cannot be "up to the chooser." In fact, the event happening can never be something "chosen" at all. It just happens. It is, like I said, a starting point. If that starting point happens to interact with other events and push those events in a direction that they wouldn't have gone without the acausal event, such a push could never have been *up to* any person or thing in existence.

In other words, if the acausal event somehow creates another "option or action" that wouldn't have occurred without the acausal event, it cannot do so in any way that can be attributed to any chooser or choice. Due to this, not only would such acausal events be incompatible with the above definition of free will, such would *potentially* be haphazard and dangerous. If they do exist and have any interaction with our thoughts or decisions, we should be scared. Very scared!

Dialogue

LIBERIUS: Ok, ok. So you address some problems with acausal events, but that doesn't mean they cannot exist.

ORION: I agree. Those were just some problems with the idea of acausality. It only addresses the nature of them if they do exist. Maybe, as some versions of quantum interpretations suggest, they truly do happen. In fact, for argument sake, I'm willing to grant they do. What does that mean for free will?

LIBERIUS: If such events exist, some events have the possibility of multiple options. This means I could have the ability to choose one thing, and if we rewind time to replay it, choose something different the next time.

ORION: This is true. The problem, however, is that it does something even more detrimental to free will. It makes those elections of options that come about through acausal events no longer up to us. In other words, in an entirely causal universe, at least our thoughts can be willed, just not freely so. In one where acausal events happen, those acausal events cannot be willed.

LIBERIUS: Why not?

ORION: Remember when we talked about acausal events not having any forcing factors? They can come in at any time and location.

LIBERIUS: Sure.

ORION: This required nature of acausal events also means that any events that come about acausally are ones that don't come from something else. This includes us.

LIBERIUS: Maybe the acausal events that happen create a structure that gives us free will.

87

ORION: Do elaborate.

LIBERIUS: Maybe acausal events alone could not grant free will, but maybe a combination of causal events and acausal events create free will. Maybe causes collide with acausal events, and that allows for us to change our decisions.

12

A Complex Mix of Causal and Acausal Events

'There's no combination of causal and acausal events that can help the free will of an individual. The causal events will always be forced in the direction dictated by the causes, and the acausal events are always events that pop into existence which a person would have no control over.'

Some folks may try to insist that free will can be derived through a complex mix of causal and acausal events. They may suggest, for example, that the brain has quantum indeterminism within it, and that the indeterminism is of the acausal sort that interacts with thought--an assumption made even if acausal events do happen to exist--and that a complex mix of acausal events interacting with causal events has the capacity to create free will.

This chapter is about examining and debunking such claims that an interplay of causal and acausal events change the factors which these events have separately.

It doesn't take much thinking to realize that neither complexity nor having both causal and acausal elements can make a difference regarding free will. No matter what scenario one can imagine, the acausal events that occur in it cannot be willed events, and the causal events that happen cannot be free. Whether you have only a few of these events or trillions of them makes no difference in this regard. Whether you have

89

acausal events crashing into entirely causal events makes no difference.

Any acausal events that occur happen entirely *spontaneously*,[27] no matter how many causal factors interplay with them after the fact. This always keeps them separate from something that can be willed, whether you have one or a million.

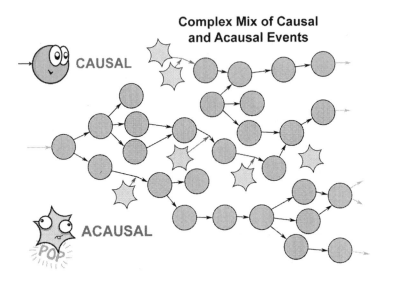

Once an acausal event occurs, only then can it interact with existing causal events in a causal way. These causal events are forced from the past events, regardless if the past event came about causally or acausally. Once an acausal event happens, the causal events that happens afterward can go no other way, based on the structures of the events (causal or acausal) that precede them.

Only after another acausal event happens can such course change again, but that changing of the course due to any acausal event is entirely separate from the willer. The person willing something has no choice where, when, or if an acausal event happens. Due to this, there's no combination of causal and acausal events that can help the free will of an individual. The causal events will always be forced in the direction dictated by the causes, and the acausal events are always events that pop into existence which a person would have no control over.

An acausal event can lead to a causal event, but a causal event can never lead to an acausal event. This means that any acausal event that occurs is always a *starting point* at that time and location. There can be no back and forth interplay between causal and acausal events. Since this is the case, any suggestion that a complex mix of causal and acausal events grant free will falls flat.

A CAUSE IS NEVER THE CAUSE OF AN ACAUSAL EVENT

Imagine a large box floating in space. The amazing part of this box is that you can throw rubber balls into it through the walls from the outside, but once the balls are in the box they bounce off the inside walls. Millions of balls were placed carefully inside of the box so they do not have momentum. Afterward a million more are thrown in at various speeds and directions. Some thrown by hand, others by machines. The rubber balls are of varying sizes and colors, but all are round and solid rubber. In accord with the laws of physics, the balls that have momentum bounce off other balls, which cause those other balls to move or change direction.

The balls also bounce off the walls of the box when they reach them, which changes their direction. None of these balls change direction or start to move without being acted on by another ball or a wall. There is minimal friction within the box.

This allows the balls to keep momentum for a long time. Once two million balls are in the box, no more are thrown in. There are so many balls, that we as observers can't know how the balls will end up once the walls absorb all of the energy to the point where the balls no longer have momentum. Once the balls putter out, where they are in the end is dictated by the balls, the energy in the balls, the walls, and the conditions inside of the box. From the initial point that all balls were in the box, these rubber balls could not have ended in any other state. If we were to replay time starting from this point, the balls would end up in the same location over and over, each time we replay time.

Now we incorporate acausal events in. Some balls inside of the box just start moving without a cause, or rather acausal events pop in that cause the balls to move. These acausal events change the end state and the balls could end up in an entirely different configuration at the end for each replay, if different acausal events happen each time. So where do these changes come from, if not the energy, balls, and walls?

The answer is: NOT the energy, balls, or walls. Not any already existing force. In other words, none of those acausal events come about through either internal or external forces. The more important part of this is the "internal" part. The "willing." To the internal part, it would make no difference if a ball acausally happens to get a ball moving, or if someone from outside of the box quickly throws a special ball (one that can leave the box once in) that enters the box, bounces off of another ball inside to get it to move, misses every other ball on its way out, and never enters again. Either way, the box, balls, and energy have no say over this rogue ball, or likewise, over any rogue acausal event that would have the same outcome as the rogue ball.

The quantity of the causal events for the balls and their interactions with the acausal events do not change this important fact. Those rogue balls are events that are outside of our control, just as causal events would either stem from events before we were born and be outside of our control, or stem from an acausal starting point and be outside of our control. Any interaction between one event that stems from outside of our control and another event that stems from outside of our control never equals to an event that doesn't stem outside of our control. The paths can always be traced back to those "outside of control" points that dictate the interaction and whatever results from such interaction.

No, complex interactions of the only two possible types of events can never (logically) reach a point of granting free will. At this point the case is closed. Free will is logically incoherent. But I won't simply stop here. I plan on addressing any possible contentions I can think of, any contrivances I have heard, and also offer further evidence, which shouldn't be needed, but why not? No, my plan is not to simply show why free will is logically incoherent, it's to stomp the idea of it to the ground like the dirty poison dipped cigarette it is.

Dialogue

ORION: A mix of causal and acausal events would run into the same problems that they both have individually. An acausal event can never be a willed event, and causal events are always due to the events that precede them.

LIBERIUS: Yes, but the event that precedes a causal event could be an acausal event.

ORION: Yep, that's true. This means, however, that the base for the causal event is on something that does not come from the willer. Something the willer has no control over.

LIBERIUS: But the causes come from a willer. So we have a combination of events, some from the willer, others not. This combo, I'd argue, can grant free will.

ORION: It's true that any acausal events that happen, once they happen, are then susceptible to causality. These acausal events, again, are never willed by us. We would have no

93

control over if, when, or where they happen. We would have no control over what they will have an effect on after they do occur. And once they do have an effect on something, we would have no control over the causal events that lead from them. No, there's no complexity that can occur with acausal events that can account for free will. The only thing they could possibly do is either be benign, or reduce or remove any willfulness that causality may allow for.

LIBERIUS: Well, let's say I choose to watch a specific movie after wavering between movie X and movie Y, each I equally want to see. It so happens that causes by themselves would lead me to decide on movie X, however, acausal events happen in combination to those causal events that happen to push me to Y.

ORION: In that case, the acausal events that pushed you to Y were not within your control. The causal events that pushed you to X were, in so far as those events can be considered part of "you," even though they ultimately stem from events outside of your control as well. Think of it this way. You wanted to watch X and Y, but imagine if an acausal even pushed you to wanting to watch Z instead. Up until that acausal event you didn't want to watch Z at all. How in control of that option would you be?

LIBERIUS: Yeah, but I wanted to see X or Y, not Z. We are talking about Y, which I did want to see, but that I wouldn't have without the acausal events.

ORION: Actually, "you" wanted to see Z even more than X or Y, only your "wanting" did not occur until after the acausal event that lead you to wanting it.

LIBERIUS: Well, okay, in the case of acausal events changing what I want to something I did not want in the first place, I can see that's a problem. But in the case of me wanting either X or Y, it's not.

ORION: You miss the point. Just as the acausal event that lead you to "want Z," the acausal event (or events) that lead you to "want Y over X" at that specific time was entirely out of your control. It's something that just happened without your consent, knowledge, power, or willfulness. In other words, Y was equally as dictated by something that's "not you" as Z was.

LIBERIUS: Hmm, okay... However...

13

Reductionism and Downward Causation

'Understanding that free will cannot (in any coherent way) exist is not tied to a reductionistic framework.'

I have come across people who claim that determinism or other notions that lead to the understanding that we lack free will are "reductive" or "reductionistic." They use the word "reductionist" as sort of a bad word. Sometimes they will use it as a way to name call: "You dirty stinking reductionist." Okay, maybe not, but it appears to come off that way at times.

Reductionism is a way to look at complex things by reducing them to their parts and the interactions of them. Some pose that free will can emerge as something "greater than its parts," and reductionism suggests otherwise.

They are mistaken that a reductionistic framework is required to understand that free will can't exist. Of course if you use reductionistic models, they could be helpful. Some of science has its basis on reductionism and works wonderfully. It's important to note that reductionism does not preclude emergent phenomena. The thinking that it does leads some reductionists down a path that nothing exists except a flow of the tiniest components possible. I address this more in the "Self and I" chapter coming up.

Keep in mind that most reductionistic frameworks do imply that phenomena that arise from the parts exert no cause on the parts themselves. Such an implication isn't needed, however, for deterministic or incompatibilistic thinking. In fact, I'd argue against such a reductionistic framework of consciousness, and in fact I'd argue against such a reductionistic framework of most things. A ball's smallest particles do not start at location Z (top of a hill) and end in location Y (bottom of a hill) due to each particle, but rather due to the roundness of the ball in which all of the particles comprise, and the angle of the hill, which all of the particles comprise, etc. The smaller parts make up larger "wholes" which have an effect on the outcome of those smaller parts (e.g. where they will end up and what they will do).

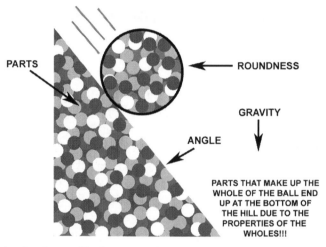

As for free will: downward causation and holistic paradigms are no different than reductionism when it comes to being incompatible with it. They equally require causal and acausal events.

Think of upward causation as the parts creating the whole and downward causation as the whole affecting the parts. In other words, the parts cause the whole (a property emerges from the parts), and that whole has an effect on the parts (changes the parts), which in turn creates an effect on the whole (changes the whole). So on and so forth.

97

Holism is the idea that the "whole" cannot be explained by its parts alone. This is not the same as the whole being "greater than its parts." When someone makes such a claim, we really need to address what they mean by "greater than." This leads to some misunderstandings. Aristotle stated, "The whole is more than the sum of its parts." However, what he meant by this is that the whole is its parts PLUS the whole. In other words, the parts make up a whole (causally), and that whole causes effects in the whole's parts (downward causation), which may or may not change the whole.

It's just another way of saying the whole can have an effect on the parts, and the parts (that the whole had an effect on) can loop back in to have an effect on the whole in the next moment. Nothing too special here.

And then there are those people that assign various levels to the process. For example, an emergent property can come about as the sum of parts, and such a property can be a part itself to another emergent property, and downward causation can interact between some or all of the emergent properties and some or all of the parts, which propagate back up to those emergent properties (wholes). Sounds confusing, huh? It's supposed to. Free will is often contrived via confusion.

So what logical difference does it make in regards to whether causality allows free will within one of these frameworks? The answer is, none what-so-ever! Whether the parts cause the whole which have an effect on the parts, or whether the parts cause the whole entirely, are just two different ways of forming a causal chain of events, the whole being an event that's factored in for some and not others. For consciousness, a "whole" might be the emergence of "thought." And such "thought" might have an effect on the smaller parts that help form other thoughts, for example, the strengthening of certain synapses in the brain.

Don't let these terms confuse you. The important part to understand is that no matter how many upward and downward interactions, and no matter how many nested parts, wholes, or levels this creates, such systems are entirely susceptible to the reasons why causality is incompatible with free will. And such a complex causal system always stems to causes outside of one's control or to acausal events that cannot be within someone's control.

It's more likely that those contriving free will due to the problems of reductionism are really against free will being a phenomenon at all. Some may claim that there are realms that are not governed by deterministic laws of "phenomenal" nature. They call this a "noumenal" realm. Such a realm, they suggest, is beyond space and time. They claim it's this realm that allows for free will. Be sure that they understand what their alternative logically entails. The alternative isn't one that allows for willing. It logically holds the same problem as acausality.

Some of these philosophers go so far as saying such "noumenal" realms have no existence for human intelligence. In other words, they are things that cannot be thought about, as our thinking is based on a world of phenomenon. This is a convenient way of saying "I dunno" therefore free will. It's a way of bypassing all logical methodologies. Suggesting free will happens within such noumenal realms is the equivalent as saying "noumenal fairies exist." Actually, it's worse than that because fairies aren't logically self-contradictory. It's more like saying "noumenal colorless pink fairies that are square circles exist."

This isn't a stance against reductionism; it's a stance against the use of logic. This book isn't about epistemology (the subject of the possibilities and best means to obtain knowledge). It takes for granted that people understand analytical logic, reason, and science as our most reliable and consistent methodologies.

As soon as someone says it's invalid to talk about logically contradictory points as not existing together, we need to throw out all knowledge. If the statements "All living dogs bark" and "Some living dogs do not bark" can both be true (at the same time, with no change in word semantics) within this noumenal realm, we have entered a realm of incoherent nonsense.

Regardless, understanding that free will can't (in any coherent way) exist isn't tied to a reductionistic framework. Free will is every bit logically incompatible with causality and acausality that employ holistic paradigms and/or downward causation. Those that contrive free will based on them thinking the opposition requires a reductionistic framework are entirely off base. I'm a proponent of both upward and downward causation. I'm not a reductionist. Suggesting that someone who concludes no free will is a reductionist is just a way to stereotype that person or the logic involved. If someone makes this claim, stop them right there. Tell them "nuh uhh…free will is equally incompatible with holism and downward causation" and explain to them why.

Dialogue

LIBERIUS: …I find your views of causality and acausality to be too reductionistic. In other words, it reduces down a cause or an acausal event, but it doesn't take into account the whole, which when complexified, can be more than the sum of its parts. Free will can be something that emerges from such a complex system.

ORION: We don't need to take a reductionistic approach here.

LIBERIUS: Aren't you breaking down objects into their parts when you suggest A causes B which causes C, and so on?

ORION: Not at all. Causality happens from small scale to large scale organization, but it also happens from large scale organization to small scale. In other words, something "bigger" that emerges from the small scale can have an effect on other small scale things. This is also called "downward causation." The important thing to remember is that the whole must be how it is based on its causal, or acausal, parts, and hence any effect a whole has on its parts must happen based on the whole that is a specific way due to its parts. Causation from parts to wholes to parts to wholes, and even those wholes being parts to other wholes, on and on with layers upon layers of parts and wholes, isn't causally different than any other cause and effect relationship.

LIBERIUS: So causality doesn't mean that the smallest particles are simply bouncing around and off of each other?

ORION: Those particles are indeed part of causality, but they are not the only thing that makes it up. Think of "color," for example. We all know that color, even though each person's experience of color can differ, is produced through specific wavelengths of light. Elementary particles, however, do not absorb or emit specific wavelengths of light. They have no color. It's only when those particles are arranged in atoms that any absorbing or emitting wavelengths of light can happen. Which means any causal happening that depends on color, for example, a darker color absorbing more light which causes the surface of an object to be a hotter temperature, or a bee being attracted to a yellow flower, does not simply happen due to the elementary particle level. It happens due to the emergence of properties that those particles create.

LIBERIUS: Then perhaps free will emerges as well?

ORION: An emergent property has to emerge based on the elements that make it up, and those properties have to cause other events based on the only way they can be. In this way, any properties that emerge are in no way free to be otherwise than what dictates them, and what they cause due to being such a property can happen in no other way either. Upward and downward causation are not a different or special concepts of causality. They are part of the very make-up of events. No such "free will" can emerge, as what emerges is never free from the constraints it emerges from. A constraint that could never (causally) be otherwise. Remember, a cause, whether upward or downward or at the same level, can never have multiple possibilities.

101

14

The Dichotomy and Existence

'If we postulate invisible fairies existing, if they exist and did not always exist, they had to come about either causally or acausally.'

The concepts of causality and acausality apply to anything in existence that did not always exist. In other words, if you postulate that something exists, that something either:

- Came about causally
- Came about acausally
- Always existed (never came about)

The third option of always existing, as you will see, cannot be an event. Events must "come about." Now mind you, events can happen *from* something that always existed. The state of something that always existed could lead to an event. Existence is a trichotomy, meaning threefold (for their possibilities). Events are a dichotomy, meaning twofold:

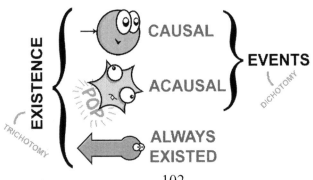

Whether something we imagine could have always existed is difficult to wrap our minds around. For example, if the universe gave birth to itself (e.g. through a black hole), does that mean it could have always existed? It's hard to fathom such an idea, specifically because we intuitively want to suggest a starting point. After all, the universe cannot give birth to itself if that universe did not exist in the first place. It appears to us that there would need to be a starting of such a cycle. Such a starting point would be an event.

So maybe, you might say, free will always existed (no starting point). Of course you would just be saying this as an attempt to escape the dichotomy. If we look further into this we will see it for what it is: nonsense. First, free will needs to be tied explicitly to thought. No one would ever say that a thoughtless thing has free will, and if they do, then we are talking about different things. That thought has to come about (either causally or acausally) or always exist. Take a guess at what happens if we suggest that the thought always existed. That thought cannot be free in any way, nor can it be willed. It always exists, and therefore cannot have a willer willing it.

Something that always exists is also not an event. The universe always existing isn't an event. The universe giving birth to itself is an event. An important distinction.

Back to the dichotomy and existence.

Now that we addressed the silliness of things that exist that never came about, we can move on to those that do come about. If something exists, and that something came about, there's no escaping the causal/acausal dichotomy. If something came about and it did not come about via a cause, it's acausal. And this means no matter what we postulate as existing. If we postulate invisible fairies existing, if they exist and did not always exist, they had to come about either causally or acausally. At least in so much as we can apply logic and reason. So whether you are applying logic to a more empirical scientific view of the universe, or not, there's no escaping this.

Logical consistency demands the acknowledgement of this dichotomy for *all* events.

Note:

Some might incorrectly criticize the use of bivalent logic for the dichotomy. That being that an event is either causal or acausal. That it's either true that event X is causal or it's false. They may cite the use of many-valued logic or fuzzy logic. They misunderstand what these are used for. They are used when the variables are not clear, are open to interpretation, or try to predict future events. They are not a replacement for bivalent logic, but rather useful tools for when we cannot use bivalent logic.

When the proposition is between X existing or X not existing, the logic required is bivalent. It makes no sense to pull in many-valued logic when there are no other possibilities to consider. We also need to be careful not to confuse a position on existence (ontology) and a position on knowledge (epistemology). Saying, for example, that there is also "maybe X existing" and "maybe X not existing" does not imply that there is a third or fourth option of "maybe-ness" that is a possibility that can exist for X. It's simply a lack of *knowing* which one of the only two possibilities does. It's all too common to conflate knowledge and existence claims. I go further into types of this problem in Chapter 17.

15
"You" and "I"

*'In reality, just as a neuron in your brain is a part that makes
up the whole of "you," everything you interact with
is a part that makes up the whole of "you".'*

The meaning of the words "you" and "I" have a tendency to blur in these discussions on free will. For this reason it's important to clarify how they are being used.

What exactly are "you"? Are you your brain? Are you your entire physical body? Are you your consciousness? Are you every component that makes up your consciousness?

Where the line seems to blur the most is that last question: *Are you every component that makes up your consciousness?* Obviously components in your physical body, including your brain, help to make up your consciousness. They are not, however, the only things. Everything you interact with is an equal partner in your conscious experience. In essence, they are all part of the mechanism that makes you who you are. There is also this play-through that consciousness appears to rely on. We can't freeze a moment in time with that moment being conscious. There's this progression of moments that make up thought. The same reason a song isn't one tone, but rather a composition of tones playing after each other. Our consciousness seems to rely not only on the very moment, but of immediate memories of its history as time flies by.[28]

If addressing the biological body, keep in mind that most[29] of the cells in your body at some point get replaced by new cells. And if we go deeper to the atomic level, most atoms that your body is composed of gets replaced yearly![30] The "you" at age twelve is indeed a different atomic "you" at age sixty, but we still say that both are or were "you." In these ways, the mechanism that is your consciousness really extends outside of the common idea of "you" that seems to be tied to the specific biological vessel.

In fact, this really goes for everything. We categorize "objects" based on a specific structure for a certain part of the universe. Really such objects are part of a continuum. Especially when we break them down to their smallest components or functions. For all practical purposes we can categorize sections of the continuum that appear distinct from other sections, even though there is this causal interconnectedness.

The earth relies on the sun, moon, forces, and so on. In essence they are part of each other, and all are part of the entire system called the universe as a whole. Yet we can still call the ball of water, land, and atmosphere that we live on "Earth." We could break the earth down into its own parts. For example, a mountain could be categorized separately yet it's a component of the earth. The earth is a part of the whole that is its solar system, which is part the whole that is its galaxy. These are categorizations used for practical purposes.

Likewise, the words "I" or "you" are categorized for practical reasons. They are categorized here as both the conscious play-through (thoughts and feelings that can be differentiated between another's) and body (in this case specific biological machinery that can be differentiated from others). I will exclude all of the external interactions which truly are a part of the mechanism that makes up your consciousness or body. Rather "your" interaction with these other things that we can categorize (other people, animals, atmosphere, etc.) separately updates the "you" I refer to in this book. Keep in mind that such distinctions are practical and therefore not arbitrary, but it's also important to see that they are lines being drawn for the purpose of their explanatory power, not because there's any other good reason to split them away. In reality, just as a neuron in your brain is a part that makes up the whole of "you," everything you interact with is a part that makes up the whole of "you." Your consciousness could not exist, or at least could not exist as it is, without all of these other parts. They all, technically, make up "you" and in this way such a "you" blends into obscurity. Into moments and "things" that intuitively we would not count as you.

It's useful, however, to create such categorical lines. It's important to distinguish you from someone else, even if you have interacted with that person and that interaction is a part of what has derived your own conscious experience. For this reason, in my usage of the word "you" or "I," I am drawing the line at our intuitive ideas of these words rather than the (actual) entire mechanism and continuum that exists to derive one's conscious experience.

Possibly, in the far future, when everyone understands that there's no free will and lose their ego, their need to distinguish a "you" will decrease and our language will change around this new way of thinking. Hard to imagine, huh?

Consciousness does exist, and the "feeling" of free will is not an illusion. The "self" is a mis-categorization, not nothingness.

A few chapters ago I addressed reductionism, and I briefly brought up that some reductionists (certainly not all) reduce things down so much that they deny consciousness existing. That consciousness itself is an illusion.

Of course the idea that consciousness itself is an illusion is self-contradictory, as to have an illusion is to have an experience, hence consciousness. Regardless of this, let's go over some points.

One argument they might have is that consciousness needs an "I" to contain it. After all, what is conscious if not "you" "your-self" or "me" "my-self"?

First, it's a mistake to think that a "self" is needed for consciousness to exist. In fact, even if feelings and thoughts just magically floated around the ether, such would correctly be defined as consciousness. The mistake here is that people think the mis-categorization of the self into a single object (e.g. in a human or a brain) does not mean that conscious experience isn't really happening. It isn't that the "self" doesn't exist in that there is "nothingness," but rather that it extends outward in a way that makes object classifications and identification for it problematic.

Think of the Internet. What specific piece of hardware creates what we call "the Internet"? Is it that special "Internet server" that exists? Is it that special cable? Or is it a large network that reaches around the globe that consists of computers, servers, software, cable lines, wireless connections, satellites, phone lines, Ethernet cables, devices, and so on? Just because we can't really pinpoint an exact "object" that is the Internet doesn't mean that the Internet doesn't exist. It's just that categorizing "the Internet" as "my computer" or "what's going on in my browser window" is an insufficient categorization.

Likewise, consciousness exists. It's the output of very specific configurations of energy playing out through time, or perhaps if you are leaning toward a more dualistic notion, something more.

The reductionist might claim that everything is just waves of energy or "small bits," and in a way, that's true. But some energy forms larger components that play into just what the "energy" does. It plays into how it flows. That means that those larger components are not illusionary, but rather they are real. As mentioned before, the fact that a ball's properties such as its roundness, and perhaps its smoothness, is one factor that allows the ball to roll. And such "rolling" moves the energy that the ball is made of in a way that such energy would not without those properties of this large scale ball. As I mentioned a few chapters ago, reducing everything down to its parts is a mistake.

The same thing with consciousness. It's quite obvious that physical bodies do things due to conscious experience and thought. Things in which the energy of the body by itself cannot account for. Things that push the energy in a direction it wouldn't take if not for the conscious experience. Like the ball's roundness, the configuration's consciousness is very much real. We might not be able to pinpoint the exact configuration, or all of the variables involved. We know that a brain, various chemicals, a complex nervous system, sensory "hardware," and the environment sensed, all seem to help. We understand that a cohesive play-out of a certain number of these "objects," with specific connections to each other, seems to be needed. Consciousness, like "rolling," appears to be something that happens through time, or moment to moment. Somewhat like each letter or word in a sentence, it strings together each moment into something coherent.

Some people suggest that if free will is an illusion, then so is consciousness. It doesn't, however, follow from free will being an illusion that consciousness is as well. In philosophical terms, this assumption is what is called a non-sequitur. Keep in mind that free will and the feeling of free will are not the same thing. The feeling of free will is *not* an illusion. It's a real feeling. The "feeling" exists as a "feeling" at the time it is experienced. Likewise consciousness, or conscious experience, exists as experience at the time it's experienced.

And if we fall back to "but who's experiencing it?" - we fall back into the incorrect assumption that a specific "who" is needed. We can, however, say that a specific biological body with a brain (that specific configuration of energy) seems to take the brunt in the downward causation of a conscious experience, as it's that configuration that we see its effect on.

So let's continue to categorize "I" or "you" as those biological containers for practical reasons. At least until we progress to a point where we no longer need to. And even if we decide not to categorize such due to its real nature, let's not pretend that means conscious experience and thought doesn't exist. Thinking so is a huge reductionistic mistake.

16

An Effect Does Not Cause
Its Cause Backward

*'An effect does not necessarily imply
the presence of a specific cause.'*

If we suggest that the universe is entirely causal (deterministic), a point of confusion that arises for some philosophers is that a number of different causes can lead to the same effect. If we had two parallel universes, except something was a little different at the start of one creating different causes, it's possible that at some point in the future, both universes will be identical in causality and lead to the same effects from that point on. Note that possibility does not equal likeliness. The point here is that different causes can lead to the same effect. This does not, however, imply that a cause can have more than one possible effect. This sounds confusing, so I'll elaborate.

Picture a deterministic universe where some play-doh (a soft, pliable modeling compound) is sitting on a table. The play-doh is in the shape of a cube. Now picture almost the same universe except the initial conditions of the universe made it so that the same amount of play-doh is shaped like a sphere. Back to the first universe, picture a person grabbing the play-doh shaped like a cube, rounding it into a sphere, and placing it back down on the table. Out of luck the sphere he makes is identical in every way to the one in the second universe scenario (every particle is aligned perfectly). In the second universe scenario, the same person sees the play-doh but since it's already a sphere he leaves it alone.

In both scenarios, a rogue machine then comes in, points its laser beam, and disintegrates the person into a pile of ashes, in which the ashes fall to the floor identically (atom for atom). A wind blows and both spheres roll off of the table and land in the exact same spot. Everything else in each universe is now aligned exactly, and the balls of play-doh are aligned. Even though there were events that had different causality, one in which someone shaped the play-doh into a ball, and another where it already was a ball, everything from that point on will be identical. There will be no difference in any future outcome if the causal structures now align and the universes are deterministic.

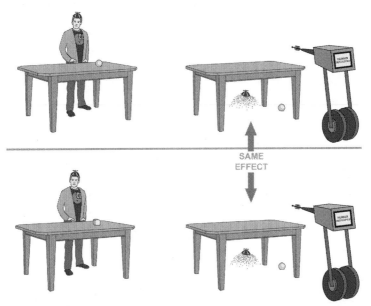

SAME
EFFECT

Now let's play time in reverse. Both balls of play-doh fly up to the table. Gravity was the same for both of them. Both roll back to the spot in which they rolled from. The wind was the same for both of them. The person's ashes materialize back to the person. The laser beam was the same for both of them. The person's hands touch the play-doh and shape it into a cube.

112

This cube shaping only happens in the first universe scenario and not the second. The causality is different at this point, yet when we play them both forward they both lead to the same output, and hence the same future output at any point afterward.

Due to this, it's possible to think of two different past situations that could lead to the same future situation.

A → X

B → X

This makes it difficult to determine the exact cause of something based only on the effect of it. If multiple causes can lead to the same effect, there could be many possibilities to consider when we only have the effect available.

This doesn't leave us blind, because most of the time we have much more than just the effect. We walk into a room with a pool table and notice the 8 ball moving toward and dropping into a pocket (the effect). We may have missed the action that occurred prior to it, but we can infer from the position of the person holding the cue stick and the position of the cue ball the most *likely* cause.

As explained previously, since a cause can only have one outcome tailored to it:

A cause necessarily implies the presence of a specific effect.

And since an effect does not cause its cause backward:

An effect does not necessarily imply the presence of a specific cause.

Confusion that arises:

Some tend to get these confused and reverse them. For example, they might suggest the possibility that the presence of an effect could necessarily imply the presence of a specific cause, but the presence of a cause does not need to imply the specific effect will occur. They misunderstand why a cause can only have one possible effect. They misunderstand why a specific

Breaking the Free Will Illusion

cause must lead to a specific effect, and why another cause could be the cause of that same effect.

$A \rightarrow X$

$B \rightarrow X$

Is not the same as

$A \rightarrow X$

$A \rightarrow Y$

In the first, A can lead to X based on the setup of A, and B can lead to the very same X given the setup of B. In the next, A can only lead to X and never Y, or Y and never X, based on the setup of A. It's important to understand the distinction between these two examples. Be wary of those that don't understand the distinction and conflate the two.

Dialogue

After much thought about Orion's claim that a cause can only have one possible effect, Liberius thinks of a brilliant idea that might throw a wrench into his argument.

LIBERIUS: You say that a cause cannot have more than one effect, because that would have to incorporate an acausal event to determine which effect it goes to.

ORION: That's correct.

LIBERIUS: How come an effect can have more than one cause then? In other words, if I push an alarm button with my hand, the same effect of the alarm going off could happen if I push it with my foot.

ORION: That's correct as well.

LIBERIUS: But that seems counterintuitive. If I were to play time backwards, the effect can lead to multiple causes.

ORION: It's only counterintuitive because you are suggesting that an effect can lead to a cause. In other words, you are

114

saying that if we play time backwards, the effect causes the cause. This is not the case at all. The cause still causes the effect, we just view that in reverse. Imagine, if you will, a long white fence. You have a brush full of black paint. You start at one end of the fence and make a long line along that fence.

Now imagine we play that time backwards. To us, it looks like the brush is painting the black line white. But if we look at the brush, it has black paint on it. We know the paint isn't coming off of the fence and on to the brush. We are just watching frames in which the previous frame was black paint going on to the fence.

LIBERIUS: Wait, you lost me.

(Orion then proceeds to let out a fart.)[31]

LIBERIUS: Uuuugh, nasty!

(Liberius plugs his nose.)

ORION: Obviously another person could have farted to create the very same olfactory sense in your nose. Both causes could have lead to that effect. This does not mean that the cause, that being me farting, could have created a different effect. Understand the difference?

(Liberius releases his breath.)

LIBERIUS: Uuuugh! What on earth did you eat today?

(Liberius re-plugs his nose.)

ORION: Going back to your button push analogy... If you pushed the button with your hand and played time backwards, you would see the reverse of your hand pushing the button. You could never see the reverse of your foot pushing the button. The cause is the hand pushing the button, not the button coming out and pushing the hand away. It matters not that your foot could have led to the button being pushed. The button being pushed is not the cause of what pushed it. A number of causes can create the same effect. This in no way suggests that a number of effects can come from the same cause.

LIBERIUS: Okay, but did you have to break wind?

ORION: Of course I did. No free will, remember?

17
Quantum Misunderstandings and Contrivances

'Not one quantum interpretation can account for a logically coherent model of free will that allows for the abilities addressed in this book.'

Quantum mechanics is the science and mathematics used to describe the atomic and subatomic levels of matter. Basically, as small as we can go. Misunderstandings occur to those with some knowledge of quantum mechanics. These misunderstandings lead people to believe that quantum mechanics can help with free will, or at least open the possibility for it.

Large books are written about quantum mechanics, with complex formulas, unintuitive results in experimentation, and various interpretations of the results and formulas. Since this is such a huge topic, the primary focus will be on the confusions that arise for philosophical understandings of causality, acausality, and the free will debate. I'll address some of the common contrivances brought up by those that have drunk the quantum Kool-Aid. Some basic knowledge of quantum mechanics would be helpful for this part, but isn't necessary. This is just a stepping off point in understanding the words and ideas people use to contrive free will, and why they are used incorrectly.

Word Confusions #1
"Determinism and Indeterminism"

The first thing that needs to be addressed is the usage of the words *determinism* and *indeterminism* as used by some in physics, particularly quantum physics. I say "some" because it appears that these terms have ambiguous meanings even within the scientific community. Most of the definitions used have similarities with the usage of these terms when talking about causal determinism and indeterminism used in the philosophical free will debate, however, there are also some important distinctions.

For some, when determinism is used in physics, it not only entails an entirely causal universe, but also a predictable one (everything has at least the possibility of "predictability"). Predictability appears to be an essential element for determinism used by *some* scientists. The same applies to indeterminism used in physics, and more specifically in quantum physics. If something's unpredictable (by any standard), it's said to be indeterministic, *regardless* if it's causal or not. In this case indeterminism means that it's impossible to 'determine' the outcome based on causality.

It becomes more a stance on knowledge[32] rather than a stance on reality or what "exists." At the quantum level, it has been shown per the Heisenberg uncertainty principle that this type of indeterminism holds true. This is because at the smaller scale both position and momentum cannot be known with precision. The more precisely one property is measured, the less precisely the other property can be measured. This appears to be a limitation of our knowledge at the quantum scale.

Causal determinism used in the free will debate, however, does not necessarily imply predictability. It only implies that every event has a cause, and due to this, future events are unchangeable as they are based on the causes that precede them. Causes derived from long chains of past events. Think of dominoes for visualization. It doesn't matter that some of those dominoes are hidden from our view.

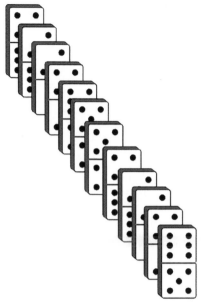

The future is "determined" by the events that cause it, re-gardless if we can actually measure the dominoes.

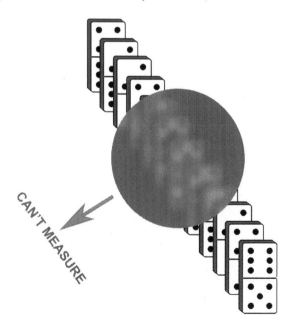

CAN'T MEASURE

Many physicists who accept the Copenhagen interpretation of quantum mechanics--more on interpretations later--suggest that we cannot know both the momentum and position of electrons because they *do not have* determinate momentums and positions simultaneously. In other words, when measuring the momentum of an electron with precision, the reason we cannot measure position with precision is because there is no cause for it. So instead of indeterminacy being due to uncertainty, it's uncertainty because of indeterminacy. This type would be true acausal indeterminacy. This type of indeterminacy contains the problems of acausality put forth in this book, and the problem with applying any acausal event to an already existing electron. It's a point of clarification needed for anyone stating there is quantum indeterminacy. Do they mean unpredictable only, or do they mean acausal and hence unpredictable? Make them take a stance on one of these, as much confusion is due to a conflation of the two.

The indeterminism that opposes the causal determinism used in the debate is one where acausal events are allowed in. If the universe has both causal as well as acausal events, it is said to be indeterministic. Acausality may imply unpredictability, but causality does not imply predictability. This sentence is important in understanding the difference between the determinism that *some* use regarding physics and the determinism used in philosophy, as well as the indeterminism used by *some* in physics compared to indeterminism used in philosophy. So much so that it bears to be repeated. For the free will debate:

Acausality may imply unpredictability, but causality does not imply predictability.

If you ever find yourself in a debate with a person that claims determinism has been disproved by quantum mechanics, the first thing you should do is question in what sense they are using the words "determinism" and "indeterminism." Chances are they are using the sense that implies an unpredictable event rather than an acausal event. Be careful of those that mix these.

120

If, for example, someone states that the uncertainty principle disproves the idea that everything is causally determined, a red flag should go off. It only disproves that everything is predictable. Whether it's causal depends on the interpretation subscribed to.

Things to watch out for:

"At the quantum level, indeterminism has been proven, therefore, determinism is false."

When talking about the causal determinism used for the free will debate, it hasn't been "disproven." Bohmian Mechanics, as just one example, is a completely deterministic interpretation of quantum mechanics. The ensemble interpretation is one example of an interpretation that is agnostic towards "determinism." And remember, for the deterministic interpretation, it does not mean "predictable."

"Since quantum mechanics *proves indeterminism, this indeterminism can supply free will."*

Even if the universe is indeterministic at base level (meaning acausal events happen), such acausal events do not help grant free will. In fact, unlike determinism, they are a more likely candidate to be a detriment to willfulness. At least with determinism, this detriment doesn't exist. Not only is indeterminism just as incompatible with free will as determinism, if such indeterminism has an effect on our thoughts, it would be damn scary.

And of course determinism (meaning entirely causal) is incompatible with free will, regardless of "unpredictability."

Word Confusion #2 – "Probabilistic"

Someone might say that a certain quantum interpretation shows that particles are probabilistic and due to this, the universe is not deterministic. What does it mean to say something is probabilistic? Can a universe be both probabilistic and causally deterministic? The short answer is yes. Probabilism does not rule out causality and may, in fact, imply it; it has more to do with what we can *know* about something rather than how something *is*. When we say something is probabilistic, we are saying that due to certain facts of reality we cannot know the complete state of that something. This goes back to the uncertainty principle and the confusions that arise with the word *indeterminism*. Probabilism in no way makes statements that an event is acausal. In fact, if we can assess a probability for an event happening that is other than "it could happen at some time or never," we probably are not talking about an acausal event. Regardless, let's still (incorrectly) pretend that we can predict a probability for an acausal event. That still leads us to only the two possibilities.

For example, we could say that an event may (probabilistically) happen within X and Y, and after the fact when it does, conclude that such event, even though we could not predict the actual event, had to come about either due to a cause or not due to a cause. The only two possible ways for the event to come about.

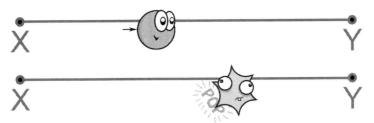

Both are incompatible with free will. But again, the fact that we can constrain a probability between an X and a Y time period means causality makes more sense, as there simply can be no such time constraint for an acausal event (nothing to cause such a constraint).

There are various quantum interpretations, or philosophies based on interpretations, that claim there are no causes at the smallest levels. For this claim, the assumption that there is no cause has to do with a non-acceptance that causes can be *nonlocal.*[33] If you are not familiar with quantum mechanics, a term such as "nonlocal" can be yet another confusing word. Basically, nonlocality means action-at-a-distance. Nonlocality is counterintuitive and has its own problems to contend with. Even so, it's still a logical possibility that in no way has been ruled out, with, perhaps, the exception of certain cases. And it certainly isn't any more counterintuitive than acausality.

Probabilism is a Position on Knowledge (Epistemology) rather than Existence (Ontology)

Notice for this topic we are talking about what can or cannot exist, and not what we can or cannot know. We say either a cause exists for an event, or a cause does not exist for an event, and then we work out what both of those imply for current existing conscious entities. In other words, if the universe was set up in a way (exists in a way) that has only causal events, or if it is set up in a way that has acausal events, what does that mean for the *existence* of "free will."

When talking about probability, however, we are addressing the subject of our knowledge. A common theme is with those that confuse or conflate these two things.

This confusion is ever so evident in the field of quantum mechanics, where there is talk about "probability waves" and "probability fields" where there seems to be this "thing" out there that spits out "probabilities."

Due to this, some people talk about "probability" as if it's something that exists, rather than a stance on our knowledge about a future state. This is false. It must be understood that "probability" is an epistemological idea, not an ontological one.

In a deterministic universe, in regards to our knowledge, a roll of a (6 sided) die would be a 1 in 6 chance for a specific result, where as in reality (or, in philosophical terms, ontologically) only a 1 in 1 chance for a specific result *exists*. Probability has to do with our ignorance of the ontological facts. It doesn't mean that there are more possibilities.

Since we cannot *know* when or where an event will happen, for example a quantum particle, but we can assess a probability based on a number of particles, some automatically assume such probability nature *exists*. Again, they confuse epistemology (our stance on knowledge) with ontology (our stance on existence).

Also, as suggested prior, probability in some way implies causes. For acausal events, the only thing we would really be able to say about them is that they may happen at some unknown point in time and in some unknown location in space, or that they may never happen at all. Remember the point about an acausal event happening to something already existing, such as a particle? It must do so with no forcing factor from the particle. In this way, the acausal event must come into existence (happen), and then effect the already existing particle. Or the particle itself needs to come into existence from nothing at all (it's very existence needs to be the acausal event).

We can observe a particle and see that its behavior appears to be acting "randomly," and then look at one thousand and, based on them, assess a probability for such behavior, but that means there must be something restricting the events within that range of probability, instead of outside of it or in the "never" category. But what could this be if an acausal event has no time or space dependant determinacy?

It's one of those things where language seems to allow for *epistemological* probabilities, but if you think about the nature of causality and acausality, *ontological* probabilities become quite incoherent. Probabilities don't "exist." They are but a tool to help us determine a range due to a lacking in our knowledge of an exactness. If causal, that exactness exists regardless of our limitations on knowledge. If acausal, determining a probability "range" of such event would be problematic if not impossible.

Double Slit Experiment

We can't talk about quantum mechanics without briefly discussing the double slit experiment. This one experiment has

124

caused a lot of controversy and many interpretations have their own way to try to resolve some of the weirdness inherent in it. Richard Feynman, a famous physicist, was known for saying "all of quantum mechanics can be gleaned from carefully thinking through the implications of this single experiment, so it's well worth discussing."[34] Much of the confusion over the "probabilistic nature of particles" has come from this very experiment.

In the initial experiment, a beam of light (light particles) is sent through two slits. If the particles were to act like particles, the beam would go through both slits, creating two light bands on the wall past the slits. This, however, is not what is seen. Rather we see an interference pattern much like a wave would make. Instead of two light bands, we get a variation of lighter and not as light bands.

To visualize this, think of a rock plopping into water and the ripples it creates. Now think of two rocks side by side instead, and the pattern of the ripples as they collide. This is the similar pattern seen on the screen.

The results of this establish what is known as wave-particle duality, which means that all particles exhibit both wave and particle like behaviors.

Another version of the experiment sends individual particles through the slits. There is a screen on the other side of the slits that shows up lighter in color when a particle hits it. The strange part is, when we shoot one particle at a time through the slits, and the pattern begins to build up, a wave pattern still forms. This has led some to interpret that the particle leaves the gun, goes through both slits and interferes with itself. A very unintuitive result indeed.

The mathematics of quantum mechanics allow us to predict the probability of where the particles will hit the screen. We cannot, however, predict what particle will end up where within the pattern. In other words, knowing where all the previous particles appeared on the screen and in what order tells us nothing about where any future particle will hit, even though the probabilities at specific points can be calculated

To some, this seems like an acausal selection event, even though the interference pattern itself is highly ordered and predictable. Some postulate variables that we don't see which (causally) dictate each particle's selection event. I'd suggest, given the ordered nature of the results and the fact that a probability can be determined, the nature of acausal events wouldn't allow for such. Remember that an acausal event wouldn't have any time or location dependency (no temporal or spatial determinacy), nor would the particle itself have any causal relation to the acausal selection event that would lead to its destination.

And if there are causal variables involved, such causes could only have the one selection effect possible based on the causal variables' states.

And of course, as already shown, neither possibility is compatible with free will. We run into the very same problems of incompatibility with causal and acausal events. The weirdness of a wave function happening even with sending particles one at a time, as well as us being unable to predict anything but probabilities, simply does nothing for the free will advocate.

But perhaps if we go to even stranger depths of this experiment we can invoke magic. Perhaps free will is mixed inside of such magically gooey quantum-ness, as the double slit experiments seem to get even weirder.

You see, as soon as we add detectors to the slits in an attempt to determine which slit they are going through, the wave pattern seems to disappear or "collapse." The particle seemingly loses its wavelike behavior, goes through one slit, and we see the pattern of two bands. The pattern we expected to see initially. This is also known as the *observer effect*[35], a term that often confuses people into thinking that the act of "them" observing the particle causes the wave collapse. This has lead to a number of pseudo-scientific claims[36] regarding the very act of us observing having an effect on reality itself, other than how such observation makes us behave.

This, however, is not the case as "we humans" don't observe anything at that scale--we can't, it's just too darn tiny--

only a measurement of it. And to measure a particle's or electron's location, the device needs to interact with it in some way. And since such a particle or electron is so very tiny, whatever we have interact with it is of comparable size. It, in essence, "causes" the collapse (or seeming collapse depending on our quantum interpretation).

So can the magic of the observer effect grant free will? Not at all. Does the fact that the wave function collapses mean anything for free will? No.

But even if we accept a little magical thinking--even if we accept that our observing the world has an effect on it in some special quantum-ooey-gooey way--it would simply be just another causal factor. There is no escaping the causal/acausal conundrum that is so incompatible with free will.

Quantum Superposition

The principle of superposition in quantum mechanics holds that something at the quantum scale can exist (partly) in all of its theoretically "possible" states simultaneously. Once measured, it gives a result of only one of those "possibilities."

The word "possible" here confuses many because it certainly suggests that any one of those states can *possibly* come about when measured. This, however, depends on whether the specific "possibility" is caused to come about (after the measurement), or if an acausal event pushes to one over another (after the measurement).

If acausal, those superpositioned states are all technically "possible." If, however, there is a cause that brings a specific possibility to the forefront, then that was the only possibility. The other options were never viable without an acausal event in the mix.

Superpositioned states cannot grant free will. The question remains how one of the states comes to the forefront of a specific reality and others don't. This, again, depends on the quantum interpretation being suggested. Either way, we run

127

into the causal/acausal dichotomy that is so incompatible with free will.

Virtual Particles

In regards to acausality, it's easy to become confused over virtual particles,[37] because they are said to "pop in and out of existence." "Popping" (or sometimes "jumping") in and out is quite metaphorical, and so is the word "particle" in "virtual particle." A virtual particle coming in and out of existence doesn't imply that it does so without a cause. It simply refers to a disturbance in a field that isn't a particle. That disturbance comes in and out of existence, much like a ripple in water comes in and out of existence, but it in no way implies that there are these magical particles popping in from nowhere, with no cause directing them, and then just disappearing.

Just as the water ripple has a cause (e.g. a stone thrown in), so do "virtual particles." The virtual particle isn't analogous to a ripple in the way a ripple forms or flows, only to the way the ripple "jumps in and out of existence" (it's there and then it's not) without implying it does so acausally.

Quantum Interpretations and Free Will

If quantum mechanics is the science and mathematics, what are quantum interpretations?

This is an important question, because quantum interpretations are not the same as quantum mechanics. The interpretations are views on the data of quantum mechanics, and what it means to our understanding of nature. They are, in essence, the *philosophy of* the data. They are not the cold, hard science. They use mathematical equations to help determine if the interpretation "works" with what we know about quantum mechanics. And there are many different competing quantum interpretations, each with their own limitations and problems. Some such as the de Broglie-Bohm theory (Bohmian Mechanics) and other hidden variable interpretations are considered deterministic, others such as the Copenhagen interpretation are considered indeterministic, and others still are agnostic[38] on the position of determinism/indeterminism. Here are brief summaries of some common interpretations and what they mean for "free will":

The Copenhagen Interpretation

The Copenhagen interpretation is one common interpretation of quantum mechanics that suggest that the configuration of a sub-atomic particle can be in all possible positions at once. This *superposition* explained prior. Such a superposition makes up what's called the *wave function*. Per this interpretation, once we measure or observe the particle, this wave function collapses into the one single position (the one we measure or observe).

The suggestion that the particle collapsing is *conscious* observer related instead of measurement related has some philosophical problems. A good thought experiment was posed by Erwin Schrödinger called Schrödinger's cat. The thought experiment addressed what Schrödinger thought as a problem with the Copenhagen interpretation being applied to everyday objects and conscious observers.

In the thought experiment, a cat is placed in an enclosed box with a vile of poison, a tiny bit of radioactive substance and a Geiger counter. If an atom decays in the substance, the Geiger counter will detect it and trigger a hammer to come down on the vile of poison, killing the cat. The thought experiment is a way to bring what happens at the quantum scale (e.g. the decay of an atom) to the level of larger objects (e.g. the cat). Per some people[39] who side with the Copenhagen interpretation, the event of such decay would need to be in a state of superposition until someone "observed" it. In this experiment, that would mean that the cat would need to be as well. That the cat would have to be both dead and alive in the box until someone opened up the box and observed it (in which case the state would either collapse into a dead cat or a living cat).

The idea of such a collapse being "observer" related has brought on a whole slew of pseudo-scientific bibble-babble about reality being dependant on conscious observers. Schrö-dinger's cat displays the absurdity of such claims. Niels Bohr, one of the main physicists associated with the Copenhagen interpretation, never intended such mis-interpretation. He said a measuring device (such as a Geiger counter) is sufficient to collapse the wave function.

I've noticed some people are prone to thinking reality is what they perceive, rather than our perceptions being part of reality. This allows them to reorder events from them-self first, and everything else afterward--hence what they "will" doesn't stem from events outside of them or their own control. Rather, reality itself stems from events *within them*, and so they can make decisions that stem only to them-self, rather than some-thing they had no control over.

Of course the Copenhagen interpretation in no way sug-gests this (though other interpretations that have a Copenhagen base to them such as von Neumann interpretation suggest such) , nor does any of the scientific evidence we possess. All of the evidence points to a universe that has existed long before any conscious creature formed within it to "observe" it. Not to mention it fails to denote where "they" came from. (I'll give a hint, they were born.) It doesn't take a genius to see the logical flaws with the conception of reality being a creation of the observer. Even a solipsistic idea that someone could be a "brain in a jar" or in "The Matrix"[40] means that there is a reality that precedes them that is different from their own experiences, but still, such would causally precede them and what they experience.

Remember a few chapters back on how existence is a trichotomy? This also would apply to the existence of any conscious observer (agent). Either the conscious observer came about causally, the conscious observer popped into existence acausally, or the conscious observer always existed. Even if we disregard everything we know about how people come to be, a conscious observer that acausally existed had no say in how the acausal event took place or their own causal setup due to it. And a conscious observer that somehow always existed, always existed in a way that they had no control over, and due to the causal variables once existing or while existing in some crazy infinite regress, must make the choices they make based on such causality or other acausal events they have no control over. These absurd ideas, even if we were to give them a tiny bit of consideration, could in no way offer the free will described in this book.

As for the appropriate way to view the interpretation, which has little to do with "observers" in the sense of conscious entities, even if we accept the plausibility of this interpretation, we need to understand what it would mean for events if it was true.

Such an interpretation wouldn't help with free will. Either the measuring/observing is part of a causal chain of events that would force one specific "possibility" from its superposition state, in turn making it the *only* real possibility that could have happened, or such "possibility" would happen acausally. It's the latter that's suggested in this interpretation with the word "possibilities" (meaning more than one possibility). We can only have multiple possibilities with acausal events, as explained earlier. Regardless, both of these ways for an event to come forth from a superposition would be entirely out of the control of the person.

Let's say, for example, that the act of measuring opens a floodgate to the possibilities in which only one can get through. Either causes must determine which event gets through this floodgate once "observed" (in which case the others would not be a "possibility"), or somehow the event just happens without a cause. But if we say that the possibilities are held in a state of superposition, that means that those possibilities exist in such position and one comes to the forefront. Remember the problem of acausality happening to existent things? It applies here to "possibilities in superpositioned states" as well.

And again, if caused, only one of the events was a possibility. Some might say that all possibilities do in fact happen. Hence some lean towards a many-worlds interpretation instead.

Many-worlds interpretation

The many-words interpretation (also known as many-universes or many-histories interpretation) suggest that for each "possible" state that a particle can be in, such leads to different histories, worlds, or universes. In other words, it doesn't collapse into one once measured or observed. All of the possibilities exist without interaction with each other, and one simply is in the perceived forefront for each universe, a process called "decoherence" in the physics world, with all of the others existing with their own history, world, or universe at the same time.

Think of decoherence as a sort of leaking of all super-positioned states (rather than just one) into the environment in which they are energetically coupled with. If we were to address the Schrödinger's cat thought experiment posed earlier using this interpretation, both states of the cat being alive and dead persist after the box is opened, but each "decohere" into their own environment (universe/world) which are separate from each other. The person opening the box will only see the one or the other (depending on the environment that particular instance of the person is in at such a moment), but the other would be happening as well, with the person in this other "universe" seeing the other result.

So what if? Could that grant free will? The answer's still a resounding no.

In this interpretation, each state must lead to the next that it causes. So even if a particle has a number of different superpositioned states (let's say three states for the sake of ease) that it can be in at a given point, it must be in all three of those states. The physics would be such that all three states had to happen, with three different universes that could not have happened differently.

I find the very idea of a many-worlds interpretation to be the most counterintuitive of them all. Even more counterintuitive than acausal events happening. First, for one super-positioned state to decohere to a specific universe over another superpositioned state, that implies causal variables that need to be there that push it to such perceived section of the environment (for "decoherence" it is coupled with a specific environment in this interpretation). And likewise, the other superpositioned states would each need their own causal variables to decohere to the forefront of their own environments.

But if this were the case, then only one would be a possibility for that particular environment, and hence suggesting the others as "possibilities" would be quite an inaccurate description. Rather, each superpositioned state would, by necessity, need to decohere into the *specific* "universe" or environment it does, due to the causes being different for each superpositioned state.

It falls into the problem we addressed with a cause not being able to have multiple possible opposing effects. If we were to say that the superpositioned states were actual different possibilities that would come out from a prior event, the only way for such multiple possibilities is if we have an acausal event. But then we run into the problems acausality would pose in regards to existing "superpositioned" states. If they are causal, only one would be a possibility for a specific environment, so saying the other superpositioned states are "possibilities" would be incorrect. If they existed, they would have to happen within the environment they were causally coupled to "decohere" into.

The whole thing can become quite confusing and convoluted. Not only would the word "possibilities" be incorrect for the superpositioned states, but for each moment there would be a number of different universes, which, from each moment of those universes there would be a number of different universes, so on ad-infinitum.

Not only would this type of interpretation offer no free will, but it would be the absolute worst for what it would mean if it were true. It would actually give a person a reason to "do nothing" in the most defeatist, fatalistic sense. For example, let's suppose there is a cause you'd find important, such as helping the hungry. If you subscribed to this interpretation, you can understand that there would be the alternate universe in which you'd be doing something to better the cause so what's it matter if you do it in this one? And if you did something about the cause, you'd know that in this other universe you'd have done nothing anyway. So in the end, it's all the same. A trap you simply cannot escape. You won't help the cause in one universe or another, so why bother in the one you are in, as the amount of suffering would be the same? It's no better than saying for every good action you do there is a bad one, a not as good one, a benign one, and any other so called "possibility" happening at the same time.

But don't worry, this interpretation of quantum mechanics is one of the most fantastical, non-evidentiary, science fiction interpretations that quantum mechanics has to offer. It's right up there with the science fiction of conscious observers creating reality, rather than reality producing conscious observers. Believing in these things is closer to religion than science or reason. We can talk about, test for, and speculate about these things, but there is no good reason to accept them over any other simpler explanation. And though more possible than the idea of free will, basing an action on a belief in such interpretation is illogical given the unprovable nature of such universes.

As a side note, it's important not to conflate the many worlds/universes interpretations of quantum mechanics with cosmological theories that there may be multiple universes. The multiple universe theories in cosmology suggest the possibility of there being other universes besides our own. For example, some speculate that a universe can be created at the other end of a black hole, or that there are many universes that have their own type of "natural selection" process that help output the physical laws of each universe. This is ultimately different than their being universes that stem from each moment (or each quantum particle in a superpositioned state), with trillions if not zillions (or more) of instances of your biological body/mind thinking and doing slightly different things all the way to extremely different things.

Though the logical problems with such an interpretation are abundant and I'm hardly scratching the surface here, it's more important to recognize that such interpretation can in no way assist with the obtainment of free will.

De Brogle – Bohm theory

Also known as Bohmian Mechanic[41] or Pilot-Wave Theory, this interpretation of quantum mechanics is often referred to as a "hidden variable"[42] interpretation. This means it's a "causal" interpretation, or in other words a "deterministic" interpretation.

For this theory, the important part for the free will debate is that "determinism" holds, regardless if the causality is nonlocal. This means that every event has a cause, and every cause is an event that has a cause.

Bohmian Mechanics is an acceptable alternative to the more widely accepted Copenhagen interpretation or other alternatives. It offers a lot of advantages and explanatory power.

It explains everything without the need for acausal events happening to existing particles, or happening at all, for that matter. That itself is a huge plus on the side of this interpretation given the problems I've addressed in this book.

Also, for the Uncertainty Principle, Bohmian Mechanics places the fact that we cannot measure both the momentum and position of a particle (at the same time with accuracy) within the realm of having limited knowledge.[43] For Bohmian Mechanics, the particle does, as a matter of fact, have both a momentum and position, unlike various other interpretations that suggest otherwise.

And last, Bohmian Mechanics doesn't require any "conscious observers," magical universes in which we only see one (rather, it takes place in a single space-time), superpositioned "possibilities," or many other extraordinary claims that some other interpretations try to make. In this way it offers an explanation that is in some ways the simpler one, which in science often equates to better.

That being said, it's not without its faults. For example, some critics find a problem with it needing to be "contextual" (which relates to particle spin), as well as some counterintuitiveness to nonlocality that bypasses Bell's Inequality.

I'm in no way trying to promote one interpretation over another; rather that it's important to note that all of them have their own problems and advantages. Due to this, some interpretations attempt to take a more minimalistic approach. For example, the ensemble interpretation.

Ensemble interpretation

The ensemble interpretation of quantum mechanics is agnostic on whether or not the universe is deterministic. In other words, it doesn't attempt to assume that certain events are acausal, nor does it assume they are causal. This point alone makes it one of the better interpretations in my eyes.

This interpretation, also known as the statistical interpretation, is viewed as a minimalist interpretation. It claims to make the fewest assumptions associated with the mathematics of quantum mechanics. Many supporters of this interpretation suggest that a key importance to it is the removal of unnecessary *"unnatural theoretical interpretations."*

Albert Einstein was a supporter of this interpretation:

"The attempt to conceive the quantum-theoretical description as the complete description of the individual systems leads to unnatural theoretical interpretations, which become immediately unnecessary if one accepts the interpretation that the description refers to ensembles of systems and not to individual systems." - *Albert Einstein*[44]

This "shut up and calculate" interpretation is the least demanding, because it assumes less.

And though it achieves this in many ways, it does have some disadvantages as well. For example, some claim[45] that it's only useful in addressing smaller ensembles that don't bridge the gap to larger classical scale objects. Since this may be the case, we might have to expand into, at the very least, thinking about some of the other interpretations that make more assumptions.

That being said, when forming a "belief" in something, it's better to take a minimalist approach and take those others with a grain of salt,[46] rather than make unnecessary assumptions.

The main quantum point

Some interpretations are deterministic (meaning entirely causal), some are not, and others are agnostic in regards to determinism. Below is a general list of some interpretations that commonly fall under determinism, indeterminism, or undecided:

Deterministic

- de Broglie-Bohm theory
- Many-worlds interpretation
- Time-symmetric theories
- Many-minds interpretation

Indeterministic

- Copenhagen interpretation
- von Neumann interpretation
- Stochastic interpretation
- Objective collapse theories
- Transactional interpretation
- Relational interpretation

Agnostic on being Deterministic

- Ensemble interpretation
- Quantum logic
- Consistent histories

Most of the interpretations have variants that can be argued for or against. Interpretations are interpretations. They try to "interpret" the results of quantum mechanics. And even the ensemble interpretation which may make the least assumptions has problems.

The important question for the free will debate when addressing each of these interpretations is: how can causality or acausality be any different than already addressed? No matter how complex, bizarre, "probabilistic," or unintuitive we postulate reality based on *interpretations* of quantum mechanics, causality must still follow from cause to effect, and acausality can have no such forcing factors. We can postulate causes interacting between different times, different directions of time, different locations, different directions of space, and even different universes. They can be affected by measurement or thought or even pixie dust. We can postulate that one of many universes or states comes in when observe or measure, but we need to know what causes it to be the specific universe or state that we observe over those others. If nothing causes it, it's acausal. If something causes it, it had to cause it in that way, and could not have caused a different state to be observed or measured. The causal/acausal dichotomy must hold if we are to be logically consistent.

Certainly we can throw out logic, but the very science and mathematics of quantum mechanics are built on logic. Not one quantum interpretation can account for a logically coherent model of free will that allows for the abilities addressed in this book.

Knowledge of quantum mechanics can help you avoid those people who just love to bring in their own misuses of terminology, poor understandings, and interpretation assumptions to contrive ideas that really have nothing to do with the actual science involved. Quantum mechanics is a very important science, and it's only harmed when people[47] contort it around in an attempt to make incoherent beliefs coherent within their own minds. It allows them to pretend there is enough reason to believe what they do and allows them to confuse others just enough so they cannot be sufficiently argued with. I urge you to study at least the basics of quantum mechanics, if only to prevent such people from temporarily stumping you with conclusions that simply do not follow from the information quantum mechanics provides. The assumptions placed around many of the interpretations are quickly becoming the newest, logic defying religions.

The confusion allows some to hold on to beliefs such as free will. If, however, they understood the nature of causal and acausal events, they'd understand that any coherent quantum fantasy world simply cannot help support a free will conclusion.

18
Determinism does not Imply Predictability

'For the free will debate, it isn't "predictability" that's incompatible with free will. It's causality that is.'

As explained in the last chapter about quantum mechanics, determinism does not imply knowledge of future events or the ability to predict them. The outcome of events can be entirely determined by past causality, and at the same time, beings with the capability of knowledge may not be able to "determine" the outcome of those events. This doesn't mean that there are not instances in which we can infer where a cause might lead. There are many, and the more we try to infer the effect that a cause will have, the better.

The uncertainty principle shows that on the quantum scale, predictability for some things at the small scale appear impossible. This unpredictability doesn't necessarily lead to indeterminism (in the acausal sense). So no matter how unpredictable something is, if it's caused, it couldn't have happened any other way, and it's entirely deterministic.

Another field of study which entails unpredictable events in entirely deterministic systems is called *chaos theory*. Chaos theory shows how small differences in initial conditions can lead to significantly different future outcomes. A goal of chaos theory is to find out the underlying order within what appears to be chaotic, disordered data.

The idea of small differences leading to significant outcomes is called the *butterfly effect*. The term "butterfly effect" is based on the initial data of Edward Lorenz, a mathematician and meteorologist who was the pioneer of chaos theory. The theoretical scenario postulates that a butterfly flapping its wings can change the trajectory of a tornado some time after. Per the theory, the butterfly's wings could create tiny changes in the atmosphere that may alter the path, prevent, delay, or be part of the cause of a tornado (or other weather related scenario).

In the scenario in which the flap was a necessary part of the cause that led to the formation of the tornado, if the butterfly had not flapped its wing at that point, or if the butterfly had not existed, the tornado wouldn't have happened.

It seems hard to believe that a single tiny thing could be a cause of something larger that appears entirely unrelated. That a single butterfly flap could have the effect of changing the weather. Per Lorenz's mathematics, it's quite the possibility.

Even in a short time period, big differences can occur from small ones. A good illustration of this is the Sinai billiards example, where you have a flat, square table with curved mass in the center. We then take one snapshot of the trajectory of a

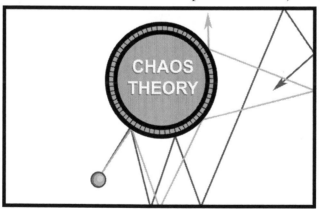

ball starting at an initial point X and hitting another point on the center mass Y, letting the ball bounce off of the center mass and walls. Then we do it again, start at the exact initial point X, but this time move the target over a very small degree to the left or right. It now hits point Z instead of point Y on the center mass. The lines seem to be very close to each other in the beginning, but as the ball bounces around, the trajectory becomes increasingly different with the two lines. The balls end up in entirely different locations due to the tiniest of changes in the trajectory.

This is a controlled model with a fairly short timeframe showing a small change with an entirely different outcome. Imagine when we complicate things. When we have multiple causes all interacting in ways that are difficult to locate or assess the trajectory of.

Back to the billiards scenario: keep in mind that though the outcomes are different in regards to where they end up and the path they take within the box, and those differences may be hard to determine ahead of time, we might still be able to (easily and reliably) predict that the ball would end up (somewhere) inside of the box, or that the path will be limited to within the box. This is important to note. For some things, trying to predict the minutia may be too difficult, though theoretically not impossible unless talking about the uncertainty principle. But we may not need to know the minutia. We might only require a general overall picture or a probability of an outcome.

In other words, just because we cannot predict everything to an absoluteness, and certain things are harder to predict than others, does not mean that we cannot predict anything at all. It's a big mistake to conflate these two things. Determinism doesn't imply predictability, but it does make it easier to predict *some* things. The acausality needed for indeterminism, however, means that any acausal event is entirely unpredictable. We cannot even predict a likeliness for such an event.

Either way, the causality on the larger scale is consistent enough to build a spaceship and land it on the moon. We can predict the likelihood that the sun will still exist when we wake up in the morning. We can predict the likelihood of a disease being cured by taking a pill, compared to it being cured if we do not take the pill. There is a whole lot of future events that can be consistently and reliably predicted, and science does just that.

Determinism may not imply predictability, but that in no way means it implies we cannot predict. We can predict, do it all the time, and can do it with great confidence and accuracy. There are, however, *some things* we either can't predict, cannot accurately predict, or are simply harder to predict than other things. Predicting the weather an hour from now is a much easier task than predicting the weather for some specific day two years from now. One has less variables to account for than the other.

For the free will debate, it isn't "predictability" that's incompatible with free will. It's causality that is. It's the fact that those causes (must) stem back to events we ultimately have no control over. Zero, ziltch, nada control! In a deterministic universe, those events stem from before we ever even exist as conscious entities. In an indeterministic universe, some of them stem from acausal events that we would have no control over. Whether we can predict the outcome of our decision matters not to the reasons why we simply don't have the ability to choose between more than one viable option or action, in which that choice was "up to us."

19
Time Possibilities

'There's no conception of time that can help grant free will.'

Time is a factor in which a rudimentary understanding is quite helpful for the free will debate. The philosophy of time is a large subject with ideas about time stemming from time existing in a real objective sense to time being only an idea that is relational to existing objects, from time existing as individual units to time existing as a whole, from time only going forward in direction to it going in multiple directions, so on and so forth. Questions about existence, directionality, relativity, and flow all play into one's idea of time and space. If a philosopher uses the term "temporal," they are referring to time. Think "temporal" (time) and "spatial" (space). Of course, most modern physics models combine the two into a single continuum of space-time.

Some sense of time seems to be a requirement of any thinking. Without some sort of time, so it appears, consciousness or mind can't exist. Thought needs to be strung together into coherent lines, and such is impossible without at least a rudimentary conception of time. Say or think the sentence *"the turkey gobbled"* and you'll realize that each moment of that sentence is meaningless without the next. If we mix up each of those sounds at each of their points in perceived time, we cannot seem to output anything coherent.

From our perspective, we perceive time as having a specific duration, and we observe the events that happen within the confines of those durations. The duration is expressed within the space that we perceive. Some philosophers claim that it's this notion of time that we derive a deterministic universe and the idea that we lack free will from. They suggest that this is an archaic conception of time, and that we should drop the notion of determinism due to this. What they fail to understand is that, no matter what conception of time held, free will cannot exist. Other conceptions of time don't preclude causal determinism and what it means regarding free will; nor do they preclude indeterminism and what that means. And if you hold that no concept of time exists, or that time is a single static moment, any notions of free will become absurd without the need to inject determinism or indeterminism into the argument.

Some ideas of time might help visualize and understand what causality can be and what it cannot within the context of them.

Here are some basic ideas regarding time and what they mean for free will:

TIME DIRECTIONS

Sequential time

- Sequential time in which the past and present exist.

PAST   PRESENT

For this view of time, each instant that occurs is created due to the instant right before it. The instance right before it still exists as that preceding instant. We can only perceive the instant that is present.

Think of this view as frames in a movie, with us viewing the last frame. That (last) frame creates the next frame which

145

will be the new present frame that we are viewing. There are no frames after the present frame.

Causality in such time are events strung from the past to the present. An acausal event in such a view of time would be a speck on a present frame without the one prior to it having something that would cause that speck. That speck would then either acausally disappear in the next frame, or propagate on through all of the next frames in a causal fashion.

- Sequential time in which the present and future exist.

PRESENT   FUTURE

For this view of time, each instant that occurs is created due to the instant right before it, but the instance right before it ceases to exist. The future already exists as well; however, we can only perceive the instant that is present at the back of the line.

Think of this view as frames in a movie, with us viewing the first frame. That frame plays to the next frame which will be the new present frame that we are viewing. The preceding frame vanishes.

- Sequential time in which the past, present, and future all exist.

PAST   PRESENT   FUTURE

For this view of time, past instances lead to present instances which lead to future instances. We can only see the present instance.

- Sequential time in which only the present exists.

⬤ PRESENT

In this view, the past and/or the future do not exist along with the present. For this view of time, each instant that occurs is created due to the instant right before it. The instance right before it ceases to exist as it becomes the next. In other words, only the present exists.

Think of this view as a single frame in a movie. The strange part about this movie is that only one frame ever exists. That frame turns into next frame. Past and future frames do not exist. The future happens due to the present frame changing to the next present frame.

Any version of sequential time is susceptible to the causal/acausal dichotomy, rendering free will impossible.

Time existing all at once

This is the idea that everything that happens in what appears to be a sequential order to us, really exists all at once, and that order is just an  illusionary perception. In other words, what seems like now to us is really happening at the same time as what we perceive as 5 minutes ago and 5 minutes after.

This view of time is nonsensical for the notion of causality, but it's equally as nonsensical for the notion of free will. Any so called choice you have would have already existed at the same time as just before the choice. It would be a static picture, and the appearance of anything dynamic, such as conscious thought, would just be an illusion. This also entails the appearance of any decisions we might make.

Non-existent time

For this view, time itself does not exist at all. Like free will, it's an illusion. It holds the same problem for free will as time existing all at once. No time means no causal succession, which means the act of a "you" willing something is nonsensical.

Circular time

This is similar to sequential time in that each event happens one after another. The main difference is that at some point time loops back on itself in a never ending circle. For this view, there really is no end of time. A beginning of time is possible as it could have taken place at any point in the loop, but it isn't necessary.

The tricky part of this type of time is that causality can seemingly lead to itself. The causal chains are still entirely causal chains, but at some point they cause the chain that leads to them causing the chain, ad-infinitum.

Like sequential time, this version is susceptible to the causal/acausal dichotomy, rendering free will impossible

- Time giving birth to itself

Time giving birth to itself is a sort of circular time. An example of this idea might be the beginning of time being created by the big bang, and a black hole in the universe that existed after the big bang created the very big bang that the black hole existed in. In this way, our universe with sequential time would give birth

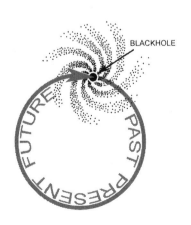

148

to our very own universe. Our own universe could also give birth to another universe, and that universe could give birth (back) to our own universe. There is a whole slew of possibilities if there are multiple universes derived from black holes.

The causal/acausal dichotomy holds in such view.

Forward/Reverse/Sideways flowing time

In this view, time does not only flow in one direction. The word "previous" is problematic here as it suggests a forward time with one event happening earlier than its effect.

If reverse time was a possibility, could it help with free will? Not at all.

Such mixed "flowing" runs into the very same problems as forward time. The events in the past would be just as forced by the events in the future, if the future event is a cause of a past event. The only difference is the time direction of the chain of events.

The later sections on Backward Time Travel and Retrocausality are a little different as they address events going backward within time rather than time itself being a different direction. The very same points, however, apply; regardless if time is flowing in a different direction or if causes create effects that happen prior to the cause.

TIME DIMENSION

Space-time

Space-time is the common scientific understanding of time. With this view, there are four dimensions. Three dimensions of space (Length, Width, and Height) and one dimension of time (Duration). Combining space and time suggests that time can be understood in the same terms as space, and many modern mathematical models make use of this.

Relativity

Along with space-time comes some interesting relativistic views of time. There are certain events that can theoretically slow time, called "time dilation."

One would be the strength of an intense gravitational field. Read up on the Theory of General Relativity if you'd like to understand this better.

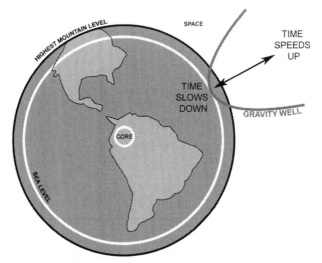

And the other would be moving really, really fast; the closer to the speed of light, the more time dilates. Read up on the Theory of Special Relativity for this.

Relativity shows us that our observations of simultaneous events are not absolute. An example of special relativity is that of a moving train car with a pulse of light going up and down between two mirrors and a person on a platform with the same setup that's not moving relative to the train car. From the

150

observation of someone inside of the train car, the pulse of light in the train car holds one time in which the pulse goes from one mirror to the other.

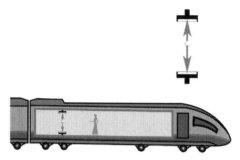

For the observer on the platform, however, the pulse takes longer to get from one mirror to the next on the train car.

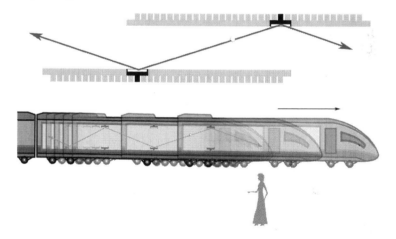

Though from the perspectives of the two observers, the other's time would have slowed down (look up "twin paradox" if you are interested). In actuality, it's the one that accelerates that slows. This has been verified experimentally. This is because an object's motion through space and time combined is always equal to the speed of light. So when your speed increases through space, time slows down to accommodate for that. For all practical purposes, the decrease is so small that we do not realize it, until we get up to those super fast speeds. When we get up to $1/10^{th}$ the speed of light or faster that's where the differences matter the most.

One very odd realization of this is that, for light itself, since it travels at light speed, it's timeless. It holds no motion through time. Of course to us, from the "platform" if you will, light seems to move through time. To the photon, however, (relativistically) time stands still.

The important thing to understand is that causality would be relative, but consistent to such relativity. Any slowing of time would be a slowing of the events happening for the *object* in motion. The causal/acausal dichotomy would hold relative to the container that these events are in. And such relativistic containers would come about via causal or acausal events as well.

Such relativity would be consistent. If we could "freeze time" as soon as the light pulse hit the top mirror on the platform, time would freeze somewhere before the light pulse hit the top mirror in the train car, depending on how fast the train car was moving. The two time bubbles are relative to each other in a causally connected way.

Time relativity does not help with the notion of free will in any way. It simply means that objects which are caused to move faster cause time to slow down to accommodate for a physical speed restriction.

Other Time Possibilities

As I stated earlier, time is an enormous topic. I did not feel it necessary to delve too deeply into some of the more obscure concepts of time. For each one, what needs to be looked at is how causality would need to work, and if it does not exist, what that means. More importantly, how thoughts can be strung together into something understandable within such notions of time. No matter how elaborate or outrageous the time scheme, free will is impossible within it. No matter what conception of time (or no time at all) you come up with, it will be either susceptible to the causal/acausal dichotomy, or be completely incompatible with any notion of free will on its own merits.

TIME TRAVEL DETERMINISM

Time travel is always fun to think about. It conjures up images of science fiction stories and movies, and allows us to imagine possible paradoxes, bizarre situations, and the future. Though certain types of time travel may be impossible, thinking about time travel is a helpful activity. It helps us understand time concepts, and also helps understand the incompatibility of free will.

Backward Time Travel

Some scientists and Star Trek fans suggest the possibility of backward time travel. A common concept of this is a wormhole from one point in space-time to another point in space-time. This would basically be punching a hole through space-time, which many scientists claim would take the energy of a star, or wrapping space/time so two points meet like folding a sheet of paper. Most doubt the actual feasibility of such travel in the future.

For this thought experiment, let's assume that backward time travel is possible. It's the near future and a time machine has been built that can go backward through time. Our time traveler is Tim. Tim the time traveler travels through time. (Say that one ten time fast.) Let's also assume time to be somewhat linear--though it need not be, but for this scenario it makes it more understandable--and that Tim can make changes while traveling.

Here we have a simple causal timeline of Tim's life prior to traveling.

PAST   **PRESENT**   **FUTURE**

Tim travels one hundred years back in time and changes something from the original causal timeline. This then creates a new timeline in which everything is adjusted based on that change.

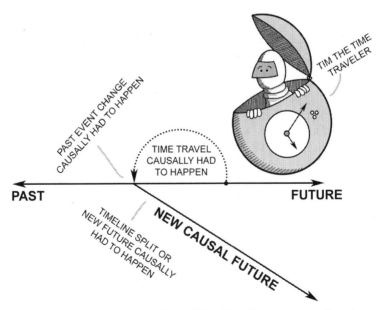

In other words, causality still holds. If a new timeline is not created, and somehow time holds the exact same course,

154

causality still holds. This notion of time travel opens the door to a slew of potential paradoxes, however.

The point of this is to show that, when understanding a lack of free will, the direction of time isn't really the important factor. What is important is how the events occur. For example, the event at the point where time splits off was an effect of traveling backward through time to that point and making the change. A cause that does not happen in a linear fashion is not any less forced to happen. And such a cause, if caused by another cause, would stem via a chain of causality, regardless if that chain was able to jump around.

Another strange conception of causality are causes that are able to travel through time in reverse. This leads us to a strange concept called retrocausality...

Retrocausality

Retrocausality is the idea that events happen both forward and backward through time, or even sideways. Some suggest that if events can happen going both forward and reverse through time, and if both type can effect a thought, that a forward event and reverse event may collide or cancel each other out, which can create some sort of "freedom."

Even if we assumed the possibility of events happening backward through time, any collisions would not grant free will. Both types of events would be dictated by the cause leading them (either forward or backward), and the collision of them would have to happen based on this. In other words, if a cause can create its effect a second earlier, that effect, though not traveling forward through time, would be dictated entirely by the cause. It would be equally as forced as a cause going forward in time. If the event collides with one going forward, whatever new event comes about through such collision (whether forward or backward) could have happened no other way. We end up in the same predicament as causality only traveling forward.

It's important to note that a cause/effect relationship flowing backward through time would have the same restrictions as a forward one. The cause could only lead to one possible effect (happening earlier); otherwise acausal events need to be added into the equation to determine which outcome out of various possibilities it would go to.

Such a type of retrocausality could theoretically create loops in the causal chain. A future cause could create an earlier effect, which could lead to that future cause if it could somehow turn around in time. Such a loop could not help grant free will.

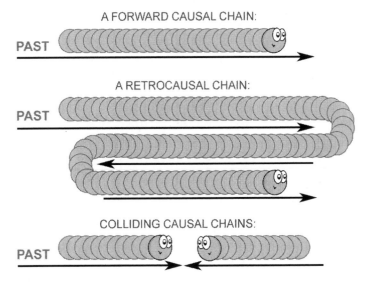

If the causality happens in multiple time directions, it must happen in those directions based on the causality and the nature of the system. It's the same reason the backward time traveler changing an event in the past would either create a second timeline or revise the current future timeline.

Of course, one should be skeptical of this notion of retrocausality since there is really no evidence of it. Regardless, it would be susceptible to the causal/acausal dichotomy, and hence cannot grant free will.

Forward Time Travel

Physicists such as Stephen Hawking endorse the possibility of forward time travel as being more feasible than backward time travel. After all, if we take the most scientifically accepted conception of space-time, we are (technically) traveling forward each moment. Forward time travel in the more futuristic sense can occur by slowing down time within the relativistic bubble you are in. For example, if we can somehow get into the orbit of a large black hole, the gravity would slow time. Or if we can build a ship that can travel close to the speed of light, that would slow time. If that can occur, you can spend a certain amount of time inside of that ship, and come out of it in the distant future.

Forward time travel does not present the paradox problem that backward time travel does. It also does not help with free will in any way. Causes within a relativistic bubble and coming out of such bubble in the future would have had to occur based on the causality of the event and the bubble it resided in.

So what does all of this time gobbledygook mean for free will?

It means that:

- There is no conception of time that can help grant free will.

- Most conceptions of time require either causal or acausal events. Even some of the more obscure notions of time.

- Those conceptions of time that do not require causal or acausal events still do not allow for a free will, as they don't allow for events, period.

- The direction or flow through any conception of time one poses is irrelevant to the causal/acausal dichotomy.

- Any conceptions of the possibilities of time travel or backward events cannot help grant free will.

Be wary of people who suggest that the no free will stance is based on a misunderstanding of time. They hold the entire burden to supply a conception of time that's not susceptible to the problems of causality, acausality, and *no time*–each incompatible with free will.

20
Large Scale Causality – The Ruling Factor

'If they (acausal events) existed, they were abundant, and had any real impact on the large scale, the world would be a more dangerous place than it currently appears.'

Even if we make the assumption that acausal events occur at the quantum scale and hence the universe is indeterministic, the causal events at the larger "classical" scale seem to override those factors to an overwhelming degree. They are consistent enough to run a computer, to hit a target with a bullet, and to navigate a spacecraft to the moon.

Imagine acausal events happening to the magnetic coating in a hard drive. It would be virtually impossible to install, store, and run software. Even if the acausal events only happened every now and again, troubleshooting a computer problem would be practically impossible. We could never know if the problem was some acausal event that corrupted the software or messed with the hardware, or a causal one such as a conflicting program or dust in the components.

The brain would have the same predicament. Acausal events would not help a brain, they would most likely corrupt it. The best case scenario is the acausal events would happen in such a way as being benign to the output of the thought (e.g. it would make no difference to the thought). If, however, acausal events had an effect on the structure that outputs thought in any significant way (meaning making a change in the output), the more acausal events that happen in it, the worse off a person could be. Random nonsensical thoughts and lapses in memory would be a common thing. Currently these types of symptoms are associated with mental diseases and disorders. It's hardly common and we recognize the genetic or environmental component to many.

Back when rifles were first designed, they weren't at all accurate. You could aim at a target twenty feet away and miss it completely. People didn't see the events that caused such a misalignment, and didn't have the technology to fix it. With a better understanding of physics, aerodynamics, and technology, most of the problems that made rifles inaccurate have been fixed. This is due to changes of large scale causality. In other words, it wasn't due to acausal events that the bullet would not hit the target; it was due to causal events. Events that were adjusted and tweaked later on to control the output. This is seen everywhere at the large scale. We attribute something working and not working properly to causal factors.

We cannot tweak acausal factors. If they existed, they were abundant, and had any real impact on the large scale, the world would be a more dangerous place than it currently appears. People would not want to fly in airplanes, that's for sure. A few acausal events messing with the engine, landing gear, navigation system, or any other vital part, and you would be in for one hell of a ride.

Who knows, maybe these do happen. If so, they are not abundant enough for us to notice. They are not the ruling factor. And we can do nothing about them.

Since this is the case, we need to treat the universe as if it's deterministic, although with an understanding that it is possible

160

it may not be. We should look for causes of illness, rather than write them off as acausal. This applies to every event we find important, including the event of *thinking*. The only things that we can do something about are causal in nature, and that's because we are part of such causal lines. Luckily for us, either the universe is entirely causal (deterministic), or causality seems to be a ruling factor at the top levels, which overrides any acausal events that may pop into existence at the quantum scale.

21
Willing

'Even though those events ultimately stem from events that are outside of the person's mind, once embedded as part of a person's thought process, they act as agents with a causal "will."'

What does it mean to say something's "willed"? What necessary criterion is needed to "will" something?

For starters, a "willer." Someone or some*thing* that's doing the willing. To say something is willed without a willer is like saying something's sung without a singer, or that dance happens without a dancer. It doesn't make any sense in language or logic. In the case of "free will," it's assumed that the willer is the person thinking a thought (the "you" or "I" that was addressed earlier).

For the person to be able to will something, they need to have the capability of conscious choice. Freedom is not a requirement of willfulness. As long as the person desires or has a reason, and then acts based on that desire or reason, we can say that the action was "willed." Willfulness has to do with intent or purpose. It matters not that the willer has no real control over that intent or purpose. There's no problem with causal events being events that are willed.

Acausal events are another story. A willer can cause willed events. Since an acausal event cannot have a willer for it, such an event can never be considered a "willed" event. Only caused events can be willed.

162

Some compatibilists suggest that, as long as an event is willed , free will exists. Since the willing comes from the willer, that's all the freedom needed for free will, they add. What these people fail to address is that everything that the willer "wills" causally extends to something *beyond* the willer, such as other external causal events, or acausal events, if they happen. The willing is entirely coerced by events that the willer has no control over. Even a willed event that comes about from another willed event does not help. It doesn't matter how many willed causes we stack in the chain, they all stem from events that are not willed, which control the entire line.

The term "willed" can be used to represent those events that are derived from an individual person's thoughts. Thoughts that stem from their brain or mind. Even though those events ultimately stem from events that are outside of the person's mind, once embedded as part of a person's thought process, they act as agents with a causal "will."

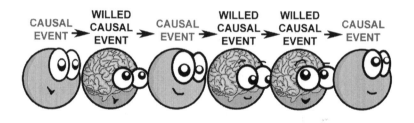

This is what I refer to when I use the term "willed." It's nothing mystical. Magic is only needed once we suggest that such will is "free" in the way that holds meaning and importance for this topic.

Some philosophers such as Daniel Wegner suggest that "conscious willing" is an illusion as well, at least for most of the decisions we make. That what we perceive as "the conscious experience of will" arises from an apparent causal path, rather than an actual causal path, between thought and action. For a scientific analysis on the experience of free will, you may want to pick up a copy of "The Illusion of Conscious Will".[48]

It is true that any perceived conscious willing stems from subconscious or unconscious events first. We'll get into that further when we address such within the context of neuroscience.

22

Should Acausality be Assumed?

'At best we should be agnostic to whether certain events occur acausally or causally.'

Quantum mechanics shows us that there is a degree of uncertainty we must contend with. We don't see certain correlations when we get down to the smallest scale and we cannot make clear measurements of both position and momentum at the same time. Does this mean that we should infer events that happen at this level have no cause?

Doing so is an argument from ignorance fallacy. An argument from ignorance fallacy claims something is true or false simply because the opposite has not been proven. Since we don't see a cause and cannot prove a cause, the claim that there is no cause is fallacious. Of course, concluding a cause when we don't see one (or cannot prove an acausal event) is fallacious as well. The important question is: which holds the higher burden of proof?

I'll be upfront in suggesting that acausality holds a high burden of proof. We may not be able to see an actual cause, but causes have much evidence. We can infer that causes do exist in the universe based on such evidence, we just cannot infer them for particular events. Acausality, on the other hand, by its very nature is hard to infer. Unlike causality, acausality cannot be objectively tested for. In other words, we cannot create acausal events to test for them, as the act of creating by its very nature is causal. We can look at events that seem to come into existence at the quantum scale and speculate that they come about without a cause because we cannot see one. But it is what it is: speculation.

We can, however, suggest how a cause could be unlikely at this small scale as the mathematics would suggest such a cause cannot be local. Bell's Theorem,[49] a well respected mathematical equation, suggests that causes (called hidden variables) would have to either surpass the speed of light (a speed limit most physicist except as being unsurpassable), or be nonlocal. Nonlocality means that one event causes another event at a distance, with nothing happening in the space between them. This at first seems counterintuitive, but the reasoning for not accounting for the possibility of certain nonlocal causes is flawed. The problems regarding acausality mentioned earlier are just as problematic.

Besides, quantum entanglement, which is the action of two particles interacting (as a joined pair) at a distance, has been experimentally shown.[50]

Since we have no evidence for acausal events and much evidence for causal events, and since acausal events are equally as counterintuitive, I'd suggest that even if the events are nonlocal, a hidden variable interpretation of quantum mechanics is just as likely as one where acausal events happen. I do, however, suggest that in this case, causality holds a burden as well. Certain experiments in quantum mechanics show that some nonlocal hidden variable accounts are even more problematic than others. In particular if the variable is non-contextual (e.g. Bohmian Mechanics is a contextual hidden variable account so wouldn't fall within the confines of such experiments). There are, however, some issues with contextual hidden variables that are similar to the issues of acausal events happening for already exiting particles.

Therefore, an agnostic stance is the appropriate stance for such small scale events. It is for this reason that both causality and acausality are addressed as possibilities in this book. This is also why I explain how neither can help with free will. This is why I support the hard incompatibilist stance, which rejects free will in both a deterministic universe as well as an indeterministic universe, rather than the hard determinist[51] stance, which assumes a deterministic universe.

My point is not that causality should be assumed at the quantum scale, but rather that neither should be assumed. And especially for the reason that "we don't see a cause."

To demonstrate why acausality should not be assumed, here's a thought experiment using large scale events that we can observe but don't see a cause for due to limitations with technology:

Let's suppose that a waterfall exists on a planet far away. We know this because we can see it with super high-powered telescopes. (It's a thought experiment, humor me.) We don't have the ability, however, to visit the planet. We can observe some unusual things about this waterfall through our telescope. The strangest part is that some parts of the liquid seem to be traveling upward when we look through the telescope every now and again, instead of where we would assume gravity should take it. Since we are unable to visit the planet and there is nothing that clues us in to why the water would start to flow upward, we have no idea what could cause such phenomenon. When it does happen, the water that flows upward seems to happen at different sections of the waterfall. We can derive no pattern for when the water flow will travel upward or what section of it will flow upward. From our perspective, the times and locations in which it does travel upward appear to be random. So much so that we cannot give any prediction to when it will happen next or what section it will happen to.

The question in this scenario is, if we don't have any proof of something causing the upward flow of water, and we don't have any proof of an acausal event leading to (or being) the upward flow of water, which one of these two is more likely? Do we give each equal ground, or would we infer a higher probability that there is a reason for the start of upward flow in a specific location, other than *it just happens*. I think most scientists, even quantum physicists, would not infer an acausal element and think a causal element very likely. Does that mean it's necessarily a causal event? Certainly not. But it also doesn't mean it's an acausal event. But this is at the larger scale where we seem to know how things work.

At the quantum scale we don't, as of yet, know (assuming we will ever know). So it's a little different. At best, however, we should be agnostic to whether certain events occur acausally or causally. Not observing a cause for an event is not the same thing as observing an acausal event taking place. One should not conflate these two.

And just because classical local causes seem to be out for certain quantum events, that does not make acausal events any more likely, intuitive, or less problematic than the nonlocal causes within some deterministic models of quantum mechanics. Therefore, until either a causal explanation or an acausal explanation can be ruled out, neither should be assumed at such a level.

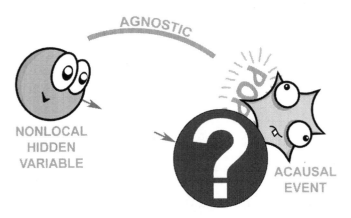

I've seen this mistake happen with both determinists who assume every event is causal, and demand such rather than conceding the possibility of acausal events, and those that accept only a very specific indeterministic quantum interpretation which allows them to assume events that are not causal. Both are assumptions due to their own preference or their own intuition on the matter, but not on anything truly solid.

I admit, my own intuition is that every event is causal. The concept of acausal events, especially influencing existing particles, is very troubling and disconcerting for me. But just because the continuity of causal events (even of the nonlocal sort) is more comforting, and makes more sense to me in some ways, doesn't mean that such is necessarily the case. Philosophy is about being as impartial as we possibly can. Let's not assume causality for every quantum event, but let's also not assume acausality.

We can think about both possible universes (using modal logic)[52] and determine what each one would mean. For the free will issue, neither is compatible with free will, even if one universe would most likely be better[53] for "willing" (the one without acausal events having an effect on our decision).

23

Agency & Experience
as a Determinant

'Agency, experience, and self-awareness are just more determinants in the causal chains of events, that must be the way they are due to events that stem outside of the control of any such agent or experience.'

Certain philosophers think that free will is compatible with a deterministic universe. Some argue that as long as an act stems from an internal psychology or thought process of an "agent," it's free.

We know that the complex mix of neurons and synapses spark the output that the brain perceives as thoughts. An important factor is that the output of those thoughts loop back and cause more brain action. Since thoughts stem from other thoughts in the brain, someone might be inclined to say that those thoughts are free, as those particular thoughts start within the person. They fail to understand. Even though there are thoughts that begin in the brain, they are forced by the thoughts that cause them, and they always stem from something the person has no real control over (either internal: genetic, or external: material/perceptual /spiritual?)

To simplify things, think of dominoes set up that lead into a box:

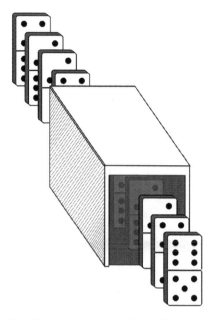

Except for the first domino inside of the box, every other domino is affected by another that is inside the box when they fall. The ones that fall inside of the box are caused by the preceding domino. This does not mean that the box caused the dominoes inside to fall. Even if the box forces the domino to fall a certain way after the chain happens (i.e. they hit the walls and go a different direction), the entire process stems from causal factors outside of the box. For example, deciding to construct the box, the construction of the box, the setup of the dominoes, flicking the first domino, are all causal factors outside of the box that cause the dominoes to fall inside of the box and in a certain way.

Another thought experiment we can imagine is a robot. The robot can gather sensory information such as video and sound, process and interpret that information based on the software and hardware it has, and then select an option based off of the information it has processed and its existing programming. Within the software, we program the robot to "like" colors that display when a low pitched hum is played, and to "dislike" colors that display whenever a high pitched whistle is sounded. It holds these likes and dislikes within an internal memory. The robot has been programmed to disregard white. We place the robot in a room full of red objects and play the low pitched sound. It processes the visual color information as something it prefers. We then place it in a room full of green objects and blow the high pitched sound. It processes that information. Next we take the robot to a white soundproof room and ask it to select the desired object between a red apple and a green apple, with no sounds played. Based on the robot's programming and memory of what it has processed previously, it will select the red apple.

Now we let the robot loose on the world where colors and sounds are abundant. The robot's sensors allow it to pick up the entire range of sound and spectrum of colors . The closer the sound comes to the high pitch, the more it dislikes the perceived colors at the time. The closer the sound comes to the low pitched sound, the more it likes the colors it perceives. Somewhere in the middle of low and high sounds, it becomes more ambivalent to the perceived colors. The computer's able to process all of the color information and sound information to create a weight for each color of the spectrum. As it goes through its life hearing sounds and taking in colors, those weights change. A month later we take the robot into the same white room and ask it to pick between the red apple and the green one. The difference this time is that we don't have an idea which one it will pick.

The colors and sounds around it for a month were so abundant that, unlike when we intentionally gave it the color and sound experience we wanted to, we were unable to keep track of the information the robot has absorbed.

We could hook the robot up to a computer and see its new weighted color data, but without doing this we simply can't know. This time the robot picks the green apple. All of the processing of the information happens within the robot, and as the robot goes along it processes information already stored in its memory from past perceptions, as well as new perceptions that happen. Once in the sound proof white room, it bases its decision on objects of color entirely by what's stored in its hard drive.

Does this robot have free will? How about by the standards of some of those other (compatibilist) philosophers?

For those who like to use the term "agency" as if that has some weight in this debate, we can say that the robot above is an "agent." It has the ability to act in the world. It compares data and weighs it accordingly. It makes decisions and acts on those decisions (e.g. pointing to or picking up the green apple).

In that sense, the robot's very much an agent. We might even say it has a "motive" to choose the green apple, that being the low pitched sounds that it picked up while looking at green or greenish objects. Later, after we analyze all of the data, we would know that the robot would pick the green apple. We could see the "like" and "dislike" spikes that correlate with the color data.

Since this is the case, and though the robot may be an "agent," I doubt anyone would think the robot was a "free agent." Stemming from an internal process does not make the process free. More importantly, any internal process would be caused by factors out of the control of the agent. The hardware and software came about causally, and the environment it perceived came about causally.

It would then be argued that the robot does not "experience." That it's not a "conscious" agent. It does not really have a feeling of "like" or "dislike" that a conscious being would, for example. It does not really experience the color red (the "qualia"[54] of red), it just maps the spectrum of light. It really does not experience the sound, it just maps the waves.

This qualitative "experience" is just another part of our internal process that the robot may not have. But for argument's sake, let's say that we were able to make an almost identical robot, except this time it truly was able to "see" the colors in its "mind's eye" as we do, hear the sounds as we do, and based on the same programming, really "feel" a like for green and dislike for red. Would we then say that the robot was "free" to like green? If we can look at all of the data and determine its preference before it even tells us?

The robot setup (hardware and software/programming) and the external environment in which the robot "experienced" the sounds and colors dictated the very specific state of its color likes and dislikes.

The robot analogy is not meant to analogize how our consciousness works, rather that "freedom" does not follow from being an "agent" or even an "experiencing" agent. These things are but mere causal determinants for the "thought" outcome. For animals (such as us humans), the hardware and software would be our biology (nature) and the environment is everything around us that our biology allows us to sense in some way, that changes the "program" (nurture). We just don't have "consciousness" recording devices attached to our brains that we can look back on with accuracy....yet.

Equally as important is the fact that agents don't always exist. They come about through other causal factors, and they do so in a specific way that, in a causal universe, could not have come about differently. And in one where acausal events pop in, could possibly be different, but not due to any control of the agent itself. And once in existence as an "agent," it's very configuration (dictated by the events that output it) and the environment that surrounds it (dictated by the events that output those) dictates every action and decision such an agent ever makes.

Some suggest that being "self-aware" is in some way separate from the agent. If this were the case, that would render the use of "agency" as meaningless rhetoric, and would also beg the question as to where such "self-awareness" comes from. If it's a property of the agent, then the very specific "self-aware" state depends on the configuration *of* the agent itself. If only part of the self-awareness depends of the agent, it yet again begs the question as to where the other parts come from. If causal (e.g. they come from something outside of the agent, such as the material universe, some non-physical realm, or even some deity), once again the self-awareness is dictated by these

174

external events. If acausal, well, you should already know how that one goes.

Agency, experience, and self-awareness are just more determinants in the causal chains of events that must be the way they are due to events that stem outside of the control of any such agent or experience. They aren't special exceptions to causality.

24

Nature vs. Nurture

'What's important here is the realization that both environmental factors and genetic factors come about through processes that stem from out of the control of the person.'

The choices people make are influenced by their environment and genetics. Some researchers suggest that the major factor for behavior is genetics, while others suggest environment takes on the larger role. These shape the public controversy of the "nature vs. nurture" debate (nature being genetics, nurture being the environment). Regardless of the degree for each, one thing's for sure: both play a role in how we behave, and determine the choices we make. The difficult task for scientists within their field is to separate out which contributions each of these play on behavior.

The Causal Elements of Environment

The word "environment" encompasses the totality of the surrounding conditions. Perceive your surroundings right now. Look around. What do you see? What do you not see? What do you smell? Is the temperature of the air cold or hot? If outdoors, is the sun or light blinding or is there a dark overcast? Are advertisements or billboards in view? Do you hear sounds or words?

Many environmental factors embed themselves into our conscious and subconscious mind. Advertisers know this. We are bombarded by what others want us to like, and then sold those things that we have been conditioned to desire.

And many of these happen on a subliminal level. Though there is a lack of evidence that subliminal messages in advertising work to the degree people think, there is evidence that subliminal messages do affect our brains. A study[55] regarding subliminal messages was published in Current Biology in 2007 by University College London researchers. By using an fMRI, they were able to show that an image does impact the state of a subject's brain even if they did not know they had seen it:

"UCL (University College London) researchers have found the first physiological evidence that invisible subliminal images do attract the brain's attention on a subconscious level. The wider implication for the study, published in Current Biology, is that techniques such as subliminal advertising, now banned in the UK but still legal in the USA, certainly do leave their mark on the brain."

There is also evidence that people respond to emotional or negative messages more easily than positive messages.[56] This ties into our biology that may help dictate which things in the environment we process and which we don't.

Even while you were floating in your mother's womb, a number of environmental factors had specific effects on you. What your mother drank, ate, breathed, or even possibly smoked, may have impacted your health to some degree. Internal environmental factors may turn specific genes within you on or off.

If the universe is entirely causal, every element in the environment was caused by something else. And that something else was caused by something else. This is why when we say the future's "fixed" or "predetermined" in a causal universe, it holds. It's not just "you" and your decisions that would be predetermined, but every factor that leads to "you" and your decisions.

The environment would simply be a part of the causal universe. If an acausal event changes the environment, of course that would be totally out of your control as well.

The words you are currently reading are also part of your environment. These words are within the environment that you are perceiving, and you are reading them, which is influencing your very brain state/mind.

The Causal Elements of Genes

Genes do much more that give a person brown hair, blue eyes, or dark skin. They can and do affect behavior. The field that studies the role of genetics in behavior is called, of course, Behavioral Genetics.

The degree that genetics plays on behavior has been disputed to this day. There are numerous indications that genes affect behavior. We can compare the behaviors of different species of birds in the same environment, for example, and understand that such differences in behavior are due to the genetic factor of the bird.

Geneticists in Tokyo have even successfully altered genes in a mouse to make it 'fearless'.[57] The mouse doesn't try to flee when it smells a cat or other predator. In other words, they turned off a few genetic switches and the behavior of the mouse is now different.

Of course, your genetics are, for the most part, out of your control. You were born, most likely from a mother and father (unless you're a clone or an alien that reproduces asexually), and you carry the specific genetic code in which the sperm and ovum hosted. You had no control over what little guy would make it through the wall of the ovum.

Your formation within the womb was dependant on these genetic codes from both parents, as well as the internal environment that may activate or turn off some genes.

For the free will debate, it isn't really important to nitpick over whether it's the environment or genetics which holds the most influence. What's important here is the realization that both environmental factors and genetic factors come about through processes that stem from out of the control of the person.

These two things are, however, important when it comes to trying to figure out the best ways to adjust harmful behaviors.

Trading Places with Hitler

Hitler is invoked all over the place in debate. "Godwin's law" suggests that the Hitler or Nazi card is played in just about any thread, debate, or heated discussion given enough time. There is also a fallacy called "reductio ad Hitlerum," which tries to refute an opponent's view by comparing it to a view that would be held by Adolf Hitler. Most of the time Hitler is brought up in an attempt to derail an argument, as a distraction, or as something that purely evokes emotion or horror due to the implication that someone's view is anything close to something that could cause such catastrophic events in history.

That being said, Hitler can be used in ways that are not fallacious. How? By defending him, of course! Not defending the horrors that were done. Not defending the suffering. Rather defending the fact that Hitler had no other choice. His genetic structure and his environment led him to do exactly what he did.

So here's a little thought experiment. Imagine you are Hitler. You are him atom for atom, particle for particle, molecule for molecule, gene for gene, and so on. You are also him at the very time and the very place he existed. You experienced everything he had since your brain started forming in the womb of Klara Hitler (his mother). You pop out and every event is identical to his in his life. You saw the same films, read the same books, ate the same food, had the same friends, and every experience was identical down to the minutia. Things that went into your subconscious and your conscious experience were identical to his. Your brain formed the very same way due to the causality of your genes and such events.

Needless to say you wouldn't do a single thing differently. Even if you believe in a soul, you'd have the same "soul" as Hitler. You can include "soul" (for whatever that might consist of) in your "nature" along with your "genes," if you care to.

Did Hitler cause great suffering? Indeed. Were the things he did horrific? Certainly. Could you have done anything differently given the same nature and nurture? Certainly not! And this goes for any of the worst people you can think of.

Nature and nurture dictates the very person you will be. Reading this book is part of that nurture. A book you would never have read if you were Hitler, as it didn't exist when he did.

But don't worry. Just because Hitler and the Nazis couldn't have done otherwise and hence weren't to blame, this doesn't mean they shouldn't have been stopped. It's a great thing that causality eventually led to them losing against people whose nature and nurture led them down a more ethical path (at least for that position).

There's a lot to be said about blameworthiness, and ethics, with no free will. This is just the tip of the iceberg.

25

Blame, Deserving, Fairness, and Equality

"This fact that being 'blameworthy' or being 'more deserving than another' is illogical has direct implications on how we view fairness and equality."

Blameworthiness

Without free will, blaming a person for something they have done is an act of absurdity. The same holds for claiming someone is more deserving of something.

Imagine a scenario where you are unwillingly knocked out by a serial tattooist. The next morning you wake up with an insulting tattoo on your forehead. That's what this nutty serial tattooist does: he finds a victim, knocks them out, and tattoos their forehead with some insulting expression. You were unfortunate enough to be his next victim.

Now imagine a person named Doug who has read the newspaper article that explained the horrible occurrence that happened to you. Doug has full knowledge that you were forced to get the tattoo on your forehead. You have begun a number of sessions to get it removed. You even cover the tattoo up so people cannot see it. Doug knows all of this.

Now imagine Doug blaming you for getting the tattoo. He says that, even though you are covering it up and in the process of getting it removed, that you shouldn't have gotten the

181

insulting tattoo in the first place. He blames you for allowing the tattoo to get on your forehead, regardless that you did not have any control over it. He says the insulting tattoo is on you, so you are to blame for it.

YOU SHOULD BE ASHAMED OF YOURSELF FOR HAVING THAT DISGUSTING FOREHEAD TATTOO WHICH WAS FORCED ON YOU!

What do you think of Doug? Do you think him rational or reasonable? Is he right to blame you?

Most people would think Doug is acting irrational and unreasonable, not to mention being a big jerk. Most, if not all, would say you aren't to blame. This is because, in this scenario, the control you have over this happening to you is blatantly obvious. You had none.

Now we take the same beginning scenario, except this time Doug doesn't blame you at all. Instead, he blames the tattooist.

Now that Doug thinks differently, what do you think of him? Do you think him rational or reasonable? Is he right to blame the tattooist?

I bet for many people, this time they think differently of Doug. They may think Doug is being perfectly rational and reasonable. They may think Doug is right to blame the tattooist.

Now let's suppose the tattooist is caught. After a number of psychological exams, it's determined that the tattooist is clinically insane. He has escaped from a mental institute. Now it appears a little murkier. Some might still agree with Doug, while others might say that the tattooist could not control himself. His disorder caused him to do those crazy acts.

And last of all, imagine the scenario in which the tattooist was caught and wasn't found clinically insane. Instead, it's found that he has been hypnotized and brainwashed to do these things whenever he receives a phone call from a woman who says the word "turkey" and then hangs up. The brainwashing started as an experiment when he was born by a corporation that had the monetary ability to engrain this hypnotic state so strongly that as an adult he would automatically pull these actions off and not know he had done it afterward.

This becomes even murkier. To many it would appear that Doug should not blame the tattooist. Of course, someone may now place most of the blame on the people that brainwashed the tattooist.

These different endings to the same initial scenario are posed to show why people blame others.

- In the first scenario, most people would say you are not to blame for the tattoo on your forehead.

- In the second scenario, most people would say the tattooist was to blame.

- The third scenario doesn't seem as obvious that the tattooist should be blamed.

- And the last scenario is even less obvious that the tattooist was to blame.

The more it appears that the person had control over their actions, the more it seems we can place blame on them. As soon as someone has no control over their actions, such as being knocked out and tattooed, the less it makes sense to pose blame.

What is really happening here is a perception of free will. The more one feels a person had the "free will" to do other-

183

wise using their own volition, the more they get blamed for the bad action. Such feelings, however, are based entirely on the illusion of free will.

It appears to not make much sense to place blame on someone that doesn't have free will, any more than it would make sense to blame you for getting that insulting tattoo on your forehead. As a side note, this is also problematic for the theist who holds that their god places blame on a person. The idea of a god in that sense will be addressed in a later chapter.

But what of criminals, you might say. Let's go back to the scenario of the tattooist. Let's say that this tattooist is not clinically insane and has not been brainwashed. Should we blame the tattooist if he did not have the free will to choose another path? No. Should we prevent him from tattooing others? Yes. Should we attempt to fix the psychology within the tattooist that thinks such behavior is acceptable? Yes. Should we punish the tattooist? A much trickier question in which deterrence and rehabilitation might require some punishment. Punishing for retributive reasons, however, should never happen. This will be addressed in the later chapter about the justice system.

And if the tattooist had a brain tumor that was causing him to do these things, well, remove it. If we cannot remove it? We should still prevent him from doing it again. Is he to "blame" in the sense that he deserves to be locked away? No, but people do not "deserve" to be knocked out and tattooed either. It's the harm that he's doing to others that needs to be prevented, regardless if a brain tumor is causing his actions. We just need to understand that he didn't have the ability to, of his own accord, do otherwise than he did.

Deservingness over Others

On the opposite end of the spectrum, suggesting that a person is *more* deserving than another requires just as much free will as suggesting they are to blame. If a person puts work into something, they are considered deserving of what they get out of it. If someone doesn't put work into something, they are considered less deserving, or to blame for their negative circumstances. These considerations imply that each individual had the free will to put work into something or not. That they could have, of their own accord, chosen otherwise.

Just like blameworthiness, we have a tendency to suggest someone more deserving when they do something (some action) that leads to something of value. We normally don't say that someone who wins some random lottery that everyone's automatically entered into is more deserving of winning that lottery than another...just for winning the lottery. We don't say, "Just because she won the lottery, she deserved to win it over everyone else." It was happen-chance. Causal luck.

On the other hand, if she built a business from the ground up and earned profits equal to that of a lottery, well then, we have the tendency to place her on a pedestal above those less fortunate. But once again, the person who built the business and the person who didn't were both brought to those very paths from events outside of their control. The states of mind that allowed the woman to build such a business came about via the same type of happen-chance.

It's important to understand that suggesting a person's to blame or to suggest they are more deserving are logically bankrupt concepts. They've been built entirely on the illusion of free will.

You may point to a person and say, "That guy is lazy! He doesn't do any work. He doesn't deserve such and such rewards." It may be true that he is indeed lazy, a slacker, and doesn't put in any effort or work. It also must be understood that he had no other viable option that he could have chosen of his own volition.

You may then say, "I, however, worked hard. I deserve such and such reward." And you may in fact have worked your buns off. You also had no other viable option that you could have chosen through your own volition.

It may be that the reward was an incentive that caused you to work hard, and for the lazy guy it wasn't enough incentive. But you couldn't have chosen it *not to be* enough incentive, and the lazy guy couldn't have chosen it *to be* enough incentive. Both are tied to past causality that they ultimately had no control over.

One is not more deserving of their past causality than another, or more blameworthy of their past causality than another. This means that one is not more deserving of the fruits of reward which their past causality *allowed for*. I know this all sounds strange. It intuitively doesn't feel right, especially given the free will psychology most have built up throughout a lifetime.

One mistake people make is in thinking I'm not advocating for incentives. I believe, at least given our current psychological states, that to motivate people, we still need incentive. This in no way means that those who work toward such incentives are more deserving of obtaining those incentives. It just means we cannot get rid of incentives that place some above others without dire consequences...yet. I talk more about this in the section on economics. Make no mistake about it; incentives are important as long as most people still have their embedded free will psychology.

For now, what is important to understand is:

- People are not blameworthy

- People are not more deserving than others

Fairness and Equality

This fact that being 'blameworthy' or being 'more deserving than another' is illogical has direct implications on how we view fairness and equality. If a person is not to blame for their actions, and a person isn't more deserving of something over another person based on their actions, it would seem that the

186

fairest actions would be those that safely[58] equalize. This can never happen as long as people hold on to the illogical notion of free will. As long as they think they are more deserving, they will shout "not fair!" as soon as we try to equalize them with someone they feel is *"less deserving"* and *"to blame"* for the negative state they're in.

This is why we need to look at this from ground up. We need to look at the base for the psychology they are holding on to. And that's the psychology that the belief in free will has engrained in them from day one. It's engrained in me as well. Our intuitive notions of fairness and equality are all wrong.

This book has a section devoted to the poor free will psychology people have. When people suggest that the debate on free will isn't important, as people will act as if they have free will anyway, they miss the point. They don't understand the psychology such a notion of free will creates. The psychology that places false blame. The psychology that grants people a false sense of worthiness over others. The psychology that makes people support unfairness as the rule, not the exception. The psychology that allows for extreme levels of imbalance and inequality.

26

An Important Base for Political and Economic Philosophy

"Economics is a balancing act between incentive and equality."

Many political or economic models have a base built ground up on the belief in free will. As long as people begin to incorporate the philosophy that there is no free will into their model, that is all that's important given the facts. I'm not asking people to accept my own economic philosophy here, only that they adjust their own based on a lack of free will. If, on the other hand, they ignore this fact, that is where I see a big problem. I assert that any political or economic model of any worth needs to incorporate this as a base structure. If it doesn't, it builds its model based on fictions. I may not fully promote my specific model of preference in this book, but I may come across as knocking down those ideas that rely on a notion of free will.

If no one is more deserving of their quality of life than another, the only fair thing is to equal everything out, *if it were possible to do so safely while holding a thriving economy.* Unfortunately, this is an unrealistic goal, at least at this point in history. Because it's unrealistic, our political and economic policies need to incorporate unfair and unequal rules. Ideally, if everyone was on board or understood the importance of productivity as well as keeping things equal, we wouldn't need these unfair rules.

Unfortunately, that isn't the case, so they are needed for a sustained economy. Too many people hold the belief in free will, and just as importantly, have a free will psychology.

There are many arguments that suggest that some people may be more deserving while others are to blame for the situation they are in. For example, some people cite cases where a person living in dire poverty or poor environment was able to work around those limitations, become educated, and become well off or even excessively wealthy. They cite these success stories and say, "If they can do it, so can anyone else." They suggest that the people that don't make it are at fault. This type of thinking is false, and yet there are people who want to inject these ideas into policy. Don't tax the wealthy any higher than the poor, they say. After all, they worked harder to get on top. They deserve what they make, and much of the poor are at fault for their own situation.

Does a person deserve to be wealthy? What does it mean to say someone is more "deserving" of something than another person? Is someone really to blame for being poor? If people are products of past causal events (or even acausal events), the notions of being more deserving or less deserving need to be dropped, as pointed out in the previous chapter.

At this point you may be saying, "But wait a second! Hold your horses 'Trick! If we distribute wealth so that someone that's lazy gets as much as someone that works hard, this will remove all incentive to work hard and produce anything of value."

And to this I agree. I'm not saying that this is what should be done. Remember the part I said about necessary unfairness. Economics is a balancing act between incentive and equality. We may need to be unfair and unequal to others to create an incentive of productivity that will help the larger civilization in the long run.

But in doing so, we also need to *admit* such unfairness. Not recognizing the unfairness can lead to an extreme imbalance. Recognition that we need to have a cap on incentives that lead to a high level of unfairness is in order. Those at the poor level are not there of any free will, and neither are those at the top level of wealth. That's where causality has led them. The trick is to create just the right incentive for productivity, and at the same time minimize the unfairness involved. A tricky balancing act indeed.

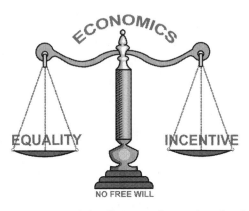

Figuring out the right line to draw that leads to enough productivity for a healthy economy while offering the most fairness is anything but easy. Someone will always end up on top while others on the bottom. Capping the top so that it cannot be an extreme top could help balance things out, without killing productivity. Incentive is based on the psychology of how a person "feels" about something. Not on the logical conclusion: that we don't have free will.

I once had a debate with someone who had more of a free market ideology. He made a statement that "If someone labors a 3, they should get a 3. If someone has a 1, the person with a 3 having to give 1 to that person would be 'unfair'."

Such a statement implies that someone laboring a 3 deserves the product or output of a 3, more than the person who has a 1. What they fail to account for is that such laboring of a 3 was brought about through a long line of past causal events that lead the person up to the ability and desire to labor a 3. They are no more deserving of owning a 3 than the person that did not labor (due to their past causality) and only has a 1. Of course, by making the person with the 3 give the person that did not labor at all a 1, all incentive for the person to labor a 3 is thrown out the window. This is due to the person that is laboring a 3 feeling they "deserve" a 3 in return, even though they were lucky enough to be endowed with the causality to be able to labor a 3.

It's also a disincentive for the person who has the 1 to labor at all. Economics becomes sort of a playing to the psychologies of individuals. The goal is to create enough productivity (through incentive) to keep things going and healthy (economically viable), and at the same time keep things as equal as possible within the context of the need for such productivity. In other words, we need to sacrifice some equality and fairness to create incentives that play to *illogical* psychologies.

In an ideal world, everyone would realize that they should be productive for the civilization they live in to thrive, which would be good for themselves as well, and at the same time understand that no one is more deserving than another, even if they are more productive.

Instead, people hold to this egocentric psychology that says "me me me" or "me and my kind." In other words, if they can get away with making a 2 without laboring, why should they bother laboring? Or if they labor a 3, why should they have to give any of that to others to equal things out?

Since we are not at the point in our psychologies to understand that everyone should be as equal as we can make them in regards to a quality of life, because no one is more or less deserving of their quality of life, we must throw selfish incentives into the equation. This "needing incentive" mindset creates competition, and forces people to either swim or die. It has no sympathy for the suffering it creates for those that don't have the causality that leads them up to be able to swim. If we don't want this suffering to occur, someone has to pay for life jackets or floatation devices, even if they "feel" it should be up to them whether they pay for it. If that person is not more deserving of what they have, why would they think they should have a total right to it when others aren't even close to being equal?

The short answer is: they shouldn't. Again, and it's important I repeat this, this doesn't mean we can force absolute equality on to people without drastic consequences. There are pragmatic reasons not to. But if we are to be intellectually honest, we must admit that those consequences are the result of poor thinking and poor psychological states. Thinking that has its base on the notion of free will. To keep our economy going, we need to tailor to this poor psychology that some are more deserving than others, at the expense of people who, logically, are not any less deserving. We need to find that point of balance between the two, at least until the majority of people hold a psychology that aligns with what's logical. At least until people begin to understand that free will does not exist, and bettering the civilization in which one lives is all the incentive needed.

Force

Should we apply force to help equal things out to the extent in which we pragmatically can? Some would suggest that we shouldn't.

To those people, I'd suggest we have to use intervention and regulation in an attempt to equalize. And if people go against such flow, yes, force may be required. Otherwise the "people have the free will to decide to sink or swim" mentality wins out and people are *forced* to sink. People that don't *deserve* to sink. There's no difference in intentionally using force to prevent something from happening and intentionally deciding not to use force, which forces the other occurrence to happen. These are just different ways to force events. It's a misunderstanding to think that *not acting* is equal to *not forcing*. Inaction is a way of letting causal events happen that can be just as harmful, intentional, and forced as an action with the same outcome.

In fact, what some would call "inaction," I would call "action." It's really the *act* of "not doing." And such action has consequences that force states on others.

Those that oppose actions of force against others are quick to point out corruption that happens within systems that require it. Those of state intervention and regulation, for example. They neglect the corruption that takes place if such intervention and regulation doesn't take place. They neglect to address what's fair in a universe where free will is logically impossible. Where one person is not more deserving than another, and another person is not to blame for the state they end up in. Where the wealthy only think that they are more deserving of their wealth than the beggar on the street. That they should have ultimate ownership rights to the wealth that they've acquired at the expense of those without basic necessities such as food and shelter.

They only have such rights because they are given such rights. Not because they should have such rights. Again, they are not more deserving of them. In an entirely fair society, a person should only have the economic comfort and lifestyle that we can afford all others to have. Since we don't live in such society, since people still hold strong to this egocentric and selfish point of view, force is needed to, at the very least, cut *the excess* and funnel it down to those in need. That means all of the excess that we can get away with and still stay economically viable.

How much excess we can get away with will have to do with how many people are still stuck with the free will psychology. The more people that irrationally believe they are more deserving than others, the more we need to bend to their irrationality at the expense of others for the sake of overall productivity and the economy. The goal is to find that line, a line that hopefully will lower as people begin to become enlightened about the lack of free will.

27

Scientific Evidence for the Lack of Free Will: Neuroscience

*'We don't feel that we have made a decision until a brain
state already happens that dictates the decision we will make.'*

Scientific evidence isn't needed to show that free will is incoherent. It's important to note this to those that reject an entirely naturalistic world view.

Regardless, neuroscience is beginning to ask the question and the results are leaning toward empirical evidence that there is no free will. Evidence beyond the (entirely sufficient) logic already provided.

One study has been conducted by the Max Planck Institute and published in Nature Neuroscience.[59] It's an updated experiment along the lines of an experiment by Benjamin Libet. Participants were asked to press a button with either their right hand or their left. They could choose which button they pressed, and when to press it. They only had to keep track of what time they felt they had made up their minds. Around seven seconds before they felt they made up their minds, the researchers were able to predict which button they would press.

How did they do this? By looking at a brain scan taken earlier than when the person felt they had made the definite decision. The prediction was not perfect, but it was definitely above chance. This suggests an unconscious element in our decision making process. An element that happens prior to our conscious choices.

This means that these brain patterns lead to the conscious feeling of choice. We don't feel that we have made a decision until a brain state already happens that dictates the decision we will make.

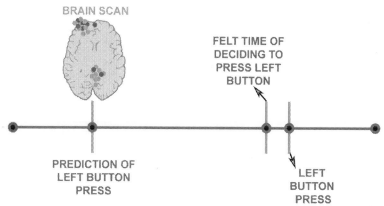

BRAIN SCAN

FELT TIME OF
DECIDING TO
PRESS LEFT
BUTTON

PREDICTION OF
LEFT BUTTON
PRESS

LEFT
BUTTON
PRESS

The "decision" itself is dictated by the brain state that exists prior to the decision. Think about the implication of this. Think about how this relates to the causality already discussed.

The brain state holds the configuration of the selection a person will decide on --> The person decides what the configuration dictates, in which they now get a conscious feeling of making such a choice, many seconds after the configuration dictates the choice.

It's clear that the brain state precedes the thought of the decision. But there is more insinuated in this. The brain state (that led to the decision) would happen from other thoughts, and those thoughts would be derived from a brain state that preceded them. It's a feedback loop. Thought adjusts brain state, which outputs new thought, which adjusts brain state, which outputs new thought. All part of a causal chain of events.

Is it possible that a decision prepared by these prior brain states can be reversed? That's still being investigated, and if so, there must be some other causal element that would do so. Regardless, the findings of such studies are not negligible. They are strong supporting evidence for what we can already know via a little bit of impartial reasoning. Free will doesn't exist.

As I was working on the second draft of this book (planning a number of drafts to clarify and perfect it), Sam Harris published his book called "Free Will".[60] If you are looking for further understanding of the neuroscience of this feeling of free will and why free will is incoherent, I recommend this short but concise book. Though not all encompassing, the information it does give, especially in the realm of neuroscience, is really wonderful.

The Burden of Proof

If you've been around science or philosophy, at some point you've heard the term "Burden of Proof." This means that someone who is making a claim has the burden of providing evidence for such a claim. It's not that simple, however. You see, depending on the claim made, some people might have more of a burden to provide evidence for the claim than others.

Some people misunderstand where the burden of proof resides when talking about science or critical thought. The burden of proof is always on the person claiming the *existence* of something. In other words, those that claim free will *exists* hold the burden of proof.

When people who believe in free will say that the burden of proof is on the person who disagrees, they commit what is called a burden of proof fallacy (also known as "shifting the burden of proof"). Within such fallacy, the burden of proof is placed on the wrong side. That being they don't need to prove their claim, but rather others need to prove their claim false.

An example of this might be someone who believes in "psychic powers." When asked what their proof is, if they say: "No one has been able to prove that people don't have psychic powers," they've shifted the burden using a fallacy. They are basically saying that the burden of proof is on you to *disprove* psychic powers, rather than them to prove them.

196

Science can prove that people hold the *feeling* of free will. This is undeniable, and no determinist or incompatibilist, as far as I know, would suggest otherwise. Science does not prove, however, that people have free will. This is an important distinction that must be made to those who try to push the burden of proof on to those that say free will doesn't exist. There is no proof of free will existing.

The feeling of free will is not evidence for free will, any more than the observation of parallel train tracks converging at the horizon is evidence that those train tracks actually converge. Free will is an extraordinary claim that requires extraordinary evidence. Evidence that breaks it away from being susceptible to various logical rules.

Even though there is no proof for free will (though plenty for the *feeling* of it), there's scientific evidence against it. And since free will is also logically incoherent, it's simply absurd to hold that free will exists, without evidence of such, with evidence against, and with it being logically impossible. The fact that the person claiming free will exists holds the burden of proof only adds yet another plus to the non-free will side.

Even though there is plenty of evidence and reasoning that supports the fact that free will cannot exist, watch out for those who try to shift the burden anyway. Not only are they incorrect as to where the burden is, it's a technique used to distract from the arguments made against free will. And even if the burden was placed on the person to "prove a negative," in the case of free will that negative has been proven!

28

Consciousness Food for Thought

'The evidence which supports consciousness emerging from entirely physical properties places the burden of proof solely on the person that claims something beyond this.'

Consciousness is a word that has many different interpretations as to its ontology (if it exists, and if so, how it exists), and once existence is assumed, what it is and how it arises. There are many different takes on consciousness, from the entirely materialistic to some sort of mind/body dualism. Of course, even if someone accepts a dualistic idea, as shown previously, the idea would not help with free will in any way. A person's idea of consciousness does, however, tend to play into their idea of free will. In other words, many people think their consciousness is something beyond material, maybe even happening in some other realm. This interpretation of consciousness creates something mysterious, which in turn assists with contriving free will.

Understanding that there is no reason to think that consciousness can't emerge through material means helps with this. In this chapter, I'll give you some things to ponder when thinking about consciousness. I'll also explain why a materialistic view has evidence that should be accounted for, while a dualistic account does not.

To get the thought process moving, I think an analogy is in order. It's in no way a perfect analogy for consciousness, but

198

rather an analogy to show how something a little more abstract can come about through something physical.

Visualize a record player (if you are old enough to know what one is) with a spinning record. As the record spins, forcing a needle along the grooves, those grooves output sound waves. The compilation of sound waves through time make a song that can be heard by those that have a brain connected to working ears.

Everything is material: the player, the structure of the grooves of the record and needle, and the sound waves breaking through the air. If we were to take away the ears from hearing the sound waves, it can be argued that those waves would still exist in the same formation. We just wouldn't have the hardware to interpret those waves as Beethoven's 9th symphony. We recognize the song when we listen to these different waves strung together through the time period they resonate during. These structures exist for a person or device that can interpret them, such as a person or recording device.

I would suggest that, on a much more complex level, it is a similar type of thing with mind and thought. The neuro-structure of the brain is the "grooves" of the record; the entire system that allows the blood flow to the brain, chemicals to happen in it, and electrical impulses to spark are the player and the needle; and the actual accumulation of conscious experience that these output through time are the sound waves that play out in a cohesive order (the music). A large difference is that the brain is also what reads that output. I have no doubt that in the future we will be able to read these brain states, record them, and play them back in some way.

The tricky part with such a simplistic analogy is that the record player doesn't experience. It does not experience the sound it produces, for example. When talking about consciousness, certain experiences are called "qualia." Qualia is the subjective experiences that our consciousness produces. Pain, color, taste, smell, and sound are all qualia. We experience the redness of a rose, for example. It happens internally, and unless others have seen the color red, it is impossible to communicate what that color is. Each person needs to experience it for themselves, and even then, we cannot know that what they experience is the same as what we experience. We infer they experience similarly because the bodies of each human are so genetically similar. Some people with color vision deficiency may be experiencing the color entirely differently, which we can test for using a color blindness test. How qualia is experienced is directly influenced by the configuration of a person at a given time. The configuration itself is forced through genetic factors as well as environmental factors.

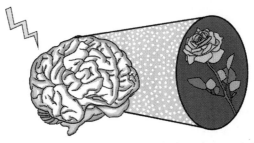

Imagine yourself turning your head and perceiving the deep blueness of the ocean. Now imagine you can freeze time the instant right before the perception takes place.

The matter that makes up your brain is configured in a specific way (chemicals, electrons, neurons, synapses, etc.), your eyes have a specific setup (maybe they are near or far sighted), and every molecule of your body is set. Your entire environment is set, including the waves in the ocean. Picture this frozen point in time as a snapshot of the configuration of the universe at that time. You unfreeze that instant and experience the blueness of the ocean. Your subjective experience of that ocean is entirely dependent on the very configuration of that preceding snapshot. If, within that snapshot, your brain was configured as a color blind person's brain, the experience of the ocean's color would be drastically different once you unfreeze time. Let's go back to the original snapshot and talk about what forces such a configuration. Imagine taking a snapshot of the instant right before the first snapshot. The configuration of that snapshot would force the configuration of the next. So on and so forth. In this way, the configuration of the state that grants the experience of qualia is entirely forced by every configuration (snapshot) before it. So what is this "qualia"? In this view, I'd suggest that qualia or experience is the series of configurations playing out, just as the song plays through the series of configurations (needle moving to different friction points in the groove at different times).

Questions regarding what qualia is and how it comes about are called the "hard problem of consciousness." In scientific terms, such questions are not fully answered. This is why there are so many interpretations from mind body dualism, to hard line physicalism, to other speculative theories using quantum mechanics.

For this topic, we only have to see that there is an undeniable connection between the grey matter of your brain and the qualia you experience. The way your brain is configured produces the output you perceive, which in turn has an effect on the brain, which in turn has an effect on the output, so on and so forth.

So why is a materialistic view of consciousness one that should be highly considered? The short answer: evidence. It can be inferred via science. If we damage the brain, that damage can alter a person's consciousness dramatically. If we remove a section of the brain from a person, they will miss various properties of their consciousness that they had prior to the removal. A tumor in the brain can change a person and even make them do things they wouldn't without the tumor. If consciousness was something other than emergent properties of the brain, why would we lose such things as short term or long term memory with brain damage? Neuroscience makes an undeniable connection from the physical hardware to conscious experience. If we stimulate a certain section of the brain, we can make a person think they are lifting their right hand, even though they are lifting their left. If we change the chemical composition of the brain, or interrupt signals using drugs, someone can be in an entirely altered state of consciousness. They may even hallucinate. This is due to changing the physical neuro-structure. The seven second ability to know what button someone will press before they do, discussed in the last chapter, is further evidence for a materialistic view of consciousness.

The evidence which supports consciousness emerging from entirely physical properties places the burden of proof solely on the person that claims something beyond this. It may be that there is some external, mystical, nonphysical component to consciousness, but it's not on the onus of the materialist to disprove such things. The onus is on the person who believes in such things to show evidence for it. All of the evidence we have points to the brain as the processor of consciousness.

It is important to note that even if one still doesn't take on a materialistic view of consciousness, any other view still cannot escape the causal/acausal dichotomy. The duelist must contend with the possible ways in which the separate "mind" or "soul" can come about and interact with the physical brain or body (and vice versa). Such non-physical events must come about and interact either causally or acausally. Logic dictates they are not immune to this dichotomy. No event is, no matter how fantastical the realm that these events are postulated to exist in is. Even within the realm of fantasy there needs to be logical consistency. Otherwise it's something even beyond the fantasy of unicorns and into the incoherent absurdity of pink unicorns that are, at the same time, colorless and not unicorns. I'll address this in the next chapter.

29
Immaterial or Spiritual "Free Will"

'If you were Hitler, you'd have the soul of Hitler. You wouldn't have the free will to decide to have the soul of someone else.'

Some theists, spiritualists (for lack of a clearly defined word), or non-naturalists believe that the *no free will* stance (for example, the hard determinist stance) is one of a strictly materialistic viewpoint. They may make the claim that a god, some other "non-material" or "spiritual" entity, or some other supernatural system, can grant a person free will.

The first thing that needs to be addressed is if these no free will stances are bottled up in materialism. Mind you that the physics of a material system is an excellent reason to take such a stance, as suggested in previous chapters. In this chapter, I want to break away from the materialistic perspective into a more phantasmagorical realm to see if such a notion is at all logical in regards to an "immaterial" free will.

As discussed in previous chapters, an event can come about via only two possibilities. Either an event is caused (causal), or it is not caused (acausal). This dichotomy applies to any and all situations, either material or immaterial. If someone claims this is a false dichotomy, they need to supply how an event can be neither caused nor uncaused, but rather something else. They will quickly realize that these two states are opposites. If an event happens and one of these options is negated, the other option must be true.

Even if an event is caused from a combination of other events that are both caused and uncaused, that particular event is caused.

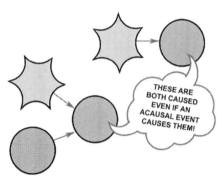

An immaterial, supernatural, or "spiritual" cause is still a cause, and an immaterial, supernatural, or spiritual acausal event is still an acausal event. To suggest that something can transcend this dichotomy is to suggest a complete absurdity. A materialistic mindset is not needed to understand this, only a logical mindset is required. We can speculate on the existence of invisible, mystical, magical, non-physical places that at some level interact with our own physical existence, but to fathom that these places can have events in them that breach the dichotomy is about as incoherent as one can get.

All of the logic regarding causal events, acausal events, and time already addressed apply to any immaterial notions of events. They are in no way exclusive to a materialistic point of view.

Let's, for example, address the notion of a soul. Within many religions, people believe that they have a body, and they have a soul. The soul is, to them, something outside of the physical universe. It's supernatural rather than natural.

The question still remains, how did such soul come about? And could such a soul have been different? If it could have been different, what could have caused the difference? We know that something can't (logically) be both the cause of a specific soul and not the cause of that specific soul (the cause of a "different" soul instead). The only logical possibility is if an acausal event came in which changed the soul into something different. In other words, if we are to say that a soul doesn't break logic itself, it's entirely susceptible to the causal/acausal dichotomy.

That means you simply have no say in the soul you have. If you were Hitler, you'd have the soul of Hitler. You wouldn't have the free will to decide to have the soul of someone else. If you were the pope, you'd have the soul of the pope. If you were a dog, you'd have...wait...do dogs have souls? If souls exist, I don't think dogs would be excluded.

A soul simply cannot grant free will.

But what if you say a soul does break logic itself? Sure, we could say such things, but it simply means that it would be something entirely incoherent. Something that would make no sense to address as anything we could even postulate as us "having." We could never identify anything as a "soul" if it could break the logical need of *identity*[61] itself.

Dialogue

LIBERIUS: Even if material free will can't exist, that is only the materialist's perspective. Something outside of our physical restrictions could grant us free will.

ORION: Interesting thought. I would hate to pigeon hole this discussion into an entirely materialistic discussion. I'd like you to explain to me how a non-physical system would work. Would, for example, a non-physical event be free from causality?

LIBERIUS: It would certainly be free from material causality, that being matter interacting with other matter.

ORION: Other than one being material and one not being material, how would, or could, causality differ between the two types of causality? What I mean by this is, would not a relationship exist between cause and effect, no matter if the cause is non-material and the effect material, or the cause non-material and the effect non-material, or the cause material and the effect non-material?

LIBERIUS: Yes, but since time as we know it is part of matter, a non-material cause wouldn't necessarily be constrained by such time. This is an obvious difference.

ORION: Am I right in saying that the non-material thing, whether it is a god, a spiritual system, or some other undefined non-material system, would need to interact causally with the willer, regardless of when it actually happens on such "non-material" plane of existence, and regardless if time has any meaning at all on such a plane?

LIBERIUS: Yes, there would need to be an interaction, but the interaction could go both ways. So, for example, let's say that a choice comes up to either drink lemonade or drink soda. It may be that the mind moves from physical willer to this non-material system. From there the non-physical system configures the information in such a way that frees it.

ORION: This configuration that you talk about, it would appear to be some sort of process. Whether the process happens in a specific time order, or the process happens going back, forth, and sideways through time, or whether time as we know it does not happen, such a process would need to be causal. At the least, the "choice" has to be a cause that affects the "process" of this non-physical system. The non-physical system would have to either process causal events, or acausal events would happen within it. It would then need to send the result back causally to the mind. How can such a process free the thought when the process must be constrained by either causal or acausal events?

LIBERIUS: You are suggesting that a non-physical process must be constrained to causal or acausal events. Maybe these events are different for the non-physical.

ORION: For example?

LIBERIUS: Maybe this non-physical system is able to separate out the choices, making each one free from any causality.

ORION: Then how does one of the choices get selected?

LIBERIUS: Well, that is where free will comes in.

ORION: So free will selects the choice, and not the person?

LIBERIUS: The person has free will.

ORION: You are acting like free will is this thing you own that goes out and selects from options.

LIBERIUS: Well, you don't own it. In this instance, it would just be a non-physical part of you.

ORION: But what leads this non-physical part of you to select one of the options, if not a causal chain of events, or an acausal happening?

LIBERIUS: I'm not saying it does not happen causally or acausally.

ORION: You did say that. But again, if they do happen causally or acausally, then why would this non-physical system be any different than its physical counterpart in regards to the logical reasoning of why those events are incompatible with free will?

LIBERIUS: Whaddaya mean?

ORION: I mean, I think you are assuming the reasoning regarding causal and acausal events only applies to material events. The reason applies to all events that happen, material or not.

LIBERIUS: Such realms would be outside of logic or reason.

ORION: If that is the case, we could make up anything in such realm. The claim of an *invisible pink square circle that is both an elephant and not an elephant* would be equally as sensible in such realm. Certainly you see the problem with this?

LIBERIUS: All we see is the physical, so we base what we know on what we can see. Maybe things outside of this don't follow the same laws.

ORION: Let's, for the sake of argument, assume it possible. In fact, let's say that in this non-physical realm, contradictions can happen. An absurdity. What can we make of it? How can we interpret what we can only view as "nonsense we cannot understand" as free will?

LIBERIUS: All I am saying is that it simply opens up the possibility of free will.

ORION: It also opens up the possibility that you have turkey will?

LIBERIUS: Err, turkey will?

ORION: Yes, every thinking decision you make goes into a non-physical system created by turkey minds. The decision goes into the turkey minds, which they do not understand. The turkeys think about a gobble, which pushes one of the decisions back to you. That is the thing you end up choosing.

LIBERIUS: Maybe, but free will is something we feel we have. That makes it more likely than turkey will.

208

ORION: No, my turkey scenario is actually more likely, as it's causal in the way we understand it and there is no self-contradiction for it. A non-physical system that is neither causal nor acausal in the sense that we know and understand these terms is closer to saying that our decisions come from turkey minds that are simultaneously not turkey minds. The point I'm making here is that we can postulate bizarre claims that we cannot know, such as floating turkey minds, and that is bad enough. To go one step further and allow for logical absurdities into those claims is beyond anything we can consider a reasonable conclusion. If logic doesn't apply, then any absurd claim can be justified. And I mean literally anything. The claim that an invisible one hundred foot tall Godzilla[62] visibly lives in my underwear can be justified.

LIBERIUS: Okay, we'll keep the discussion in the realm of what is logical.

ORION: Otherwise we'd need to get into the topic of epistemology, which addresses appropriate standards of knowledge. A much longer topic. Agreeing that free will is illogical, and believing that it exists anyway, is problematic to say the least. Anyone can believe anything they want, I'm simply saying that believing in free will is illogical, meaning such free will is incoherent. That, I believe, should be sufficient to show why a belief in it is an irrational belief.

30

The Incompatibility of
Future Omniscience

*'You cannot choose apple pie if a deity already
knows you will choose cheesecake.'*

Some theists pose a deity that is omniscient, meaning "all knowing." Part of this omniscience is the ability to know the future. These same theists make the claim that this deity grants us mortals' free will. Unfortunately, they are blind to the incompatibility of this. This incompatibility is different than the determinism reason; however, an understanding of it is helpful in understanding the determinism reason.

Let's, for the sake of this chapter only, assume such a "future knowing omniscient" being exists. Why would this prevent free will? The short answer is that we mortals would be predestined[63] to do what this deity already knows we are going to do. Let's look at two lines. One line representing the past, present, and future that the deity knows will happen, the other representing the past, present, and future path that we will take.

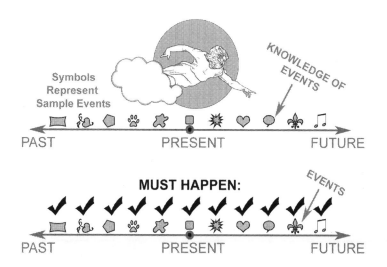

Since the sample events must align with the knowledge of those sample events, the person is forced to one specific path. It simply cannot be that our future is different than that of the omniscient being's knowledge.

For example, such deity would know that you were going to choose cheesecake for dessert next Friday at the restaurant. Since this foreknowledge already exists, when Friday comes around and you are given the dessert menu, you may think you are choosing between multiple viable options such as apple pie, a banana split, cheesecake, or not having dessert at all; but the truth is only one of those options is viable. You cannot choose apple pie if a deity already knows you will choose cheesecake. If you do, then that deity was incorrect, and therefore not omniscient. The only viable option is the cheesecake, even though you feel like you could have chosen otherwise. Free will is just an illusion.

It must be noted that this does not mean the deity forces you to such decision, or that the foreknowledge itself forces you. It simply means that if such absolute foreknowledge is possible, the future is "set in stone." There is no doing otherwise. It must happen in a way that aligns with such knowledge. In other words, what will happen in the future is static rather than dynamic. This is similar to determinism but does not necessarily posit causality as the reason for the static future. Instead such future is just one's fate.

Even though such a deity is a logical absurdity (e.g. how could such a deity ever know it was all knowing?), the idea of such a deity helps to illustrate the point as to how the "feeling" of free will can exist without free will actually existing. This same feeling pertains to the causal and acausal incompatibility of free will as well. Even without such a deity, the feeling of free will does not equate to free will. What catches a lot of people is the counterintuition of this. It is like watching a brilliantly done magic trick in which you cannot figure out how the magician is doing it. The difference is that this magic trick plays over and over again, and you can never see the causality to figure out the trick. It's a trick you have seen since you were born, and everyone around you has always thought it real and not a trick. You never even questioned it as a trick.

One last point in regards to such fatalistic positions, and one of utmost importance. The nature of such fatalistic or predestined positions is different than the nature of something being determined through causal events. In the causal event scenario, you are part of that very causal process. That means what you do is an important part of the process itself. Fatalistic conceptions, however, have a tendency to lead to a mindset that what we do is irrelevant to the outcome. What happens is dictated by god's will, rather than our thoughts and actions that come about through causal events.

In that way, it's more likely to lead to a (dangerous) defeatist attitude. One that simply does not follow logically from deterministic thinking. It's important not to conflate the two ways of thinking. Regardless, such a "future omniscient" being is incompatible with free will.

Dialogue

Endymion sees Liberius and Orion having a discussion and enters into the conversation.

ENDYMION: Hey guys, what are ya up to?

LIBERIUS: Hi, Endymion. Myself and Orion were having a discussion regarding free will. Orion does not believe people have it.

ENDYMION: Is this true, Orion?

ORION: It is.

ENDYMION: Do you believe in god?

ORION: No.

ENDYMION: Well, that might be why you don't believe in free will. You see, free will is something that God has granted us.

ORION: I see. Well, instead of side tracking on to the topic of whether or not a god or gods exist, for the free will argument I will grant you your god definition. Is your god omniscient?

ENDYMION: Yes, God is all-knowing.

ORION: Does this mean that God knows the past, the present, and the future for us mortals?

ENDYMION: It sure does.

ORION: Does God know what you will say and do five minutes from now?

ENDYMION: Of course, like I said, God knows the future.

ORION: Understood. Can you do something different than what God knows you will do in five minutes?

ENDYMION: You misunderstand. I have the free will to decide what I will do five minutes from now, God just knows what I will decide based on my free will.

ORION: I see, but you did not really answer the question. If God knows that you will choose to eat cake five minutes from now, can you decide not to eat cake?

ENDYMION: Well, no, but that does not mean I did not have the free will to choose the cake.

ORION: Could you have chosen ice cream or anything other than the cake? Again, if God knows you will eat cake.

ENDYMION: The question is not whether I could, but rather whether I will. If God knows that I will not, then I will not. God just knows what I will freely choose.

ORION: But if the knowledge that you "will not" is absolute, doesn't it also follow that you "could not" choose ice cream?

ENDYMION: I don't understand. I have already explained that I could choose the ice cream; it is just that I won't choose it.

ORION: If it is known absolutely that you won't choose ice cream, how is it possible that you could choose it?

(Endymion pauses for a moment, frustrated.)

ENDYMION: Okay, okay, I see your point. If God knows all future events, then every event is already predestined. I don't have the free will because I must decide exactly what God already knows.

ORION: Exactly, any accurate future knowledge, if it exists, must be followed exactly. If future knowledge is possible, it is entirely incompatible with free will.

214

ENDYMION: Okay, how about a god that is not omniscient of future events?

As he did with Liberius, Orion explains to Endymion about why any sort of spiritual events would still need to be either causal or acausal. If God interacts with, or creates something else that interacts with, humans, that thing would be a cause. He explains that an event is either caused or it is not, and that both of these options are incompatible with free will.

Endymion doesn't really understand this and walks away, annoyed with the discussion.

31
A Blaming and Punishing Deity

'If a person doesn't have free will, it doesn't make any sense to blame that person.'

As addressed in a previous chapter, blaming a person that doesn't have free will is absurd. This is something that a theist who believes in an omniscient, omni-benevolent, creator deity must contend with. Would it make sense for such a deity to punish those that do not have free will?

Imagine you are a scientist that created a small robot. You program that robot to trash the inside of your home, even though you don't want your home trashed. You are confident that the robot will follow its programming flawlessly. You set the robot in your home and turn it on. You leave the house. The robot then, per it's programming, proceeds to wreck the inside of your home. It throws things around and breaks them. An hour goes by and you walk into your home and find everything trashed. This infuriates you. Luckily for you, you created the robot with a sensor that can feel pain and the ability for it to suffer. You blame the robot for trashing the inside of your home, so you want to punish it. You then proceed to cause the robot pain as punishment.

Does the above scenario strike you as odd in any way? It should. First, you knew that the robot would destroy your home. Second, you created and programmed the robot to destroy your home, so it had to. Third, you put the robot in your home and turned it on. After all of this and after the robot tore up your home, you blamed the robot for its actions. You not only blamed the robot, but you punished it with pain. Any rational person should see the absurdity of this.

If a person doesn't have free will, it doesn't make any sense to blame that person. Knowing this, it's bad enough if you do blame the person. But actually creating the thing that has no free will, understanding what you created has no free will, and then blaming that very thing for its actions, is one step further from absurd. It is deliberately harmful. A creation for the sole purpose of harming that creation.

Such a god wouldn't even need to be all knowing. As long as that god knew you didn't have free will, as we can know this by understanding the causal/acausal dichotomy, and that god still punishes you for your actions through intentional suffering or pain, there is something very disturbing about such an entity.

This is not an argument against god, but rather a certain type of god that relates directly to our lack of free will. This can be bypassed by imagining a god that does not punish retributively. It's something that many theists need to contend with. Especially those that suggest their god would allow a person to be sent to hell (or any place of torment) for their wrongdoing. As a punishment. Wrongdoing that they could not have, of their own accord, done otherwise.

32

How Thought, Logic, and Knowledge come about Causally

*'It simply doesn't follow that an act of free will would lead
someone to use logic and reason, or that causality
cannot etch out a path to the use of such.'*

Certain philosophers claim that holding such ideas as determinism is self-refuting. They believe that to obtain certain types of knowledge (those beyond observation) requires free will (what some call "conscious volition") and a specific method of validation. Others claim that the use of logic is self-refuting in a deterministic universe. Some even suggest that thoughts cannot come about. As you will see, there is no foundation for this way of thinking.

Thought and logic without free will:

Some people suggest that if determinism is true, we are all mindless robots. In a sense, we may be robots (or at least mechanistic), but hardly mindless ones. Conscious thought does come about, regardless if such thought was forced by preceding events. Not only that, but such conscious thoughts are events that cause other events.

This book is an output of thoughts. Those thoughts are part of the chain of events essential for you to be reading this book, and for you to be thinking about the information within this book. Thoughts affect other thoughts. So yes, the universe may be atoms banging about at its lowest levels, but by doing so they output qualities that, due to the nature of them, affect things differently. A brick dropped in water will sink; a brick dropped on a hard surface will stop at the top of it and maybe break. Two different qualities based on the configuration of atoms of a liquid versus a solid with two different results for the brick.

Likewise, thoughts happen through a complex interaction of events, and such thoughts interact differently than other configurations such as bricks. It's an error to suggest that, if determinism is true, thoughts cannot happen. Thoughts come about through those deterministic processes.

An actual argument that I've come across is: without free will, one cannot conclude the lack of free will using logic, as such conclusions come about causally (or not freely). This makes the conclusion that there is no free will, according to this person, self-defeating.

Even if this were true, it would not render determinism false, but rather knowledge impossible. All knowledge. This would include any knowledge that determinism is false as well.

But it's not true.

The conclusion that logic or reason cannot be used in a causal universe is a misconception. I think it stems from deterministic analogies such as billiard balls colliding. The comparison is that if our decisions are causal, and so is one billiard ball hitting another, that they are equivalent. Therefore thinking, or using logic, doesn't really exist. This misses the qualitative factors of each thing. For a person, thinking is *part of* the causal process. Using the methodology of logic is *part of* the causal process. How the thoughts and logic come about are separate from what the thoughts and logic do.

To understand this we need to discuss thought a little more. Thought happens from the processes of the brain (or mind, if you prefer). Just as a computer program displays a character in a video game through an entirely causal process, so does a brain or mind think. Thoughts are the product of causal processes. A character displayed on a monitor is the product of causal processes. What makes thought fundamentally different is the feedback loop. Thoughts cause other thoughts, which make adjustments to information stored in memory, which causes other thoughts, etc. Also, thoughts compete with each other. The thought that "I want that cake," which comes about causally, might compete with the thought "I am overweight and should not eat that cake." Both thoughts are causally taken into account, and the one that wins out is the one that the configuration of the brain or mind allows. A configuration that has come about causally as well.

Logic is comprised of methodological processes. As long as causal thoughts are confined to the accurate use of such methodologies, those thoughts are considered "logical." We determine the strength of logic by its consistency, usefulness, reliability, intuitiveness, and explanatory power.

A rather silly argument I have heard from a philosopher stated that, if the universe is deterministic, it wouldn't make sense for a determinist to debate with people. His reasoning was that if the universe is deterministic, then it would be like arguing with a rock. In fact, this philosopher stated "you wouldn't tell a rock rolling down a hill to roll left or right, so it doesn't make sense to debate with someone who believes in free will." The philosopher makes a large mistake. He equates rocks with humans because they share the characteristic of both happening causally and both taking only one specific path if the universe is deterministic. He also conflates the types of interactions that affect these two things. This equating does not logically follow from these shared characteristics.

It is quite obvious that yelling at a rock will not causally make that rock go left. The only way thought can affect the rock rolling down the hill is if the thought leads to the person placing a block in front of the rock. Of course, a thought is not needed as even a branch falling from a tree can block the rock. The point is in regards to the nature of what affects the rock. The interaction between two thinking and communicating humans is different than the interaction between a thinking and communicating human and a rock that does neither. Hearing or reading words create an effect (a change of brain state) in the brain of the person that hears or reads them. So, unlike the rock, if a person tells another person to go left, depending on what is in the person's mind at the time, they may do that. Those words may be a cause of that action. It matters not that those words came about causally.

Causal forces lead to people that understand logic, science, or mathematics and apply such methodologies, and causal forces lead to people that accept less consistent and reliable standards and apply those instead. An interaction of language communicating animals is part of these forced events that can adjust a mind in a certain direction.

Knowledge without free will:

I am not going to get deep into the topic of epistemology, that being, understanding what knowledge is, understanding what the best standards are to obtain it, understanding how we know what we know, and so on. That is yet another book sized topic.

What I'm going to explain is, no matter if free will exists or not, it makes no difference to the question of whether knowledge can be obtained and how. All of the problems inherent in epistemology exist regardless of these facts.

So, for example, someone might claim that if determinism holds, then what a person thinks she knows is determined by past events. And since they have no control over those events, they cannot know if those events have led them to real knowledge of something. This thinking has a deep misunderstanding of how we gather information. Even if we had some mystical free will, or if determinism did not hold true (which would just inject in acausal events), we have the very same problem. We still have to gather information about something, and try to parse the truth of that information. And we can still be wrong about it.

Whether a misunderstanding of something comes through a causal chain of events of gathering misinformation, or we gather such misinformation using free will (whatever that would mean), we still have the problem that it could be wrong. And if we use a methodology and base that on the consistency of the results of such methodology, we still need to learn such methodology and apply it.

Whether we learn it or apply it due to past events, or we learn it and apply it of our own volition, we still are learning it and applying it. And we still can do so based on the results we perceive of it. And we can still do so using methodologies that we know are consistent and reliable.

It simply doesn't follow that an act of free will would lead someone to use logic and reason, or that causality cannot etch out a path to the use of such. It simply doesn't follow that an act of free will would allow someone to automatically know and understand if they have made a mistake. Even if some magical free will was possible, that wouldn't imply they were free to always be correct. If it did, then we could dismiss such notions of free will on the fact alone that almost everyone (more likely everyone rather than almost everyone) is incorrect about something they think they are correct on.

33

Knowing the Future

*'The predictive capabilities of science
have been proven over and over again.'*

In a *deterministic universe*, it's true that if we knew, or if we could know, all of the variables, we could theoretically find out what was going to happen in the future. Since, at the quantum scale, there are situations in which it appears we can't know all of the variables, we are limited. We can, however, know or may able to find enough of the variables to make looking for them worthwhile.

The idea that, by knowing all the variables, we can predict future outcomes was posed by a thought experiment called Laplace's demon. The though experiment was published in 1814 by Pierre-Simon Laplace.

The idea of the demon is that if such an entity could know the exact momentum and location of every atom in the universe, it could know the future outcome precisely from that point on. Laplace also believed such an entity would be able to know the past based on that information, which I think he was mistaken on. (See prior chapter regarding effects not causing causes backward.) For this discussion, the more important part is the future knowledge. Proponents of specific quantum interpretations such as the Copenhagen interpretation point out that all variables cannot be known. They miss the point of the thought experiment. It is not to determine whether something could have all of the current variables, it is to question if something did have all of the variables, could it determine the future based on those variables if the universe is causal?

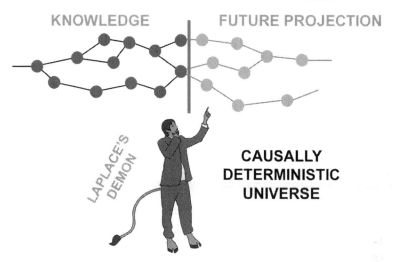

The point that Laplace's demon makes in regards to free will is the one suggested all along for a causal universe. If the universe is causal, and the demon could know all of the variables, the fact that it can predict the future based on those variables and where they will lead to suggests that:

- Any thoughts a person would have would be known by the demon.

- Any actions a person takes would be known by the demon.

- There can be no free will.

Now mind you, the butterfly effect throws a wrench into the situation for humans. A small mistake in data or calculation can lead to a drastically different outcome, as you are aware from the chapter "Determinism does not imply predictability." As stated before, this drastic outcome can even be in the short term. That being said, the long term is even more difficult to project.

This is why we can predict the weather with much more accuracy in the short term than the long term. Figuring out if it will rain in a certain area a few hours from now can be done with much more accuracy than figuring out if it will rain a few weeks from now. The farther out into the future, the more causal events we need to try to account for. The more causal events we need to account for, the more we can miss. One slight miss can throw a future projection off to extreme proportions. As our technology grows, and as we begin to understand underlying causality, we better our chances of getting the initial causes and future projections correct.

Unlike Laplace's demon, there will always be gaps in our knowledge of causes, even if the universe is deterministic and we can locate nonlocal hidden variables. The goal is to make those gaps ones that we can jump over.

For the most part, we already make those jumps. Science has a great predictive capacity, and for this reason alone it makes such methodology one of our best standards of knowledge. For example, astronomers doing mathematics predicted that there would be a thermal radiation left over from the big bang if the theory was correct. Later on, this cosmic background radiation was *accidentally* found by Arno Penzias and Robert Woodrow Wilson as they experimented with the Holmdel Horn Antenna. They detected it, and it matched exactly the astronomers' predictions.

The predictive capabilities of science have been proven over and over again. A theory of gravity might predict that if an apple falls from a tree, it will be attracted toward the center of the Earth. We might predict the likelihood of a natural disaster occurring, or a pandemic spreading. Even in quantum physics, where certain things appear unpredictable, we can predict probabilities of outcomes.

And by now it must be clear, that for anything that is any way predictable, such predictability must be due to causality. There simply is no such thing as a predictable acausal event.

The fact that we can and do make these predictions is simply more evidence of the prevalence of causality within our universe.

••••••

A Fun Quandary to Think About

Here's a thought experiment which entails a device in a deterministic universe that is able to determine every atom, momentum, and location, and based on that could project a future outcome. This device will output a sheet explaining exactly what you will do at a specific time in the future. The thought experiment, however, adds something else into the equation. It gives the sheet to you, who will read the paper and attempt to go against what the sheet determines you would do.

The quandary: It would appear that you would be able to do something different than what the sheet determines. In which case the sheet would be wrong. The problem with this thought experiment is that it assumes the machine would be able to produce such a sheet.

If the device (causally) determines that you will go against the output of the sheet (it factors itself in as a causal agent), it could process an infinite loop and never be able to create the paper. If, at some point in its looping process, it determines wording that you would not causally go against, only then would the loop be broken and it could give you an actual output on paper.

In other words, if the causality only led to you going against what you read, you would never get to read such a sheet. The device would be stuck in a loop as it factored that in.

To give you a basic idea of why it loops, see this example of a "program" trying to determine Y:

1) X = the number this program will predict Y will be
2) Y = any number that is not X
3) If X = Y, goto 4, else goto 1
4) Print Y

No matter what number X is, X will never equal Y, because the criteria is that Y does not equal X. 1 through 3 will loop forever, or until the Y criteria is changed to accept X. The program will never be able to run 4 to print the output of Y.

In other words, the flaw is not with the future being fixed, but rather the program itself, because part of the programming is the variable that you will choose something different than what the program outputs. This creates a loop in the program. Only if the program can determine (based on the causality) that you will not do differently than what is on the sheet can it actually come to a conclusion and print out the sheet. Number 2 is the glitch in the program that prevents X from equaling Y, and that Y would be you going against X in the initial thought experiment.

I bring this to light to show that, if the predictive device is a part of the causal predictive process, then that process must factor in that device. This, however, could potentially lead to problems with being able to output a prediction for such circumstances.

34

Morality, Ethics, and Responsibility without Free Will

'... the ethical system would act as a causal element that could lead a person to or away from a specific action.'

Perhaps the largest problem with suggesting that people lack free will is one that has nothing to do with whether they have it or not, but rather on the ethical implications if they don't. What does it mean for morality or ethics? How about ethical responsibility?

Some use an argument from adverse consequences fallacy to suggest it would be harmful if we didn't, at the very least, believe we have free will, and therefore the free will stance should be believed. Obviously, free will doesn't follow from an implication of harm if it doesn't exist, so such a belief will still be faulty. The question is: should it be believed anyway?

I'd argue that the conclusion of such adverse consequences if we don't believe in free will is unfounded. As will be suggested later, there are more reasons to conclude adverse consequences by holding on to the false belief of free will and the psychology embedded into a person who holds (or even held) such a belief.

The problems with morality, ethics, and responsibility do need to be addressed, as understanding the lack of free will is an important base for these.

Morality, ethics, and responsibility are tricky subjects in philosophy, with various meanings, systems, and ideas.   For simplicity's sake, I'm going to use ethics interchangeably with morality. The word "morality," however, seems to contain a lot of extra baggage that the word "ethics" doesn't, so I'll use the word "ethics" as the primary placeholder.

Also keep in mind, such tangents regarding whether morality or ethics are subjective, inter-subjective, or objective, though important questions, hold little value regarding what the lack of free will means for ethics.

I don't intend to espouse an entire ethical system here. That will be held for another book I'm planning. In such a book I intend to go through all of the little nuances of an ethical system and why some are better (more reasonable) than others. The only point I'm making in this book is in regards to ethics and what the lack of free will means for them, and why ethics are still viable within the no-free will framework. Responsibility is of key importance and needs to be addressed thoroughly as well. It'll be shown that:

- A lack of holding one responsible does not make for a lack of ethics.

The below definitions are for *one type* of ethical system in which free will isn't needed. Keep in mind that the lack of free will is compatible with a number of different types of ethical systems as long as they don't inject that one can be held accountable after the fact. Whatever the ethical system proposed, one thing that must be accounted for is that there is no free will. Those ethical systems that are based on a notion of free will, or based on claiming people blameworthy after the fact, need to be abandoned.

One Example of an Ethical System that Does Not require Free Will

Ethics, for this (consequentialist) example, can be defined as the conscious discerning between consequences that are good or bad, negative or positive, harmful or helpful, or benign (none of these) in which a thinking creature can understand actions that would lead to or prevent these values and align accordingly. It's the philosophical study of how to reach an inherent value state and the *conscious* causal alignment with such. If, through such study, we determine that action X leads to what is a positive (or good) value, we have determined that action X is ethical. If we consciously align with action X, we have acted ethically (per such system). If, through such study, we determine that action Y leads to what is negative (bad, harmful, etc.), we have determined that action Y is unethical. If we consciously align with Y, we have acted unethically. It doesn't matter that the conscious thought comes about through some means beyond the person's control.

It's not my goal in this book to address how such "value" is determined (again, another book, and yes, I plan on detailing this out). Or how there are varying degrees of ethical and unethical actions for this example. The more important point is that the lack of free will doesn't prevent or minimize the study of value or the understanding of actions that lead to or away from such value states. Free will is not a requirement for such an ethical system.

For this example, if kicking a puppy for fun leads to a consequence that is a negative value *(again, how we might get to that won't be addressed here, that depends on a number of considerations that will only sidetrack the point)*, and if we are using a system that determines the ethic based on the consequences *(there are other ethical systems – see deontology and virtue ethics)*, it's unethical. If we know that it's unethical to kick the puppy for fun, but we do so anyway, we are acting unethically (per such system). And if we know it's unethical to kick the puppy for fun, so we don't kick the animal, we are acting ethically.

As you can see, free will is not needed for a system of ethics. The larger confusion arises between ethics and responsibility. These aren't the same thing. I repeat, these aren't the same thing. Whether someone has the freedom to act this way or that, or they don't, is independent of whether they would understand that such actions they do would be negative or positive (good or bad, etc.) and if they causally have a concern over acting ethical based on such a system. Even entirely mindless events can be deemed as "bad" or "negative." For example, a tornado that takes out homes and kills or injures numerous people most would deem as bad. Of course we would never deem a tornado as immoral or unethical. This is because the tornado doesn't have the capacity to acknowledge the distinction that what it is doing is causing "bad consequences."

When talking about ethics, a consciousness is required; one that can understand that its action can lead to some value state, and then act accordingly. In this way, the ethical system would act as a causal element that could lead a person to or away from a specific action.

Whether or not we should be held responsible after we have already acted ethically or not is where the debate on free will truly enters the picture. It pertains to the next part *only*, the most important part for this "free will" business: responsibility.

Responsibility

If we don't have free will, we cannot have ultimate control over whether we act ethically or not (if we understand an ethical system and allow it to enter our being), and if we have free will, some suggest we can have this control. This control is what I'll call *ethical responsibility*. Not having free will places restrictions on responsibility, accountability, blame, guilt, worthiness, and so on. After all, we blame people when they lie, cheat, steal, or murder, but if they didn't have the free will to choose, of their own accord, other options, they shouldn't be blamed for their action. For many, this is the downfall of not having free will. What they think is a downfall is a misunderstanding of what it means.

One might think being able to place blame on a person is a good thing. This has more to do with the vengeful attitude people are raised with as well as environmentally subjected to. This doesn't mean we cannot create action as deterrents. We may do so at the cost of being fair to the individual, but we also have to look at what is fair to everyone else, and balance those out. The chapter on the justice system will go over this.

The above definitions are how I am using them. I am not suggesting that other brands of ethical systems that are not my own can't be equally as helpful, only that there is a difference between ethics and responsibility that needs to be addressed. In other words, someone can act ethically, and still not be responsible for those actions–per how I group these terms.

Obviously if you define morals or ethics as encompassing ethical "responsibility," your definitions are different than my own. This is fine, but then you need new words for what is meant by the conscious understanding of good or bad, negative or positive, and so on, as actioned by a person who thinks about these attributes, and a new word for the thoughtful alignment of these attributes. It would be fallacious to incorporate responsibility into the definitions of these, and due to that incorporation ignore these as having separate importance.

This seems to be a common thing for those claiming that ethics cannot exist without free will. They combine the items into one large blob called "ethics," even though a person can act unethical but not be responsible for such action. A person can hold the ethic that it is bad, wrong, or negative to cheat someone out of their money, consciously decide to cheat someone out of their money anyway and then do so, which would be an unethical act (not aligning with the best output), and not be ultimately responsible for the action (though we could rightfully hold the person as a risk to the wellbeing of other individuals, and do something because of that).

A Lack of Free Will and Ethical systems

In this book, as I mentioned, I'm not presenting the details of my specific ethical system. I'm only displaying the restrictions that a lack of free will should impose on such systems, or any system held. In certain sections, I allude to ethical standards held by me. The important part is in regards to what a lack of free will means for those standards. The next chapter will go into more detail as to why an understanding that we lack free will is so important to the ethical system we align with.

The separate meanings of morality/ethics and moral/ethical responsibility are essential for a cohesive understanding of any proposed ethical system.

The Duty to Act Ethical

Keep in mind that there is a difference between "being held responsible" and "having a sense of responsibility." We need to clear up an ambiguity for the word "responsible." One can lack free will and still be instilled with a sense of moral duty or obligation. They can have this feeling of duty (sense of responsibility) and at the same time understand that they should not be held accountable (held responsible). When I say a person is not responsible, I am in no way suggesting they can't or should not have a sense of responsibility. One can hold a (perfectly consistent) sense of responsibility solely based on their understanding of what is ethical and their understanding of the importance of such ethics to future outcomes.

In fact, I'd suggest that a duty to act ethical is one that can and should be instilled whenever possible. It's incorrect to suggest that (not) having ethical responsibility is the same thing as (not) having a duty to act ethical. An important distinction needs to be made as holding one ethically responsible is logically inconsistent where as holding a sense of ethical duty prior to, leading up to, during, and even after action, is not. There are good reasons to hold such a duty, and free will is not a requirement for it. Free will is, however, a requirement if one wants to blame another for acting unethical.

A sense of ethical duty is one of the most important traits a person can hold; as such a duty causes the willful output of ethical action, leading to, in the case of the consequentialist ethical position above: positive events and to the reduction of harms. One can derive a sense of ethical duty by understanding the effects that acting ethical and not acting unethical have on the world. This understanding is a helpful causal element to consciousness that doesn't, in any way, require a belief in free will.

Be wary of those who conflate responsibility defined as *worthy of being held accountable*, with responsibility defined as *duty: the social force that binds you to the courses of action demanded by that force*. These are two difference usages of the word, and the one that requires free will is the former, not the latter. Being instilled with a sense of duty and obligation comes from knowing that ethical actions exist, regardless if one has the free will needed to be held accountable. Not being held accountable is not a logical reason to act unethically. Such conclusion does not follow from such premises.

This is a common misunderstanding people have when they learn that people are not ethically responsible. They may say something like, "If I'm not ethically responsible, it would be okay for me to stab you with a knife" or any number of silly sentences. They disregard the fact that such action may be considered an unethical act, regardless if they are to be held responsible after the fact. They disregard the fact that, if they did do that, they must not have been causally instilled with a sense of ethical duty. They also disregard the fact that laws would be in place to deter people that hold no sense of ethical duty from harmful actions such as this. The criminal system will be addressed in the next chapter. It'll go over deterrence for those people that hold no ethical duty, and the purpose of rehabilitation and imprisonment for when they break the law.

Dialogue

LIBERIUS: Without free will, there can be no ethics.

ORION: Why not?

LIBERIUS: Because, if everything is determined by causal events, we would have no control over how we act. And as you stated, acausal events cannot help with this control.

ORION: Please explain what control has to do with ethics?

LIBERIUS: Without it, I cannot help but act ethical or unethical due to past events.

ORION: I'm not disagreeing with that, but according to that statement, you will be acting ethical or unethical even though you cannot help it.

LIBERIUS: Okay, maybe ethics exists, but we cannot freely act ethically or unethically.

ORION: But can we un-freely act ethically or unethically? In other words, can our willful action align with what is ethical?

LIBERIUS: Yes, but we have no control over those actions.

ORION: We are back to the word control. At this point, we are just trying to see if something can be ethical, and if so, if we can act ethically—without control. Once we clarify that, we can address this "control" issue you keep bringing up.

LIBERIUS: Okay, I think I see what you are getting at. An ethic can exist and someone can act in accord to that ethic, so yes, they can act ethically. But without the control to be able to act ethically or not, those ethics are meaningless.

ORION: Great, now that we agree with the point that ethics can exist without free will, we can address control. When you say control, what do you mean by it?

LIBERIUS: The control over doing something ethical or unethical. So, for example, if I don't have control over whether I stab you or not, then what meaning is there in saying that such action was unethical?

ORION: The action was unethical probably based on the suffering it causes and/or the social rules it breaks, which is defined by the ethical system. You acted unethically because you were consciously aware of this ethical system yet you did it anyway. Control has nothing to do with these two things. In fact, causality (or acausal events) would have lead up to you acting unethically.

LIBERIUS: But if I was driven to it by past events, how can I be held responsible for acting unethically.

ORION: Ahh, responsibility. Now that's something else. I wanted to clear up that you can act unethically before we moved into responsibility for such actions. What you are saying is: one cannot be held responsible for the actions they have taken. To that I'll absolutely agree. The fact that you have infused responsibility with ethics leads me to think we should address what responsibly really means.

LIBERIUS: So you agree that, without free will, we cannot be held responsible?

ORION: Of course we cannot be held responsible. If we act unethically, we do so based on our causal factors (or acausal factors) that precede the unethical act. Part of those causal factors are, however, the thoughts that we have in our mind.

LIBERIUS: But the thoughts that we have in our mind come about causally as well.

ORION: Yes, they certainly do. How fast you learn, Liberius. And those thoughts can causally understand and act ethically.

LIBERIUS: Even though they are not ethically responsible?

ORION: Yes, even though they are not ethically responsible.

LIBERIUS: Doesn't this mean that people shouldn't bother acting ethically? After all, why should they care if they are not responsible?

ORION: No, not at all. That reasoning just does not follow. Being responsible for one's actions doesn't equate to caring, and not being responsible for one's actions doesn't equate to not caring.

LIBERIUS: But whether they care or not is determined by preceding events.

ORION: Exactly, and if someone acts ethically (or not) is many times dependent on whether they care about being ethical (or not). Free will cannot make a person who doesn't care about ethics act ethically. For me, for example, my past events have led to me caring, and since I care, I'd like others to care as well. I'll urge others to act ethically, in hopes that my urging will be part of the causality that leads someone to act ethically. If no one cared about acting ethically it wouldn't matter what ethical system was ever put forward, and it wouldn't matter if people had free will. If they didn't care, free will wouldn't push a person to care. Of course causal events could, and free will isn't needed for that.

LIBERIUS: Yeah, but if we cannot hold people responsible...

35

Ethical Systems and Compatibility with the Lack of Free Will

'It's clear that belief in free will is not benign to the ethical systems people hold.'

The lack of free will is more compatible with some ethical systems than it is with others. This is important when assessing ethical systems. To demonstrate this point, I'm going to analyze a few positions.

Let's take the three positions below for example:

- Ethical Egoism: The position that ethical actions are those that act in accord to one's own self interest.

- Ethical Altruism: The position that people have an ethical obligation to help and serve others, even at expense of one's own self interest.

- Ethical Utilitarianism: The position that one should treat one's own self with no higher regard and no lower regard than one has for others.

These three positions are consequentialist positions. This means that they are ethical positions which hold that the consequences of one's actions are the basis for ethical judgments. It's important to note that consequentialism is distinct from deontology and virtue ethics, systems that will not be addressed in this book. They may be addressed and criticized in a future book about ethics that I currently have in the back of my head. These three consequentialist positions are only brought up to demonstrate why the lack of free will aligns closer to some models than to others, which is the important point to understand for this particular topic.

As already explained, the lack of free will means that we should abandon the idea that we are more deserving or less deserving over another person. We may be lucky to have something over another person, but we are not more deserving of that something. Another person may be lucky to have something over you, but they aren't more deserving. Let's assess what this fact means for the three positions provided:

Ethical Egoism doesn't necessarily cause a detriment of others. It may be that one's own self interest aligns with helping others. Maybe donating to charity gives one a sense of satisfaction, and so it's in one's own self interest to give to charity. On the other hand, it may be at the detriment of others if one's self interest is at the expense of those others. Since free will doesn't exist and one's self interest is not deserved any more than another's wellbeing, ethical egoism does not mix all that well. It makes no sense to say that X should be bumped above Y at the expense of Y, when X is not more deserving of such bump and Y doesn't deserve the negative that such a bump would cause. We can see how a belief of free will can help keep ethical egoism alive. It's a perfect way to say that X deserves more than Y. If free will existed, X did such and such using her own free will while Y decided not to do such and such even though Y *could have done it.*

Ethical Altruism certainly doesn't cause a detriment to others. The problem, however, is that those others aren't more deserving than oneself. To sacrifice the wellbeing of one's own self interest to benefit another suggests that the other is more deserving. Certainly an act of altruism wouldn't be unethical if a person accepts the consequence to themselves, but given that free will doesn't exist, one cannot say that an altruistic act that sacrifices oneself is necessarily *more ethical* than not acting altruistically at an equivalent expense to oneself. If Y is not more deserving than X, it makes no sense to say that X should give to Y what they are not more deserving of at an equivalent expense to X. X may decide to, but we shouldn't assume that the action is a *more* ethical stance than not.

This brings us to Ethical Utilitarianism. The position that one should treat one's own self with no higher regard and no lower regard than one has for others. The lack of free will seems to be most compatible with this sort of ethic compared to the other two. It doesn't suggest one is more deserving than another in either direction. Since everyone is a product of the causality that produces their will, or of acausality that is not willed, the most ethical action is one that doesn't project blame or deserving on to oneself *or* on to others.

This is just one small example within a consequentialist framework. There are many other things, within the realm of ethics, that the understandings surrounding the fact that there is no free will implies. It's clear that belief in free will is not benign to the ethical systems people hold.

36
The Justice System

'In a universe that has no free will, there is only one reason for a legal system: to protect others.'

Since a criminal is not to blame for the crimes they've committed, our justice system requires an overhaul. To some degree rehabilitation is already stressed, but it's hardly the primary focus for many justice systems throughout the world. There's an undertone of blame and retribution. The more horrible the crime, the more people want to see what they call "justice" done, which to them really just means "revenge." Justice systems tend to align with these desires. Many people still have an eye for an eye mentality. Of course this will happen, it's human nature. Emotions run high and people want vengeance. They want the person that caused the crime to experience the same pain or suffering that person may have put another person through. This is part of the mentality that lacking the belief in free will helps us move away from.

Most people wouldn't feel the same way about a person that intentionally kills another than they feel about someone that accidentally kills another. In legal matters, it's the difference between degrees of murder and degrees of voluntary or involuntary manslaughter.

There is something about intent that makes all of the difference in the world. We need to examine what this "intent" really is. For example, let's suggest someone intentionally kills someone else because their entire family is held hostage and will be killed unless they do so. The person can opt not to kill the one person, but if so, his entire family will be killed. The person rationalizes and decides that it would be better if he killed, and so does. Chances are most people would understand such rationalization and give at least some leeway. This is because the circumstances leading up to the decision are right there. They are visible. They don't need to look much further than the causality of only having two horrible options.

The events that lead up to other criminal actions are equally as forced. They are, however, not as obvious. They are hidden from sight. Motives driven by embedded psychologies that the person had no control over.

In a universe that has no free will, there is only one reason for a legal system: to protect others. There are three main ways to go about this when dealing with criminals: 1) Rehabilitation 2) Imprisonment and 3) Deterrent. I will also tack on a 4th, the more controversial "death penalty" and look at it from the light of this book.

I will address each of these separately, though each of these relate to each other in various ways. For example, imprisonment may be a deterrent as well. Or a deterrent may help to rehabilitate.

First, it must be noted that just because a person is not to blame for an action does not mean that they are not part of the cause of an action. As a cause, the person who commits the crime needs to be addressed. Is it likely they will commit the crime again? What other things are likely to happen based on our response to the criminal? What response would lead others to commit the same crime? What response would prevent that from happening? Where is the line between fairness to the criminal, and fairness to people affected negatively by the crime?

Rehabilitation

A primary goal of the criminal system should be to focus on rehabilitation. Whenever possible, we should humanely rehabilitate the offender to such a degree that the offender will not recommit the offense again. This is easier said than done. It's not my contention that this can happen in all cases. It's only my contention that this should be the primary *focus* of a justice system.

There are obvious instances where as a person is beyond rehabilitation. There are also instances where there are not enough resources to rehabilitate. Many people don't want to pay for criminals. Due to this, we lock criminals away in facilities that do nothing to rehabilitate them. In fact, these facilities often turn small offenders into larger ones. A process of reverse rehabilitation. Prison life hardens them.

Imprisonment

Until such time that a person is rehabilitated, that person may need to be kept incarcerated. This is solely for the protection of the rest of people in society who are following the laws put in place.

It's sometimes argued that if we cannot blame an individual, we cannot incarcerate a person. One, however, doesn't follow from the other. You may say incarceration is a form of punishment, and to the person being incarcerated it may very well seem that way, but how something seems and what its purpose is can be two separate things. A prison can indeed strip away a feeling of freedom that the person may have if they are not in prison, but that shouldn't be an objective of imprisonment. The only objective is the protection of others, and it just so happens that the best way about this is through such imprisonment. The negativity of "being imprisoned" is just a side issue to the solution, and as long as there is no better solution in sight, it needs to be dealt with.

But just because the criminal doesn't want to be imprisoned doesn't mean that letting them loose is a better option. We don't allow attacking dogs loose just because they are not free to decide not to bite, even if they hate being in the cage. At the same time, we can feel some compassion for their pain, and

understand that they are where they are out of sheer bad luck of having the properties they causally possess that makes them a danger.

Deterrent

If we use punishment as deterrence, it doesn't mean that such punishment was deserved. It doesn't mean that the person is being held responsible in the sense that they are to blame. It's simply a proactive means to a desired end. One based on an agreed upon ethic. It means that we understand human psychology. We understand that if we impose punishment X for negative action Z, X reduces those accounts of action Z. It's similar to the economic position in which we need to have a balancing act between unfairness and fairness for the sake of productivity.

Is it fair to the person that does negative action Z? No. However, assuming we let negative action Z go by without any deterrent, and assuming negative action Z harms others, it's also not fair to those others that are harmed due to the lack of deterrence of negative action Z.

This is the balancing act we need to play. The harshest penalty would indeed deter the most, but it would also be the most unfair to the person that did action Z.

For example, we could put people that go over the speed limit to death. That would certainly cause less people to speed. It would also be an entirely imbalanced equation for the individual that does speed, as well as that individual's family and friends. So we need to balance out the importance of staying within the speed limit for the rest of society, with the punishment (e.g. a fine). How much potential does an action have to be harmful than another action? Was it an accident, or consciously intentional? If intentional, can the person be rehabilitated to prevent further similar intentional acts (note: punishment can be part of rehabilitation)? Will a fine reduce the amount of speeders? Will taking away their license? If they will drive without a license, should we incarcerate the person?

There are options other than taking the harshest penalty available. To put it another way, it's inherently unfair to punish a person who is not responsible for what they are being punished for, but it is also inherently unfair to others affected by the negative action that such punishment would deter. Since we have to be unfair, it only makes sense to be unfair to those that cause problems with the functioning of a civilized society to prevent the negative actions from arising in the future. This is the path of least harm, even if it must apply some harm to enforce it.

Deterrence against repeat offense is just as important as deterrence for the general public. This type of deterrent can be part of the rehabilitation process (above).

Also, consistency is important for deterrence. One might suggest punishing people for crimes they didn't commit would deter just as much as punishing people that did commit the crime, therefore a case cannot be made for deterrence without free will. That is not the case. If, for example, we place a small child in time out for the trouble that that child's brother caused, it does the reverse of rehabilitate and deter. It allows the brother to keep getting away with the action, and it says to the small child that it doesn't matter what they do because they will get in trouble anyway. Also, if it gets out that we are punishing people that have not committed the crime, all impact to deterrence is lost, and we are guilty of a crime ourselves.

Deterrence is important even for those that don't break laws, but that still act in a way that one might find unethical. For example, if someone keeps picking on another person by calling them names, that's not against the law. It may, however, be a behavior that is unacceptable to you or others. You may, at that point, do something (legal) that deters the person from acting that way. Maybe it is as simple as stating your disapproval to them. Or maybe you don't help the person when they request help. Or maybe you ignore the person when you are around them. Any action that might get the person to reflect on their actions as the cause of your own. Actions in which they dislike. This can all be done with the understanding that the person did not freely choose to pick on that other person. It can be done with an understanding of the psychology involved, and an action that deters such psychology. Such deterrence may also rehabilitate the psychology of that person. One need not place blame on the person to take these actions or to understand the importance of them.

The criminal system's use of deterrence is similar to this type of action. Ideally, it would use just the right amount[64] of punishment to deter the crime to an acceptable degree, preventing the unfairness the crime would cause to the people being harmed by such crime, without going into excess unfairness to the criminal.

The Death Penalty

The death penalty is a controversial topic in and of itself. When, if ever, it is justified to end a criminal's life is a question that is up for much debate. That being said, I'd argue that if a criminal is dangerous even in an imprisoned state (e.g. to other inmates, guards, etc.), and if there is no chance of rehabilitation, it may be an appropriate response to, as humanely as possible, put that person down.

But it can never, ever, be about punishment. It can never be about placing blame on that individual for what they have done. Rather, it's simply the response that will protect others who equally don't deserve the wrath of what this criminal may put them through.

People who sit in a room behind a glass wall to get that feeling of vindication by watching a killer be put to death just cannot get past what the killer has done to a family member. It's psychologically understandable. They think the killer "deserves" what he or she is getting. When something that horrible occurs, it's difficult not to let one's emotion override their rationality.

I think, given a few generations of people who are raised in the understanding that free will doesn't exist, that these types of psychological needs can be weeded out. They will become just as sad as having to put a dog down due to it biting someone. People will understand it may be needed, but feel a sadness for the individual, understanding they would be the same if they had all of the same variables.

Retribution – An Illogical Desire

If a person doesn't have free will, retribution serves only one purpose: to make those who hold people responsible feel better. This feeling that it's 'justice' to cause harm to someone regardless if it has a protective purpose to others. To harm the person who causes harm just because they have done what they have. This is an entirely psychological response based on the feeling of free will.

As emotional creatures, it's hard to tell people they are wrong in doing this. If you do, you are almost sure to get a response such as "You'd feel the same way if someone were to do something to someone you loved!" And they could be right. I was raised with the belief in free will, and my psychology still has those remnants. Most people today, even those who have eventually learned that free will is impossible, still possess deep psychological needs for retribution. People love movies in which the bad guy "gets what's comin' to 'em," and that usually doesn't mean they simply go to jail.

But this psychology is wrong. We need to progress past mere beasties that say, "Ugg, me no like, me hit you with club." We can use logic and reason to conclude that those bad people did not have any other viable option that was up to them. They could not have, of their own accord, done otherwise. They need to be fixed, prevented, deterred, or any combination of these things. Retribution is not needed, nor does it make any sense without free will.

Dialogue

LIBERIUS: *Yeah, but if we cannot hold people responsible*, we cannot blame them for breaking the law.

ORION: This is true.

LIBERIUS: So you agree? Can't you see what a horror that would be? We couldn't prevent crime.

ORION: Whoa, slow down there, cowboy. You are over-reaching on what "we cannot blame" means.

LIBERIUS: No, it would be unfair to imprison a person for a crime!

ORION: It would unfair to everyone else not to. You are looking at one side of the coin. The purpose of the justice system should be to protect others.

LIBERIUS: What about retribution?

ORION: If we can't blame people, we shouldn't look to obtain vengeance on them.

LIBERIUS: So you think some serial killer doesn't deserve to be punished?

ORION: A serial killer requires preventative measures, and maybe even attempts at rehabilitation when possible. But no matter how harsh of a crime someone commits, they were driven to such crimes by events out of their control. That doesn't mean we shouldn't incarcerate, or (maybe) even punish. As long as the *purpose* of the incarceration or punishment is to deter or prevent further crimes.

LIBERIUS: But again, if the serial killer couldn't have done otherwise, it would be wrong to incarcerate or punish them. They should be let free!

ORION: If we can be sure that the serial killer would never harm another individual, I'd agree with that assessment. That isn't the case most of the time. We recognize that a serial killer has a compulsion in them that will cause them to do harm to other people. And here is the important part: those other people don't deserve to be a victim of the serial killer. By letting the serial killer free, such action causes people to be victims of the serial killer.

LIBERIUS: You're arbitrarily placing the line at the victims' wellbeing rather than the serial killer's, when neither is "more deserving" of their wellbeing than the other.

ORION: It isn't arbitrary at all. One person is the machine that is going around harming others, and the other isn't. It makes more sense to stop the harmful machine rather than allow it to keep harming others. We can't blame a mad, rabid dog for biting, but we can stop it. It isn't arbitrary in the wake of the people being bitten. And in the context of an ethical system, stopping the dog or serial killer is most likely the most ethical action we can take, regardless of the fact that they aren't to blame. We simply must consider that the dog and serial killer could not have, of their own accord, done otherwise–therefore our hate and retributive thoughts aren't reasonable, even if they still exist.

LIBERIUS: So people are stopped merely for the utility of others? But you mentioned punishing may even be okay.

ORION: That too would be for the utility of others. Creating a deterrence. If people think they could incur a fine for speeding, such a fine is a "deterrence" because it punishes the behavior. We don't have to place blame on the person for the behavior, in fact they might not even have been aware they were speeding. They could have been listening to tunes on the radio not realizing they were stepping on the pedal too much. But getting a ticket is a causal element that could adjust behavior, such as watching the speedometer next time.

LIBERIUS: But they didn't have an option not to speed at the time.

ORION: Correct, and that is why such punishment should never be about the act that they had no control over, but rather about a recognition that such behavior can be causally adjusted in the future. It needs to be about causally aligning the outcome of future events with what is best for society.

The Illusion

37

The Free Will Illusion

*'Since this information is missing from our thoughts,
our brain has a tendency to fill in the gaps.'*

If free will is an illusion, why does the illusion exist? How did the illusion form or what is it derived from? There are a number of possibilities regarding such questions. This chapter will touch on a few of these. These are to be taken as food for thought. I invite the reader to analyze what I say here and decide for themselves what ideas make the most sense. No matter what we speculate regarding how the illusion was derived, one thing we can know for sure: it is only an illusion.

The first observation is that we don't consciously perceive all of the causal events that lead to our thoughts. We don't perceive the subconscious events happening. We don't see that there is a balance or imbalance of chemicals such as serotonin in our brain. We don't know or understand the neuro-structure of our brains and what causes some synapses to spark while others lie dormant. We don't understand that all of the memories of the past stored in the structure of our brain play an important role in having the simplest of preferences from disliking certain types of music to liking certain types of foods. We don't focus on all of the perceptual inputs our brain receives. We don't have a realization of the workings of genes that are hard coded to create a propensity for one thing or another. There are so many causal factors to account for. All of these things happen in the background, and they dictate every decision we make. For each decision, we are limited to a few things in which we are aware of. We may be aware of the emotional response we have when selecting to pet a puppy over a tarantula, for example. What we aren't aware of is many of the past events that create memories that give us the emotional response at that time.

Since this information is missing from our thoughts, our brain has a tendency to fill in the gaps. It says that you chose something over another thing, but it doesn't suggest that you couldn't have chosen that other thing. It's a shortcut our brain takes to fill in the gaps of all of the information we are not aware of. It's the path of least resistance.

To understand illusions such as this, it is important to see how our brain fills in gaps. Examples of our brains filling in information is in the form of optical illusions. A common optical illusion is Kanizsa's triangle where there is a triangle with an equal section taken out of each side. Then add circles with a pie slice taken from them. If those empty slices align with the spaces, our mind fills in lines and creates a triangle on top of another. Also the triangle appears brighter than the surrounding area, even though it has the same brightness. This is called a contour illusion.

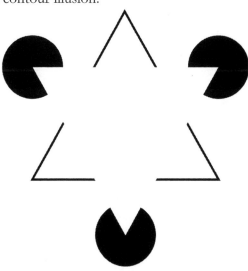

Other illusions have to do with color, audio, and so forth. A key aspect of many of these illusions is our minds' ability to create something that isn't there. Again, to fill in the gaps. The feeling of free will falls into the category of our mind filling in gaps. Gaps of missing information regarding the events involved in a decision.

Such a feeling may have also been an evolutionary advantage. Indeed, the illusion to be able to choose between multiple options would grant the creature that thought it a distinct survival advantage. For example, instead of taking the immediate perceived path, the feeling would allow the animal to go through the options, and maybe even choose an option that would help in the longer run over something that would give short satisfaction in the short run. The feeling that the animal could choose more than one option could lead it to an option it otherwise would not have been led (causally) without such a feeling. An option that would assist in ensuring the animal's survival over those animals that acted on the first impulse given.

Just because the feeling of free will would be a distinct evolutionary advantage doesn't mean that believing in it is an advantage for humans. It also doesn't mean that evolutionary advantages are a good thing. People that claim that we should act a certain way or that we should believe something because that is how we evolved are using a version of the naturalistic fallacy. This is when a person claims that what is natural is inherently good or right, and what is unnatural is bad or wrong. The illusion of free will almost certainly came about via a natural process, but so did most diseases on the planet, and we don't revere them.

Having hundreds or thousands of offspring is an evolutionary advantage, especially when only a teeny-tiny percentage of them will survive. But that's simply a numbers game with a large death toll.

Thinking or feeling we have free will may have assisted with our survival of the fittest instincts, but as humans who have traveled to the moon, believing in such thinking is an ancient byproduct of such feelings. It's no more needed than wisdom teeth. As intellectual creatures we can make choices and at the same time realize such choices are not freely willed. The illusion, that feeling we have, is a barbaric remnant that we can bypass with just a little bit of critical thought. The belief in free will is detrimental if we want to escalate the human race to caring beings with perspectives that span to all life.

38

Brains in Vats and the Feeling of Free Will

'If a brain in a vat would think it has free will even though it doesn't, and the idea of free will is logically incoherent, such intuition about having free will should not override the reasoning against it.'

If you've read or worked with philosophy at all, chances are you have come across a version of the brain in a vat thought experiment. It has been used in varying degrees to support philosophical skepticism, solipsism, and uncertainty of knowledge. I'm going to use the thought experiment to address this feeling of free will. Here's the gist of the brain in a vat thought experiment:

A mad scientist removes a brain from a body and places it in a vat of liquid that keeps the brain alive and thriving. He then connects the neurons of the brain to a supercomputer. This supercomputer sends electrical impulses to the brain that are identical to the impulses that a brain in a body would received if it were able to experience the "real" world. The brain in the vat has the exact same conscious experience that a person experiencing the real world would have. In this way, the brain in a vat does not know it is only a brain in a vat. It thinks it is walking around, feeling the rays of the sun, and experiencing the pain of sunburn. It interacts with other people who it thinks are real; it eats dinner, has sex, and thinks all of the complex thoughts of a person. It may even think about the

256

brain in a vat thought experiment, if those electrical impulses were sent by the supercomputer.

In this thought experiment, the computer takes the place of all of the external factors that cause a brain's neurons to spark in a certain way. For example, seeing three objects in front of you, thinking to yourself that you will pick up one of those objects and leave the other two, reaching your arm out and seeing yourself picking up the object you decided on. Each one of these is experienced inside of the brain. For the brain in a vat, the computer causes the experience to happen. In such scenario, the brain does not feel any differently about its free will. It thinks and feels as if it is a full person freely making the choice to pick up the one object and not the other two. It thinks that it could have chosen one of the others if it wanted to, even though it could not. The computer dictates that it couldn't, but the feeling of consciousness the brain experiences entails the feeling of such freedoms.

I don't think anyone would suggest the brain in a vat has free will or free agency in this thought experiment. So why would it be such a surprise to suggest that you wouldn't have free will either? The brain in a vat could theoretically have every experience and feeling that you possess. The main difference, unless of course you are a brain in a vat and don't know it, is that the largest causal factor for the brain in a jar is the computer attached to it, while the largest causal factor for the person is the body and environment that occur based on causal events that precede them.

Thought experiments such as these can help us understand that there can be a drastic difference between what *is*, and what is *felt or experienced*. How we "feel" about something is not necessarily a good determiner that the feeling is correct. There is something to be said about intuition, and there are many situations that we are placed into in which we must rely entirely on it. When it comes to beliefs, a more analytical approach is in order. If a brain in a vat would think it has free will even though it doesn't, and the idea of free will is logically incoherent, such intuition about having free will shouldn't override the reasoning against it.

You may say that we also can't know if we are a brain in a vat or not, as the brain also thinks it is perceiving reality that same as you are. This is true, however, unlike free will, there is nothing that contradicts that we really are perceiving reality. Us not being a brain in a jar not only has logical possibility to it, but us being a brain in a jar has no evidence for it. Us having free will does not, however, have any logical possibility--in either case.

The irony is that the only way free will could ever be possible is if we were in such a solipsist nightmare, and we were being fed incorrect information regarding everything we "know" about language, science, logic, and reality. In that case we couldn't make a case for a single thing, including free will and colorless purple square circles.

Brains in jars are useful thought experiments. They are not a reason to dismiss reason. We need to accept some axioms about the universe we experience if we are to navigate within *it*. And that includes the acceptance of logical consistency.

THE PSYCHOLOGY

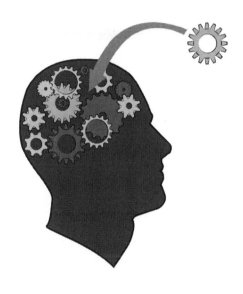

39
Psychology

'I explain how psychologies that look down on the idea of a lack of free will are like dead worms and appetite loss. These psychologies exist, but are illogical, irrational, and unnecessary.'

This psychology section is separated from the philosophy section for a reason. A person's psychology should not have much say on their philosophy. Logic, science, and reason should have the overwhelming say. Reason and logic should trump a person's psychology when such psychology opposes it. And even more so if the actions that stem from such psychology have harmful consequences.

Nevertheless, people have entirely psychological problems with the idea that they don't have free will. It's my intention to explain why such psychologies are unfounded, unnecessary, and problematic, and to suggest resolutions that attempt to break away from these built-in psychologies. Everyone has their own psychology. I have mine, and it doesn't always follow the most rational or logical path. Large spiders freak me out, even harmless ones. Seeing dead worms outside after a rainstorm makes me lose my appetite. I worry over things that are trivial. These are psychologies that are unnecessary, but they're part of me regardless. This doesn't mean I don't see them for what they are: illogical, irrational, unnecessary deep rooted thinking. For this section, I don't bring to the table an exact logic of what your psychology should contain based on the knowledge that we lack free will. Instead I show what it could contain. I explain how psychologies that look down on the idea of a lack of free will are like dead worms and appetite loss. These psychologies exist, but are *illogical, irrational, and unnecessary.* An important difference is that free will psychology is not as benign as temporarily losing one's appetite. It has real world problems that affect others in large ways.

A lack of free will is nothing to be fearful of. It's nothing to find repulsive or to worry about. In fact, it can lead to a psychology that is helpful, empathetic, and ultimately more rational. The first step is to recognize our psychology for what it really is.

40

Psychological Recognition

'If you hold the psychological feeling that you deserve something over another person due to an action you took, you can still understand that such is only your psychology speaking.'

Understanding the nature of causality helps with the recognition that what we experience is filtered by subjective psychological causes. Recognizing our subjective biases helps keep a more objective perspective, to the extent that an objective perspective can be obtained. For example, we may think that dogs are cute, and at the same time think pigs are ugly. These thoughts are based entirely on our psychological make-up that has been set up inside of us. Due to this psychology, we may give a different value to dogs than we do pigs, even though pigs may be more intelligent and just as feeling as a dog.

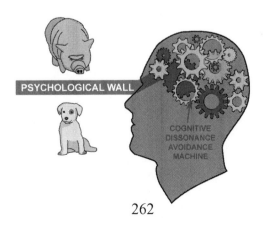

Our environment, which includes our upbringing and experiences, dictates this. If someone were to place dogs into places that inflicted much suffering, many people in countries where dogs are pets would be outraged at the cruelty. Entirely different psychological events happen in these people's brains when pigs are put into the same situation that causes the outrage for the dogs. These differences, if the person were to think about them, conflict with each other. The individual's psychology allows the person to keep them separate and miss the conflict. They allow people to disregard some things but not others; even though those things being disregarded may be much worse than the things the person cares about. Everyone does this to some extent. I do this.

Understanding causality is a stepping stone to recognizing these inconsistencies. It may not prevent people from thinking the dog is cute while the pig is not, but it may help them understand that there is a reason they think it. One that is dictated by their psychology, not by a rational standard. Once they have this understanding, decisions can be made that override such psychological positions. In other words, we can have the psychology, but having such doesn't have to imply that we base our beliefs, the laws we support, and how we act on those psychologies.

If we can see our psychology for what it is--something created through past causal events that don't necessarily create consistent or logical thought--we can start to realize that the causality of our psychology is not the best thing to base our beliefs on.

Nepotism is another example of basing beliefs on psychology. Favoritism is granted to friends or relatives, regardless of merit. Someone might save a family member at the expense of ten people they don't know. Some may even save their pet at the expense of ten people. They rationalize what they love, over the logic that effects people or other animals they aren't affiliated with. The nature of human psychology is not something we should revere. It's something that we are better off controlling. And when we don't have control over it, we need to understand it for what it is, and not allow our actions to be based on it, unless it happens to align with what is rational.

The psychology that the feeling of free will creates doesn't align with what is rational. If you hold the psychological feeling that you deserve something over another person due to an action you took, you can still understand that such is only your psychology speaking. If you think through it, you can logically conclude that you are not more deserving, and therefore (if you are concerned with fairness and equality) you shouldn't take something at the expense of another person who is not less deserving.

If you hold the psychology that someone is blameworthy due to a bad action they've done, you can still understand that it's your psychology speaking. If you think through it, you can logically conclude they couldn't have, of their own accord, chosen a different action. You can feel a sense of sympathy for them instead of this attitude of *"let's harm them back as they deserve what they have coming to 'em,"* and you can help to fix the types of events that caused it in the first place.

The belief in free will means that people can reward themselves at another's expense and they can place blame on those others. No wonder people are so reluctant to even consider that free will might not exist. Free will is the ultimate excuse for egotistical actions. Of course they will resist changing such a belief that goes so much against their psychological intuitions of self worth and worth of others. Of course they want to feel like they deserve what they have and that others deserve what they don't. Of course they want to feel as if they are special, and that special-ness is due to them and not due to something out of their control.

This is what needs to be recognized as psychology, not what is rational or logical. This is what people need to separate out, even if they can't make these feelings disappear due to it being so deeply embedded into the structure of their brain. The recognition that these feelings should not have control over their beliefs and actions. Beliefs shouldn't be based on how someone "feels" about something. How someone feels should be based on what they believe, which should be based on logic, reason, and evidence. The problem with this is, once someone believes something for so long, it's quite difficult to change that feeling even if that belief changes. This is no reason not to change the belief. It's a reason to recognize the distinction between the two, and separate out your actions accordingly. It is possible to separate these out, at least to the degree that relates to what you believe.

41
Anger

'It's easy to see how much free will psychology has been embedded within the world. Anger, real anger, is rampant everywhere. Anger derived from the ability to hold others responsible.'

Anger runs rampant in the world. The psychology imposed by the belief in free will is responsible for a lot of this anger. The lack of free will challenges the rationale for such anger. Resentment and indignation that people hold toward others are there because they believe those others had the ability to choose, of their own accord, something different than they had chosen.

Keep in mind that being angry is different than being upset. Being upset that something has happened doesn't suggest free will, but being angry at the something that caused the happening does. Being upset that your car has broken down is different than being angry at your car for breaking down.

And yes, we do at times become angry at non-conscious objects such as the car. We may even swear at and kick the car. This doesn't mean it is rational to do so, and we know it. We know the car is not blameworthy. When it comes to other people, however, most don't seem to know it.

Once free will psychology is embedded within a mind, it's difficult to extract out. I know free will doesn't exist, and that I and others aren't to blame, yet such psychology is still embedded in my neuro-structure. When I think about it, I try to not let it get to me. But like the psychology I have of dead worms grossing me out, I get angry. Most of the time I get angry at myself rather than others. But I do so, irrationally, to my own detriment. Getting angry causes harm and takes away from where the focus needs to be to resolve problems. Sure, in some situations anger can change things for the better, but not in most cases.

Most anger causes suffering in the world. The worst of anger is when violence arises from it. This can be anything from violence due to a domestic dispute, to an entire group of people having hate and anger for another group and inflicting violence due to that.

Once people begin to understand that others are not blameworthy, they can take the best actions to resolve the ethical problems. The anger is not necessary, unless such anger happens to be the best action. And even then, it should not be real anger, but rather a projection of anger. Real anger at another person implies that you think the person not only should have, but could have of their own accord, done otherwise than they did.

THEY COULD HAVE AND SHOULD HAVE DONE OTHER THAN THEY DID!

It's easy to see how much free will psychology has been embedded within the world. Anger, real anger, is rampant everywhere. Anger derived from the ability to hold others responsible.

267

Imagine a world where people understood that others were not blameworthy. A world where they can focus on fixing actions that lead to poor consequences, instead of focusing on being angry at people that cause poor consequences. A world where reason trumps psychology. Not only would such existence be more logical and rational, but it would also be more peaceful. We can begin to empathize with people that we didn't empathize with before. People with opposing positions. We can understand the causality that has led them to where they are, the position they hold, and the actions they do. If we don't like those positions and actions, we could oppose and counteract them without anger.

Easier said than done, I know. That doesn't mean we cannot start with baby steps that will lead to this better way of thinking for future generations.

42

"It's Just Too Depressing"

*'There is no reason to take a defeatist
attitude in the light of not having free will.'*

"It is just too depressing to think I don't have free will."
"Life loses all meaning and purpose without free will."
"Why should I bother getting up in the morning without free will?"

I'm not making these quotes up. These are real psychological responses that I've heard. People are so engrained with the idea that they have free will that the mere thought of not having it repulses them. No wonder they contrive its existence. They seem to think if they lacked free will that it follows that one must become a defeatist. This simply doesn't, however, follow.

The truth is they probably have never given enough thought into why free will gives them such "meaning and purpose," and why actions without free will wouldn't give them just as much "meaning and purpose" or reason to do things.

The question that needs to be asked is: Would an action be less meaningful if it came about through a process that stems outside of an individual?

To assist with understanding this, let's use an example of an action someone may consider "meaningful":

Billy Bob likes to donate a certain amount of money to charity to feed starving children. Billy Bob finds the action of

269

helping starving children one of the many things that gives his life meaning and purpose. He says it gives him great satisfaction to know that he's helping to reduce the suffering of the world. Billy Bob thinks and feels that he is using his free will when he decides to donate the money.

Let's look at the above example and list off three bullet points:

- Billy Bob's donation helps starving children.

- Billy Bob says he likes to donate because he gets satisfaction from helping to reduce suffering.

- Billy Bob thinks he donates using his free will.

Bullet point #1 – Billy Bob's donation helps starving children: It is apparent that, regardless if Billy Bob has the free will to do so or not, if Billy Bob donates, the donation helps starving children. The lack of free will does not undermine this.

Bullet point #2 – Billy Bob says he likes to donate because he gets satisfaction from helping to reduce suffering: This one needs to be looked at a little closer. Billy Bob "likes" something because that is what his psychology dictates. We'll come back to this.

Bullet point #3 – Billy Bob thinks he donates using his free will: It has already been explained that, regardless if he does so using his free will or not (or if he thinks he has free will or not), if he donates, bullet point #1 is not affected. The question is, why should it affect bullet point #2? The answer is that it shouldn't. He is still reducing suffering, and if that is really the *reason* for his satisfaction, that should not change if bullet point #3 changes.

So what's the real reason that Billy Bob's satisfaction might change once he realizes that he is not donating of his own free will? This is the big question, because the answer seems to be something different than the real reason Billy Bob says he has satisfaction. If his satisfaction does change, it's not due to the reason Billy Bob cites of "satisfaction of helping the reduction of suffering," but rather something more self absorbed. Billy Bob wants *all of the credit*. It's not about the starving children, but rather Billy Bob's own ego.

It's important to recognize that in this instance the prevention of children starving is the ethical reason to help them (given a consequentialist ethic). The lack of free will shouldn't remove the desire for this. If it does, I would argue that the psychology of the individual is flawed to begin with, and that this flaw stems from the false belief in free will and the bloated importance of it. It is this egocentric point of view that causes a veneer of *what appears like* the desire to act in an ethical way, rather than the desire to do the ethical thing because of the positive outcome it produces. It is this psychology that prevents people from truly caring. To be more concerned about what others think of them.

Removing the idea of free will can help minimize or adjust this egocentric point of view. This doesn't mean you can't be proud of the causality you have. There is no reason not to be glad that something good happens through your consciousness. It's enough to think of yourself as a positive cog without placing yourself on a pedestal.

Then there is this other attitude of "why do anything at all." It is a fatalistic and defeatist view that some minds slide into when someone suggests they do not have free will.

Take a look at the below two actions:

- Not doing anything due to an understanding that you lack free will

- Doing something after understanding you lack free will.

The difference between these two things is entirely psychological. The first is derived via a free will psychology. One that places an overpowering importance on this non-existent thing. Not having free will does not turn a person into a rock. It doesn't mean that they are not complex, thinking, decision making machines that can understand that certain actions are better than other actions.

There is no reason to take a defeatist attitude in the light of not having free will. Of course if you do, you had to, but it must be clear that it is not due to any rational reason. Your causal alignment was one of misunderstanding and misinformation regarding what a lack of free will means and doesn't mean.

The lack of free will does not mean that a person's actions aren't important. It does not mean we cannot and do not interact with our environment. It does not mean we don't have complex feelings and thoughts. It does not mean that the state of the world is unimportant.

Understanding that we lack free will and what it means can purify many processes. Processes that have been diluted with a mix of free will nastiness. The second bullet point in the Billy Bob example would be done regardless of this need for credit. It would be done for the purity and benefit of an outcome that is not egocentric. Once we abandon free will, we can begin to repair the psychology that places such an unnecessary importance on free will. And even if we can't fully get rid of such psychology due to the long term, deeply embedded effects of the illusion, we can make sure to teach others early on. Instead of indoctrinating them to align with the illusion at an early age, we can start them on a path that recognizes the illusion. We can allow them to see the inter-connective nature of the universe rather than split themselves out into egocentric bubbles. We can break them free from an unnecessary and harmful psychology. One that you and I may still hold parts of deep down, even if we admit to our irrational tendencies as to not inflict them on others.

<u>Dialogue</u>

Realizing that his ideas of free will appear to be wrong, Liberius makes an emotional plea with Orion.

LIBERIUS: If you were to convince me that I didn't have free will, I'd find myself depressed and without meaning. It would be better for me to keep the belief in free will.

ORION: Why should the idea of not having free will depress you? What qualities does free will offer you that makes your life ultimately better than without it?

LIBERIUS: Free will allows me to make my own choices and be master to my own self. It makes me a free agent rather than controlled by my genetics and environment.

ORION: You answered what free will does, but you didn't really answer why those things are important, or why they should make your life of better quality to believe in them?

LIBERIUS: Because having personal control is better than not.

ORION: Let's examine this statement further. You use the term "better" in which ways?

LIBERIUS: Ways that are more desirable.

ORION: Does having control always lead to a desirable outcome?

LIBERIUS: Well, no, but it could. Having control itself is more desirable.

ORION: Assuming that it's true that having such control is more desirable for you, we need to look into the matter more deeply. Does it cause you physical pain not to have such choice?

LIBERIUS: No, but knowing I don't have control could cause a mental anguish of sorts.

ORION: Surely there is a good reason for such anguish. For example, if you knew that not having such control would cause needless suffering in the world, we can see why such mental anguish would occur. What is the reasoning behind such mental anguish? I don't believe in free will, and I do not have mental anguish due to it. Maybe I should, but if so, why should I?

LIBERIUS: Because without it you can't have ultimate control over your own future.

ORION: We seem to be working in circles here. You are suggesting that not being able to have ultimate control over your own future should cause mental anguish. But what is the reasoning for this? In other words, is there a basis for such anguish, or is such anguish something that just comes about due to a psychology and unneeded dependence on having ultimate control?

LIBERIUS: I'm trying to explain to you the basis but having difficulties. Allow me to rephrase in a way that's more understandable. If I know I don't have free will, then I know I'm not responsible for my actions. I also know I don't have control. It saddens me to know I might do something horrible and be unable to control it. If I have control, I know I have the ability to avoid doing something horrible.

ORION: What if we can know that you will never do something horrible? In fact, what if we know you will do much good? Would it still depress you to know you do not have the free will to control all of the good you will do?

LIBERIUS: It may, but for argument sake, let's say it doesn't. It's only when I don't know if I will do something horrible and have no control over it that it depresses me.

ORION: Okay, let me ask you a different question. Is it possible that, by believing you have free will, the very belief might be a cause of something horrible to happen?

LIBERIUS: That's a possibility, but at least it would be something I think I could change.

ORION: How would you go about detecting the problem to change it?

LIBERIUS: I could try to observe the factors that seem to be leading to it, and change those factors.

ORION: In a world without free will, could you be caused to try to observe those factors that seem to be leading to it, and change those factors entirely through such causal process?

LIBERIUS: Yes, but I would have no control over whether I was caused to do so or not.

ORION: True, but what if you, of your own free will, chose not to. What if you freely did not have the desire to detect the problem and change it?

LIBERIUS: Then it would be my choice not to.

ORION: And what if you didn't have free will, but causality led you to have the desire to detect the problem and change it?

LIBERIUS: Then it would *not* be my free choice to.

ORION: And which of these options would have a better result?

LIBERIUS: For that example, not having free will would be the better result. But those scenarios could be reversed.

ORION: True, but the point still remains. Not having this so called free will would not necessarily lead to the better result.

LIBERIUS: Maybe, but your scenario asks what if I chose not to. But because I have free will, I would choose to.

ORION: Why?

LIBERIUS: Because if I didn't, I would be held accountable for that decision. Without free will, there is no accountability, so why should I?

ORION: Who would hold you accountable and what happens if you are held accountable for something you shouldn't have done, via your free will, of course?

LIBERIUS: Other people would hold me accountable, and I might be punished in one way or another due to that account- ability. For example, I might be socially avoided if I do some- thing people don't like.

ORION: It's interesting how you inject the causality of an external factor to dictate what is supposedly freely chosen by you. Regardless, what if people avoid you, and yet recognize that you are not accountable. What if they avoid you simply to avoid actions they think you may take based on what you have already done? Just as they would avoid a biting animal without thinking that animal has free will. Would not your response be the same?

LIBERIUS: Possibly.

ORION: So deterrence can happen without placing blame or accountability on the person.

LIBERIUS: If they avoid me, they are holding be accounta- ble.

ORION: One does not follow from the other. A preventative measure does not necessarily mean that accountability is being applied to the person. A car is not held accountable for break- ing down, but we certainly can avoid driving a car that is likely to break down, or take the car in and get it repaired before it does. We understand that the car has no control over the age or quality of its parts.

LIBERIUS: We are not cars.

ORION: Agreed. The point is, we are not making an attempt to punish a car when we refuse to drive it, when we bring it in to be fixed, or when we junk it. There are practical reasons for doing those actions. Likewise, there are practical reasons to avoid people who do undesirable things, or as mentioned previously, to create deterrence, or to incarcerate to protect others or attempt to rehabilitate people that are harmful to others. We can do all of this without holding the person accountable for something that they could not have, of their own accord, done otherwise.

LIBERIUS: Okay, even if they don't hold me accountable, without free will I couldn't avoid doing the thing that made me the outcast in the first place.

ORION: This is true, but being the outcast could make you causally do the thing that will make you accepted again. With free will, you could have the free will to do the thing that would make you an outcast or not do that thing. But that would already be based on which option you want or desire prior. Perhaps you are saying you prefer having the free will to decide what you want as well, but what exactly would that be based on? If nothing, then is seems you'd have just as much of a chance, with your so called "free will," to decide to want to do the thing that would make you the outcast. And if you say the chances aren't the same, you are already conceding that you have some wanting of what you will want. With a regress leading to something outside of you.

LIBERIUS: Well, perhaps free will is about the ability to go against what I want or desire.

ORION: Okay, let's say that's possible and go back to the option that you "want." Now let's say you decide, of your own free will, to go against what you want and choose the other option. Since you didn't want to go against it, otherwise that would be an overriding want and not you going against a want, you run into the very same problem. You override the want, but for no good reason. Does that sound like a worthy kind of free will?

LIBERIUS: But if I have a good reason to override what I want, then having the free will to do so is important.

278

ORION: If you "have a reason," that reason causes the override of the want. You simply don't need free will to have such a reason. If you want to override a want because you have a reason to, then you "want to" due to that reason. As you can see, the lack of free will doesn't imply that you cannot do what you want, or do the actions that are best. Causality can (and often does) simply dictate those things. And if it doesn't dictate those things, no version of "free will" can dictate them for you.

LIBERIUS: I'm sorry, Orion, but I'm just letting you know how I feel on the matter.

ORION: I understand and can truly empathize. I'm just trying to explain that the psychological disgust you feel when provided with the fact that you do not have free will is a response that has been built up throughout a lifetime of intuitively feeling you possess certain "free will" abilities that you don't. There is every reason to attempt to build a better and more helpful psychology based on the fact that it doesn't exist. And if that can't be entirely done, we need to, at the very least, recognize it and educate those at an early age who don't yet have such psychology already deeply embedded.

43
A Shift in Attitudes

'The irony is that understanding that we are not free frees us from the specific chains that free will dogma places on us.'

Understanding that there is no free will is important, not only because it's the truth, but because it's needed for a significant shift in attitudes. Raising humanity's conscious awareness of this fact, when done properly and in a way in which people truly understand the implications, can increase the compassion and empathy people have for others. It can help people begin to heal the guilt they carry as they understand that those past events could not have happened in any other way, or (if posturing acausal events) in any other way in which they themselves could have controlled. People can start mending the blame that they put on to others for compassion and understanding regarding the causality they had. People can begin to see that the best route to fixing problems is not to place blame, but rather to try to understand the events that created the negative in the first place. The irony is that understanding that we are not free frees us from the specific chains that free will dogma places on us. The only cure from these chains is for people to shift their psychologies based on a better understanding of nature and reality.

Such changes, if they occur, will be part of such chains of events. It's my hope that this book will be part of a causal chain of events that leads to such a shift. It is my hope that people who read this book will pass on the information within it on. Every person has a part to play that will either lead to an increase in harm, or lead to solutions that reduce harm in the world. As someone that waivers between pessimism and optimism, it's hard to say which will prevail in the end. Surely if people keep going on blindly, ignoring our most reliable methods of logic and science, the future seems bleak. If we go on with archaic standards imposed by evolutionary illusions, we'll keep on consuming and reproducing while ignoring the causal chains that lead to harmful events.

A shift needs to take place in the minds of the masses. A revolutionary shift that would change our entire way of being.

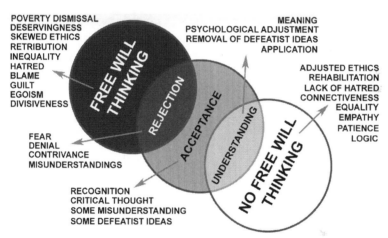

Once you start to understand the implications involved with not having free will, you can see how such an understanding would change everything about the way we interact with others and the universe. Our entire nature, if we allow it, will be different. But for this shift to happen, this understanding needs to become a widespread understanding. It needs to be encompassed in everything from the shows we watch, to the magazines we read, to the funny words on our t-shirts. Everyone needs to play a part in explaining why there is no free will, and just as important, explaining what such really means. The topic needs to move outside of the realm of academia into the public mind.

With the Internet, this has begun to happen. I can see a shift just starting to take hold as more and more people become educated on such matters.   More famous philosophers and scientists are writing books claiming there is no free will. And it's easy to go on the Internet and look up information as websites, blog posts, and social media are giving both great information, and mis-information (e.g. some of the critics). For further info from me on this topic, please visit my website at:

breakingthefreewillillusion.com

44

Studies with
Inconclusive Conclusions

*'I'd wager that finding a test group of real (self-proclaimed)
hard determinists or hard incompatibilists (specific people who
don't believe in free will) would bring forth entirely different results.'*

S tudies have been done that, at first glance, appear to link
deterministic thinking with immoral or aggressive action.
The studies in and of themselves aren't flawed (well, some are),
however, what they suggestively conclude is. These studies
don't really link purely deterministic thinking with unethical
action. What they really link is a *free will psychology* and a misunderstanding of deterministic thinking with these actions. In
other words, they make an attempt to "induce a disbelief in free
will" in people that (most likely) believe in free will and who
already have a psychology based on free will. They don't, in any
way, induce an in depth understanding of what it really means
to lack free will, an understanding necessary to adjust the
psychology of the individual. In other words, it's not a lack of
believing in free will that leads to the results, but rather the
confusion of possibly lacking free will along with an ignorance
of what it really means and psychology that aligns with such
ignorance, and a predisposition to free will.

An example of one of these studies was a study done by
Kathleen D. Vohs of the University of Minnesota and Jonathan
W. Schooler of the University of British Columbia. Thirty

college students were given math problems to solve on a computer. They were all informed that there was a computer glitch where, if they don't press the space bar, the answer would pop up. To avoid this, they were asked to hit the space bar. They were also informed that no one would know if they had or not. Some of the thirty were given a passage to read claiming that most educated people do not believe in free will. The study shows that members of the group asked to read the passage were more likely to let the answer appear (i.e. cheat).

It's easy to see the problem with this type of study. It's a quick questioning of a belief with no time to adjust one's prior set psychology based on the new information.

It would be like trying to induce a disbelief in god by having theists read an article, and then without them obtaining any information regarding what such a lack of belief would entail or time to parse it out for themselves, run the experiment. First off, you simply cannot create a true disbelief that quickly. If anything, you would just create a temporary confusion, which when being tested for, may lead to a less theistic response to the test. This would not mean a real lack of belief in a god was induced. Second, you have done little to adjust the psychology deeply embedded from the past theist thought.

For the initial study, if we were to go back to those "induced lack of free will belief" subjects a week later, would they still have this lack? If not, is a temporary confusion reliable to attribute to someone that truly considers him or herself a "determinist" or "incompatiblist"?

These studies say more about the psychology people hold due to a belief in free will than they do about people that actually lack this belief through an understanding of nature. Such a psychology can be changed through educational and thoughtful means. This is the point that is missed in these studies. I'd suggest it's not due to the lack of a belief in free will that a person cheats, but rather due to the initial belief in free will that created a psychology based on such untruth. The same belief also curves what a person does, so without it, the psychology created by long term effects of such belief says "why not cheat" or "if I don't have free will, nothing matters." This is the psychology built upon an untruth. This is the psychology of a person who has created a strong sense of importance in having free will. This is what these studies test.

What needs to be compared is the "induced disbelief in free will" that these studies attempt to give with an actual disbelief in free will. In other words, studies such as these need better control groups if they are attempting to make a claim on the psychology of someone that truly disbelieves in free will. I'd wager that finding a test group of *real* (self-proclaimed) hard determinists or hard incompatibilists (specific people who don't believe in free will) would bring forth entirely different results. These are people that have thought about and parsed the topic. These are people that have not incorrectly placed the "why bother" fatalistic, defeatist attitude to such understandings as do those who have initial perceptions built on an already existing free will psychology.

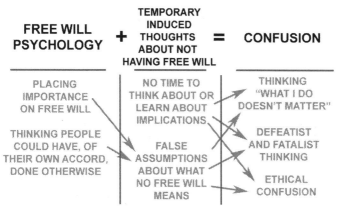

I'd suspect most people who have concluded a lack of free will usually have gone through a long and thought out process that entails a thorough understanding of why and what it means. This is because it goes against what they naturally feel. So before someone points to these studies and says "see what happens when people don't believe in free will," we need to study a group that actually disbelieves in free will for more than the temporary, poorly thought out state that was studied.

It's more likely that a quick confusion between the subject matter combined with a psychology based on free will causes more cheating or aggression or whatever the study tests for.

All is not lost with these studies. They do show us something important about how we transition ideas in people. If we do so recklessly, we get reckless results. It's for this reason that I find the parts of my book that explain the psychology just as important as the undeniable logic.

If you ever come across studies like these, ask yourself: Does this study truly induce a lack of belief in free will. If so, does this study give the test subjects enough time to build a psychology based of this new revelation or educate them on what it means? If not, what is the current psychology based on? An illusionary importance of something they had always thought they had: free will?

Until these tests start using wider control groups of people who have held that free will doesn't exist for a while, they make no case for holding on to the false belief in free will.

Which brings me to other studies done that take participants and try to assess a lack in belief in free will by seeing if they aligned with such things as: "What will be, will be—there's not much you can do about it," "Chance events seem to be the major cause of human history," and "No one can predict what will happen in this world," mixed in with some appropriate sentences that address determinism rather than fatalism or unpredictability.[65] The fact that the people doing this study depict these as options that address people who don't believe in free will for rational reasons says a lot about the people doing the study and their misunderstandings surrounding the topic.

In other words, they don't bother to split out the different types of disbelief in free will. The fatalistic ways, the randomness ways, and the more rational deterministic conclusions. Of course fatalistic ideas or thinking things just happen spontaneously will lead to "why bother" or "what's it matter" types of attitudes.

It would be similar to doing a study on theists with a criteria such as them saying yes to "would god want you to kill the infidel?" as a criteria for the assessment that they are "theists" (rather than certain religious zealot theists). And then, based on other parts of the actual study, noticing some bizarre tendencies of theists compared to non-theists . Not only is a category error happening (e.g. theism doesn't fall under the umbrella of such religious zealots willing to kill for their god, but rather vice versa), but it's dishonest.

If an honest study wants to be performed that does not run into these problems or category errors, this is what I suggest needs to take place:

1. A survey should go out to a large group of people asking a number of random questions. Among those should be direct questions like "Do you believe in free will?" and "If no, for how long have you disbelieved in it?" and "Are you a Hard Determinist or Hard Incompatibilst (if you don't know what these are, write that)?" and "Do you think your actions are fated by God?". These are questions that actually determine a person's *real* position on free will.

2. Once the survey comes back, attempt to pull in an equal random number of people who say they don't believe in free will and an equal number of those that do believe in it for the study. Don't let the participants know which questions pertain to the study and don't assess who is being pulled for the study by any other answers in the survey.

3. Run all of the same tests

4. Compare the results:

   • Compare the results of those who believe in free will with those that do not.

- Compare the results with those that do not believe in free will for a short period of time with those that do not for a longer period of time.

- Compare the results with those who know what a hard determinist or hard incompatibilist is and who label themselves as one or the other, with those who don't believe in free will but don't know these or use such labels.

- Compare the results of those who think they are fated by God with those who think they don't have free will for other reasons.

Once an impartial study of this sort has been accomplished, I think the results would really say something of importance. Not only that, but it would also split out those who lack free will for good reasons and those who do so for bad reasons.

And obviously other impartial groups who are not associated to the first repeating this sort of study would help to validate such results. I think many of the current studies are done by people who are not impartial[66] to the topic. We don't need to ask indirect questions that only vaguely relate to what a person may "believe" or not.

But let's get the way we go about such studies right, because the wrong ways are allowing people to read into something that is just not there. And it's doing so at a great expense of the benefits that a rational understanding of the lack of free will would provide to the world.

MEMES, STEPS,
AND SUMMARY

45

The Importance of Memes

'Memes are simply a useful way to think about how thoughts get from person to person.'

Now that you (I hope) realize that free will doesn't exist, and now that you understand that causal elements are the important factor for what a person thinks, let's address memes. The word "meme" was first introduced by Richard Dawkins, an evolutionary biologist, in his book "The Selfish Gene"[67] in 1976. The idea was to make a correlation to genes and the way they propagate through a process of natural selection. For the memes, however, they are closer to a sort of "unit of information" that gets propagated through natural selection. A similar (but not the same) notion of social evolution called the mneme appeared in 1904, prior to Dawkins' usage, by biologist Richard Semon.

At its basic level, a meme is a thought or thoughts that propagate themselves and are subject to selective pressures. They are transmitted from mind to mind through various means. This book is a meme. Whether it will be a successful meme (a stronger one) or not, only time will tell. It's my hope that it will, and I'll do whatever is in my power to make sure the ideas are spread to as many people as possible. This topic is too important to let people hold on to the illusion.

So what is meant when we say a meme is subject to selective pressures? When talking about genes and evolution, those selective pressures are in the form of the traits that the genes give and the environment in which those traits either help the creature survive until it is able to procreate, prevent the animal from living long enough to procreate, or are benign. For example, frogs that have spots that help them blend into the plant life are more likely to survive to procreate and pass on their genes, while frogs that have a pattern or color that make them stand out may be noticed and eaten by predators before they have a chance to procreate, unless they have some other genetic quality such as being poisonous, in which case other animals develop a propensity not to eat the bright colored frogs, as the ones that do don't survive to procreate. This is basic survival of the fittest. When talking about memes, they have some similarities (and hence the name), but they are ultimately different.

First thing to note is that memes are not a scientific finding. Memes are really just a way to think about ideas and how they spread. The meme idea is a helpful tool to conceptualize the transfer of information from one host to another.

Don't take the connection between genes and memes too literally. It's just there to give you something to relate to. It's closer to an analogy. A meme doesn't have the same type of structure a gene has. They aren't eaten by other memes, but rather other memes override them. Weaker memes never get to the point where they can embed themselves into a mind. Stronger memes root themselves deeply into a mind, compelling a person to pass that meme on and "infect" others. Memes are susceptible to their environment, which would be the mind of the people that perceive them. Some are allowed to propagate and grow strong within their environment (the mind); others get torn apart by their environment, or wither away.

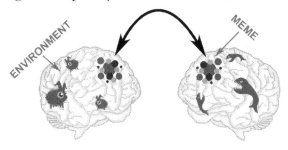

Some perceive memes as mere intangible ideas. In some ways this is true. I'd suggest that this isn't exactly the best way to view them, however. Think of them more as software changes within the hardware of a mind that have the ability to affect other minds. Sort of like a computer virus, but not necessarily a malicious one. Depending on the meme, it could be malicious, or it could be helpful. If there were computer viruses that made your computer faster and more reliable without any security concerns, you may purposely try to "infect" your computer with it, or at least it wouldn't bother you if your computer was accidentally infected. The difference between memes is that they are usually built up. In other words, they can lie dormant until other memes or ideas come in that support them. The more that come in, the stronger they can become. They battle with some memes and team up with others that are already in the software of the brain (or mind, if you prefer). The stronger ideas survive and get propagated. The weaker ideas don't get propagated, so tend to die before or when a person dies.

If we were to apply memes to the physical (which is unnecessary but helpful for understanding them), a meme is just a memory store of the brain that is coded with information that has come from perceiving the ideas of others. Memes are not in any sense a far stretch of the imagination as some would have you believe. No, it isn't an idea that is linked explicitly to the evolution of genes. Unlike genes, there is no specific DNA type code script for memes. It has never been suggested that there was. Memes are simply a useful way to think about how thoughts get from person to person.

You can help propagate important memes. Think of it as advertising the world that you want to live in. The next chapter will help you propagate the meme of this book, if that is something you might consider a positive action (which I hope I have convinced you it is). It'll allow you to be a positive gear for the no-free-will enlightenment of humankind.

46

Steps to Take with the Knowledge Acquired in this Book

'Understand, Change, Adjust, Observe, Spread'

There are two key aspects to this book: the reasoning and the psychology involved. This chapter, on the other hand, is about suggested steps to take once you have acquired such knowledge.

Step 1: Understand the reasoning fully

No writing is perfect and no philosophy is flawless. I've made every attempt to minimize down ambiguities and language barriers. This doesn't mean I've been successful in its entirety. Clarify any points not fully understood about the reasoning. Go over areas that don't initially make sense to you. Take notes. If you are reading this on an eReader, use it to take notes in certain areas. It's not only important that you understand why free will is illogical, but it's also important that you understand it enough to be able to explain it to others, or to understand the arguments for when you come across someone stating "Quantum mechanics can give free will" or "I don't think free will an entirely material or physical thing." If you cannot explain to them why their thinking is fallacious, they'll keep on contriving their free will, because their desire for it overrides all others. If

293

you can't remember all of the arguments, point them to this book or give them a copy. Show them or highlight the spot that they are contriving.

If you understand the logic involved, you'll know what to point out. By understanding it, you'll not only reinforce your own lack of belief in free will, but you'll be more capable of defending your position when it's criticized.

Oh, and let me know which parts you couldn't understand. I can always make enhancements to further editions. No book is without flaws of some sort or another, no matter how many times an author goes over it or how much editing went into it.

Step 2: Change your psychology

This step is on par with understanding the logic. Our psychologies are dictated by our past causality. You now have different causal events in your mind, but if you don't make an effort to override your current psychology with the suggestions in this book, you could be led down an unnecessary avenue of fictions that have no connection to the knowledge regarding the lack of free will. This book is here to remind you to make that effort. I hope it's a strong enough causal link. Here are some suggestions to keep you reminded:

- Keep a sheet of paper in your wallet the size of a dollar bill. It can be blank, or you can draw a symbol on it, or a short note. As long as you relate the paper to changing your psychology, it will remind you whenever you see it.

- If you are the type of person that likes tattoos, place a symbol, an image, or a word on your body that will remind you.

- Come back to this book at a later date and read through it again.

Here are some points and goals to keep in mind about your psychology:

- Be motivated by incentives, but be fair. Understand that you are *not more deserving* than others.

- Understand that the things you do have an effect on other people. You may not be able to avoid some negative effects, but you can still understand the ones you create and try better next time. Awareness is the first step to change.

- If someone does something you don't like, understand they are *not to blame*. Hate the event, not the person. Better yet, don't hate at all if possible. Look for possible underlying causes and solutions.

- *Don't blame* yourself if you don't make a goal; rather examine the causes of why you didn't make your goal and strive to do better next time. Remember, there was nothing you could have, of your own accord, done differently. The thoughts you have right now, however, have an impact on how your causality will play out in the future. Rebuild the goal if it's important to you and try again.

Step 3: Adjust your ideology

Adjust your ideology with the base "lacking free will" understanding. Without this base, your ideology doesn't have a logical foundation and will be built on the notion of free will intuited, or that others teach.

Any ethical system you have needs to incorporate the idea that free will does not really exist. If it doesn't, it is a flawed system. Rethink it.

If you carry political or economic ideology that places blame on a person, you should rethink it. If your ideology excessively rewards people due to their actions, in which that reward might take away from others, you should rethink it.

Change your ideology about the way the criminal system should work. Try to reduce or purge retributive stances and lean toward more rehabilitative stances.

If you hold some other idea, look deeply at its foundation. Does it rely on some sort of free will? Work out what happens when that changes. Changing your ideology may be difficult, especially if you are in deep with your ideological affiliations-- religious, political or otherwise. You can do it! It may, however, take some time. Don't rush things.

Step 4: Observe and become aware of causality

This may start to come naturally after you have done the first three steps. The reminders in step 2 can help you to remember to keep an eye out. When you see something good or bad, don't overlook how those things came about. See if you can figure out causal elements extending into the past. Don't insist you know, but try to infer possible causes and likelihoods of them based on sound evidence. The more we understand possible causes, the more we can decrease negative outcomes and increase positive ones for future events.

Keep in mind that this includes what people do, even those considered horrific. A terrorist or a serial killer has a lifetime of causality which includes genetic and environmental variables. Sure, you can simply hate them, and I am not saying you necessarily shouldn't. You can also hate a tornado that kills your family. Even though that is the case, the hatred of the tornado is of a different sort. You don't blame it for coming about, you recognize the conditions of why it did. It's the same thing for a dog that bites you. We may still put that dog down if we determine it a danger to others, but we can hardly blame the dog for its temperament (or rabies).

Become aware of the causality that leads those events. Ask yourself what can be done to prevent such an outcome in the future.

Step 5: Spread the knowledge on to others

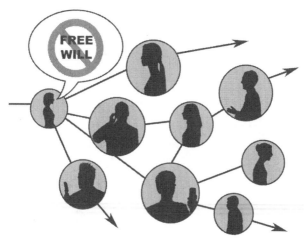

- Spread your knowledge on to others. It will do humanity less good to have the knowledge locked solely in your own brain for your entire life. You are important. You know the importance of memes. Here are ways to spread the meme:

- Bring up the subject into conversation where you see fit. Utilize the arguments in this book to explain the logic and the psychology to others. Come up with your own analogies and ways to illustrate points.

- Refer this book (or other books on this topic) to others. Give them as gifts to people that have an open mind. If you know someone that is stubborn, give it to them as well to help them see another side. Even if they disagree and hate the book, the information lodged in their memory may be reinforced at a later date. People do not change mindsets immediately. Sometimes it takes a long, drawn out process until they finally say "ahhh, now I get it."

- Talk with people online. Create a YouTube account. Go on to forums. Explain what you know. You'll be surprised by the contrived responses explained in this book, and you will have the tools to counter them. Create articles, videos, or podcasts.

- Create a website dedicated to the topic. If I am still alive when you are reading this, point people to my website, and let me know about yours. Part of my mission is to spread the information. The more hands in on this the better.

- Blog about it.

- Create or spread around imagery, infographics, or logos. I made this logo to brand Breaking the Free Will Illusion:

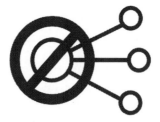

The three smaller circles on the logo represent multiple viable options. The options that someone with "free will" would be able to take. The mid-sized circle represents the "willer". The person, self, or entity that would have the illusion of possessing this fantastical ability. And the thicker circle with the line through is the breaking of the illusion. It's basically saying that such ability is impossible.

- Host a meet-up group to talk about this topic, or join an existing one.

- If you have a different way to explain the content in this book, do it. Write your own book, play, movie, podcast, video, etc. Don't get me wrong, I want my book in the hands of as many people as possible. What author doesn't? But I'm equally as concerned that the *information* itself gets into the hands of as many people as possible. The information is what is ultimately important.

47

Book Summary

To sum up, an event can either be caused, or not caused. If it's not caused, you cannot be the cause of the event and hence that specific event cannot be willed. If the event is caused, you can cause the event, but not freely so. Any combination of caused or uncaused events cannot grant free will. At most, they can grant willfulness in an entirely causal universe; or partial willfulness in one where some events are not causal. This willfulness can never be free. It is entirely dictated either by past causal events that always extend away from the willer, or a combination of past causal events and acausal events that come into existence with no control from the willer. Free will, even though we feel we have it, is logically incoherent. It's simply not a possibility. Therefore this ability we experience is an illusion.

It's fine to sustain the feeling, but we can do that and at the same time understand that it's only a feeling and that those feelings should not dictate our philosophical, ethical, and political outlooks. We also must incorporate this fact into our psychology and actions. The stakes are too high to keep holding on to the illusion, or even to derive new definitions of "free will" when such can cause so much unnecessary confusion. I hope reading this book was a strong enough causal factor for you, now or even at a future date when you think about it some more. If it was, then the events that have led me to want to propagate this understanding were well worth it.

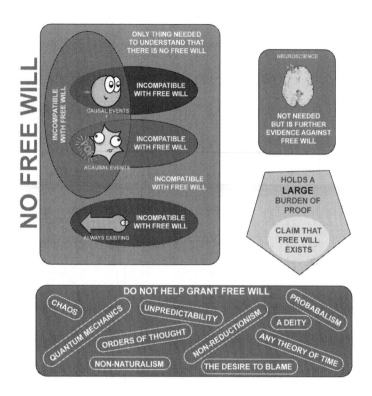

Dialogue

Liberius walked home after his talk with Orion. As he walked along the sidewalk, the discussion they had whirled in his head.

LIBERIUS: No, Orion is wrong. I have free will and that is that.

The thoughts started rolling around again as he thought about the logical flaws in his free will position. *No, I will not let these thoughts control me. I'll choose free will of my own free will!*

The desire residing in Liberius to have free will caused a rejection of the reasoning proposed by Orion. He was forced by the past causality that led to a psychology unwilling to except the truth; to cling dearly to the illusion.

That was until many years later when he started thinking about the topic again, and all of the memories of his conversation with Orion rushed back in.

Author's Causal Bio

The appreciation for philosophy had been causally imprinted within me, 'Trick Slattery *("Patrick" on birth certificate)*, since I was a teenager. It all started in January of 1971 when I deterministically popped out of my mother and met my family. A loving, open, and friendly atmosphere allowed me to pursue abstract, unordinary thoughts. An introverted personality led to much introspection. Events occurring within that environment led up to the curiosity, analysis, and ultimately the non-acceptance of certain popular norms.

At some point prior to college, as I flowed along the river of events, an interest in philosophy and art clung to my consciousness. Contemplation and drawing were my pastimes. These two things worked well together. One would allow for creative expression, the other for analytic thought; a combination that allowed me to think about analytical concepts both visually and creatively. These events lead up to me aligning my academic and personal electives to their study. These interests also started a process of self teaching that extended way beyond academia.

Methodologies of logic were studied and became indispensable tools. Such studies caused by a desire to understand the truth about reality. Such desire caused by antecedent events stemming as far back as one can imagine. Still not broken away from shy introversion, I would go for long times within my own head, without the need to hear others. Ideas would play ping pong matches using critical thinking paddles. Internal debates strung along by competing conceptions derived from complex causal patterns. The characters within the dialogues in this book are really an extension of such ping pong matches.

I don't remember the exact point that I realized free will was a fiction. The thought process began at some point in my early twenties. At that point, I didn't know much about the free will debate in philosophy. I just knew that events were forced by causes, and that an event without one couldn't help with free will.

I didn't know what the terms "determinism" or "indeterminism" meant. I didn't know that other philosophers had addressed causality, free will, and the question of responsibility. I just had a basic idea derived through my own internal thought processes.

It wasn't until after I had written a philosophical post for a website that I actually began to examine the topic seriously. On the website I had a drawing of a basic timeline with lines representing causes going from past to present in an attempt to illustrate what I was thinking. It was rudimentary at best, and I thought it was original. At least until someone pointed me toward others who already concluded what I had. After that, I was hooked. I began hopping into online debates about the topic. I began to learn the terminology involved. I was forced to. It became one of my favorite topics to debate on forums and websites.

People who were into philosophy, as well as others interested in the topic itself, would offer their input. The arguments people made for having "free will" seemed to never end, and one thing began to happen. I began to see patterns of flaws and fallacies people were making on both sides of the debate. I also noticed my own flaws as well as poor word choices. Every debate I had would cause me to think hard, to break down the logic, to analyze each aspect, and to research the facts. A causal process that honed my understanding surrounding the topic.

I would also research what the philosophical and scientific authorities had to say on the topic. The authorities on this topic varied greatly from extreme ends to in-the-middles. I realized that my own philosophy based on the topic aligned much closer to some than others, and that my overall stance really was not influenced much by any of these "authorities." The stance of authorities came as afterthoughts once others used them to contrive free will. They were, however, causal springboards for different ways to think about and address the topic.

As I debated with people online, very intelligent people would hit me from every angle with illogical ideas surrounding how free will is possible.

I noticed people starting to throw this authority or that authority in my face, and many didn't really seem to understand what such authorities were saying. It also appeared to me that many of these authorities on the subject were contriving the notion of free will. Or they were propagating the idea that letting people know they did not have free will was dangerous. But who was I to challenge them? An unknown. A nobody. But then again, so were they at some point.

It frustrated me that they overlooked the simplicity of the causal/acausal dichotomy, over complicated it to the point of obscurity, or redefined free will in a way that was not free, or not will, or neither--at least in the ways that were important to so many other topics. They are part of the causality that has led to me writing this book in a way that is simple, straightforward, logical, and tailored to layperson speak. Also in getting past that I was an "unknown." So what. I had valid and sound points and criticisms to make.

As my understanding of the topic strengthened, others things changed within me. How I perceived the world around me changed. I began to recognize that people are not to blame, nor are they more deserving than others of anything. Any real hate in me dissipated as I recognized that if I was in the shoes of those I hated, with the same causal setup, I'd be who I hated and wouldn't have had the means to be different. I'm grateful to have the causality that lead to such change. I'm not, however, more deserving of it, and I wish such causality for all.

Thank you for taking the time out of your busy life to read this book. I hope you enjoyed it and that you take the thoughts in it to *heart* and mind. – 'Trick Slattery

~ END ~

One last thing…

If you enjoyed this book or think it would be of use to others, would you be so kind as to *rate it* and write a short review on Amazon? The more good reviews it receives, the more hands it'll causally find its way into.

Also, if you believe the book is worth sharing, would you please take a few seconds to let your friends know about it and share it on any social media site you have? If it turns out to make a difference in their lives, they will be grateful to you. As will I.

Also, don't forget to sign up for the infrequent newsletter at: **http://breakingthefreewillillusion.com/**

And check for extra book content here: **http://breakingthefreewillillusion.com/book-extras/**

The rest of this book is all of the "back of the book" boring stuff such as endnotes, bibliography, some base syllogisms, and so on. Real snoozer parts. Read these parts at your own risk! I don't recommend them to the sane.

Philosophy regarding Free Will is not just for Academic Elites

Complex philosophical terminology and technical jargon discourage people from taking an interest in topics that are of great importance to everyone, not just academic elites. Sometimes this terminology is unavoidable, but every attempt should be made to make the content palatable for the largest audience.

Philosophical Terms for the Free Will Debate:

Since I made every attempt to make concepts as simple and readable as possible to the layperson, there are many terms I may have left out on purpose. Others that I have left in I made sure to give clear definitions of. Since I want people to read up on the topic and decide for themselves, below is a handy list of useful terms that can be referenced for further reading on the topics of free will, and causality/acausality. I also plan on creating articles for each of these terms on: breakingthefreewillillusion.com

Free Will

• Libertarianism

• Compatiblism

• Incompatiblism (libertarian and not)

• Hard Incompatiblism

- Determinism

- Soft Determinism

- Hard Determinism

Causality/Acausality

Three types

- Necessary cause

- Sufficient cause – the only possible type

- Contributory cause

Aristotle

- Accidental Causality

- Essential Causality

- Aristotle also categorized four types of causality to answer the question "why" for a cause: Material Cause, Formal Cause, Efficient Cause, Final Cause

A Brief List of Some "No Free Will" Folks:

Want to look up some names of people who held or hold the non-free-will stance, or who play a part in history for this topic? Here is a short starting list:

Slattery, Trick - Born 1971 - Me! - Philosopher, Writer, Artist
Harris, Sam - Born 1967 - Philosopher / Neuroscientist / Writer
Pereboom , Derk - Philosopher
Pearce, Jonathan M.S. - Philosopher / Author / Teacher
Wegner, Daniel - Born 1948 - Philosopher / Psychologist
Strawson, Galen - Born 1952 - Philosopher
Hawking, Stephen William - Born 1942 - Theoretical Physicist / Cosmologist
Greene, Joshua - Psychologist / Neuroscientist / Philosopher
Cohen, Jonathan - Philosopher
Blackmore, Susan - Born 1951 - Writer / Lecturer / Skeptic / Broadcaster

309

Ortega, George - Quality of life researcher / Author / Host of 'Exploring the Illusion of Free Will'
Minsky, Marvin - Born 1927 - Cognitive scientist in the field of AI
Russel, Bertrand - 1872 - 1970 - Philosopher / Logician
Ginet, Carl – Born 1932 - Philosopher
d'Holbach, Baron 1723 - 1789 - Philosopher
Churchland, Patricia - Born 1943 - Philosopher
Libet, Benjamin - 1916 - 2007 - Scientist
Einstein, Albert - 1879 - 1955 - Theoretical Physicist
Darrow, Clarence Seward - 1857 - 1938 - Lawyer
Laplace, Pierre-Simon - 1749 - 1827 - Mathematician / Astronomer
Locke, John 1632 – 1704 - Philosopher
Spinoza, Baruch - 1632 - 1677 - Philosopher

* If you wrote a book or made strident public efforts to promote the understanding that there is no free will, and people can easily look up your work, let me know if you aren't on this list. I may be able to add you to a later edition. The list above is hardly an extensive list and important people are no doubt missing from here.

Syllogisms

It's often helpful to organize and break down thoughts into syllogistic form. If you're not familiar with the term "syllogism," don't fear. It's simply a logical argument put into the format of two premises and one conclusion. The conclusion is inferred from those premises, given that the premises are accepted.

Here are a few syllogisms I quickly put together that may help to simplify some of the key concepts that were addressed in this book. The content of this book supports the premises and conclusions of these syllogisms, and in regards to word usage, they are quite rough. I placed these syllogisms in here as a helpful tool to organize and structure some thoughts about some key concepts. They are a work in progress and could always be worded better. These only constitute some of the more prominent arguments. Not all have been placed in syllogistic form here. These syllogisms are **not** meant as sole arguments, and shouldn't be taken as such. I debated keeping them in here as it bothers me when people take base syllogisms out of the context of the book, evidence, and points that represent or show their premises.

Definitions

• Premise 1a: There are people who believe they have free will, and that the free will they have gives them the ability to choose between more than one viable option or action, in which that choice it up to them. (Chapter 3)
• Premise 2a: No person has the ability to choose between more than one viable option or action, in which that choice is up to them. (C1m, C1q, C1x)
• Conclusion 1a: There are people that hold a false belief about free will.

Events

- Premise 1b: Things happen.
- Premise 2b: All happenings are events.
- Conclusion 1b: If something happens, it's an event.

Causal/Acausal Dichotomy

- Premise 1c: An event that happens *not due to a cause* cannot happen *due to a cause* (the event must happen acausally).
- Premise 2c: An event that happens *due to a cause* cannot happen *not due to a cause* (the event must happen causally).
- Conclusion 1c: All events that happen are either causal events (due to a cause) or acausal events (not due to a cause).

- Premise 1d: Once an acausal event happens (if acausal events are possible), it can cause another event.
- Premise 2d: Multiple causes can lead to one effect (event).
- Conclusion 1d: A causal event can happen due to causes that stem from a combination of causal and acausal events.

- Premise 1e: All events that happen are either causal events or acausal events. (C1c)
- Premise 2e: A causal event can happen due to causes that stem from a combination of causal and acausal events. (C1d)
- Conclusion 1e: All events that happen are either causal events or acausal events, and if causal can stem from a combination of both events types.

Thought Events

- Premise 1f: If something happens, it's an event. (C1b)
- Premise 2f: All thoughts happen.
- Conclusion 1f: All thoughts are events.

- Premise 1g: All thoughts are events. (C1f)
- Premise 2g: All events that happen are either causal events or acausal events, and if causal, can happen due to a combination of both event types. (C1e)
- Conclusion 3g: A thought is either a causal event or an acausal event, and if causal, can come about through both event types.

Cause and Effect

• Premise 1h: An effect is an event that occurs due to another event (cause).
• Premise 2h: A cause is an event that creates or forces another event (effect).
• Conclusion 1h: All effects must have a cause and all causes lead to an effect.

• Premise 1i: All effects must have a cause and all causes lead to an effect. (C1h)
• Premise 2i: Acausal events do not have a cause.
• Conclusion 1i: No acausal events are effects.

• Premise 1j: A cause that can lead to both X and *not* X fails to denote a cause that led it to one state over the other.
• Premise 2j: If there is no cause for one state over another, yet it goes to one state over the other, it happened acausally.
• Conclusion 1j: A cause (the same cause) cannot lead to both X and *not* X, as an acausal event would be required.

• Premise 1k: A cause cannot lead to both X and *not* X, as an acausal event would be required. (C1j)
• Premise 2k: To claim a cause can lead to effect X and *not* Y and effect Y and *not* X is to claim the cause can lead to both X and *not* X.
• Conclusion 1k: A claim that a cause can lead to effect X and *not* Y and effect Y and *not* X is a false claim.

• Premise 1l: A claim that a cause can lead to effect X and *not* Y and effect Y and *not* X is a false claim. (C1k)
• Premise 2l: No acausal events are effects. (C1i)
• Conclusion 1l: A single cause cannot hold the potential for multiple possible effects.

• Premise 1m: An event that happens which is not an effect is acausal.
• Premise 2m: A single cause cannot hold the potential for multiple possible effects. (C1l)
• Conclusion 1m: For an event to have possibly been different, it must be acausal.

Acausality

• Premise 1n: Acausal events are not forced by a cause to a specific time.
• Premise 2n: Acausal events are not forced by a cause to a specific location.
• Conclusion 1n: A cause is needed to force an event to a specific time or location.

• Premise 1o: A cause is needed to force an event to a specific time or location. (C1n)
• Premise 2o: An acausal event happens without a cause.
• Conclusion 1o: An acausal event happens without respect to a specific time or location.

• Premise 1p: Already existing objects or things exist in a specific time or at a specific location.
• Premise 2p: An acausal event happens without respect to a specific time or location. (C1o)
• Conclusion 1p: An object or thing cannot control an acausal event's occurrence to its specific time or location.

• Premise 1q: A person, brain, or mind does not cause an acausal event.
• Premise 2q: A cause is needed for something to come about due to something else.
• Conclusion 1q: Acausal events that happen within a person, brain, or mind, do not happen due to that person, brain, or mind.

Willing

• Premise 1r: Something needs to will a willed event.
• Premise 2r: A willed event requires a willer to cause it.
• Conclusion 1r: Willers are required causes for the process of willing.

• Premise 1s: Willers are required causes for the process of willing. (C1r)
• Premise 2s: Acausal events do not have a cause.
• Conclusion 1s: No acausal event is a willed event.

Freedom

• Premise 1t: A person must be able to, of their own accord, do otherwise to be free (in the sense of the free will semantic established for this book).
• Premise 2t: A person that is caused to do something cannot do otherwise.
• Conclusion 1t: An entirely caused person is not free.

• Premise 1u: A person must be able to, of their own accord, do otherwise to be free.
• Premise 2u: An acausal event that would lead a person to do otherwise happens independent of their own accord.
• Conclusion 2u: Acausal events do not make a person free.

• Premise 1v: An entirely caused person is not free. (C1t)
• Premise 2v: A person with acausal events is not free due to them. (C2u)

• Conclusion 1v: Neither an entirely caused person nor a person with acausal events is free.

Blaming / Holding Responsible

• Premise 1x: Causal events (that lead to choice) cannot happen otherwise.
• Premise 2x: Acausal events (that lead to choice) cannot happen of someone's own accord.
• Conclusion 1x: A person cannot, of their own accord, choose otherwise.

• Premise 1y: A person should only be blamed or held responsible if they could have, of their own accord, chosen otherwise.
• Premise 2y: A person cannot, of their own accord, choose otherwise. (C1x)
• Conclusion 1y: A person should not be blamed or held responsible.

Being More Deserving

• Premise 1z: A person should only be held more deserving of something over another person if they could have, of their own accord, chosen otherwise, and if the other person could have, of their own accord, chosen otherwise.
• Premise 2z: A person cannot, of their own accord, choose otherwise. (C1x)
• Conclusion 1z: No person is more deserving of something over another person.

Again, it's extremely important not to single out these "back of the book" syllogisms as *the* arguments being made. They are meant as just another tool, but they help formally *reflect* some of the more in-depth thoughts that this book represents. It's important to look at all of the data, evidence, thought experiments, and reasoning that goes against our strongly engrained intuitions on these matters.

Annotated Bibliography

Breaking the Free Will Illusion for the Betterment of Humankind:

Visit my website here:
http://breakingthefreewillillusion.com

The Anthropic Principle:

Carter, B. (1974). "Large Number Coincidences and the Anthropic Principle in Cosmology". IAU Symposium 63: Confrontation of Cosmological Theories with Observational Data. Dordrecht: Reidel. pp. 291–298.

Other interesting reads on the anthropic principle:

Ikeda, M. and Jefferys, W., "The Anthropic Principle Does Not Support Supernaturalism," inThe Improbability of God, Michael Martin and Ricki Monnier, Editors, pp. 150-166. Amherst, N.Y.: Prometheus Press. ISBN 1-59102-381-5

Ikeda, M. and Jefferys, W. (2006). Unpublished FAQ "The Anthropic Principle Does Not Support Supernaturalism." http://quasar.as.utexas.edu/anthropic.html

Neuroscience and Free Will:

Chun Siong Soon, Marcel Brass, Hans-Jochen Heinze & John-Dylan Haynes (2008) Unconscious determinants of free decisions in the human brain. *Nature Neuroscience*

http://www.nature.com/neuro/journal/v11/n5/abs/nn.2112.
html
http://phys.org/news127395619.html

Libet, Benjamin (1985) Unconscious cerebral initiative and the
role of conscious will in voluntary action. *Behavioral and Brain
Sciences*, 8: 529–566.

http://en.wikipedia.org/wiki/Benjamin_Libet

Harris, Sam (2012) Free Will

Wegner, Daniel (2002) The Illusion of Conscious Will
Chapter   3   page   68
Chapter 5 page 165

Dr Bahador Bahrami (2007) Subliminal Advertising Leaves Its
Mark   On   The   Brain
http://www.sciencedaily.com/releases/2007/03/07030812193
8.htm
http://www.ucl.ac.uk/media/library/notaware

Anthony Cashmore on Free Will:
http://phys.org/news186830615.html

Information regarding neuroscience, the lack of free will, and
how the law needs to change due to the lack of free will:

Greene, Joshua and Cohen, Johnathan (Nov 2004) For the law,
neuroscience changes nothing and everything.
http://www.wjh.harvard.edu/~jgreene/GreeneWJH/GreeneC
ohenPhilTrans-04.pdf

Genetics

Kobayakawa et al. (2007) Innate versus learned odour processing in the mouse olfactory bulb. Nature, Volume 450,
p503-508

http://www.nature.com/nature/journal/v450/n7169/abs/nat
ure06281.html
http://www.s.u-tokyo.ac.jp/en/press/2007/24.html

Intuitions Regarding Free Will:

Eddy Nahmias, Stephen Morris, Thomas Nadelhoffer, and
Jason Turner (2005) Surveying Freedom: Folk Intuitions about
Free   Will   and   Moral   Responsibility
http://www2.gsu.edu/~phlean/papers/Surveying_Freedom.p
df

Nichols, S. and J. Knobe (2007) Moral responsibility and
determinism: the cognitive science of folk intuitions. Nouse
41:663-685.
http://onlinelibrary.wiley.com/doi/10.1111/j.1468-
0068.2007.00666.x/full

Sarkissian, H., A. Chatterjee, F. De Brigard, J. Knobe, N. S.,
and S. Sirker (2010) Is belief in free will a cultural universal?
Mind & Language 25:346-358.
http://dingo.sbs.arizona.edu/~snichols/Papers/Is_Belief_in_
Free_will_a_Cultural_Universal

Causality:

The Metaphysics of Causation
*First published Sun Feb 2, 2003; substantive revision Mon Aug 13,
2007*
http://plato.stanford.edu/entries/causation-metaphysics/

To learn a little more about Aristotles four causes, in which as I
explained in an endnote, fall under the umbrella term "cause"
as used in this book:
Aristotle, *Physics* 194 b17–20; see also: *Posterior Analytics* 71 b9–
11; 94 a20.
Stanford Encyclopedia of Philosophy 2008.

http://plato.stanford.edu/entries/aristotle-causality/

Burden of Proof

This is an appropriate video on the burden of proof by Qualia Soup
http://www.youtube.com/watch?v=KayBys8gaJY

Holism, Downward Causation, and Reductionism

Stanford Encyclopedia of Philosophy article: "Holism and Nonseparability in Physic"
http://plato.stanford.edu/entries/physics-holism/

Dossey, Larry. Reinventing Medicine: Beyond Mind-Body to a New Era of Healing. (ISBN 0-06-251622-1) HarperSanFrancisco. (1999)

Campbell D.T. (1990): "Levels of Organization, Downward Causation, and the Selection-Theory Approach to Evolutionary Epistemology", in: Scientific Methodology in the Study of Mind: evolutionary epistemology, E. Tobach and G. Greenberg (ed.), (Erlbaum, Hillsdale, NJ), p. 1-17.

Donald T. Campbell, "'Downward Causation' in Hierarchically Organized Biological Systems," in F.J. Ayala and T. Dobzhansky, eds., Studies in the Philosophy of Biology: Reduction and Related Problems (Berkeley and Los Angeles: University of California Press, 1974), 179-186; 181.

Robert Van Gulick, "Who's in Charge Here? And Who's Doing All the Work?" in Heil and Mele, eds., Mental Causation, 233-256.

Interdisciplinary Encyclopedia of Religion and Science: "Reductionism" http://www.disf.org/en/Voci/104.asp

Quantum Physics

Bell, J.S. (1987)   Speakable and Unspeakable in Quantum Mechanics, pg 100, Chapter 12 – Free Variables and Local Causality
http://www.scribd.com/doc/6916838/Bell-John-Speakable-And-Unspeakable-In-Quantum-Mechanics-Cup-1987KT225S

Einstein, A.; Podolsky, B.; Rosen, N. (1935). "Can Quantum-Mechanical Description of Physical Reality Be Considered Complete?". Physical Review 47 (10): 777–780.

Bell, J.S. (1966). On the problem of hidden variables in quantum mechanics. Reviews of Modern Physics. 38(3). 447-452.

Simon Groblacher, Tomasz Paterek,   Rainer Kaltenbaek, Caslav Brukner, Marek Zukowski, Markus Aspelmeyer, and Anton Zeilinger   (2007) An experimental test of nonlocal realism
http://arxiv.org/pdf/0704.2529.pdf

Radek Lapkiewicz, Peizhe Li, Christoph Schaeff, Nathan K. Langford, Sven Ramelow, Marcin Wiesniak, & Anton Zeilinger (2011) Experimental non-classicality of an indivisible quantum system
http://vcq.quantum.at/fileadmin/Publications/Experimental

Other resources

Pereboom, Derk (2001) Living without Free Will

Dawkins, Richard (2006). The Selfish Gene (30th Anniversary edition). New York City: Oxford University Press. ISBN 0-19-929115

End Notes

1 The word "feeling" can have many different usages. For example, an emotion could be a "feeling." So can the sense of touch be a "feeling." It can also be used as sort of an intuitive sense: "I have a feeling we are not alone in this dark room." When it comes to the "feeling" of free will, it's used more in the intuitive sense. It is an inclination. The person feels they have this ability. They don't really conclude it, as they do not need to structure an argument that leads to it. The simply feel it or intuit it. They then may conclude it based on the feeling afterward, but of course such a base is never reliable.

2 The word "intuition" is similar to the word "feeling" used and addressed in the above endnote. It implies an ability to acquire knowledge without inference and/or the use of reason.

3 "Reasonable" or "reason" in the sense used here is a *discursive reason*, meaning the faculty of drawing inferences. And though this book isn't in regards to appropriate epistemological standards (standards of knowledge), it's assumed that logical inductive and deductive methodologies are appropriate. At the very least, it must be understood that identity and non-contradiction are accepted, and the use of modal logic in so far as we can assess "if" possibilities (e.g. if B then X, if *not* B then Y) is as well. If not accepted, I'd suggest there is a base epistemological problem on the part of the person who does not accept these, which another book may be needed to address.

4 *Cog in the machine* is an idiom that denotes someone is one part of a larger system.

5 When I say free will can be "taught," I mean it in the sense that other people reinforce the idea that we have it. Many times they talk about it as if it's a given. The words just flow in everyday conversation.
   Person One: "Did you mean to do that?"
   Person two: "Yes, I've done it of my own free will!"
or

Lawyer: "Someone held a gun to his head telling him what to do. Obviously his action was not of his own free will!" (Assuming, of course, that it would have been of his own free will had he no gun to his head.)

6 Retributive punishment must be separated from "punishment" in the general sense. There may be utilitarian reasons to "punish." For example, to create deterrence or to prevent the person from further harmful acts. Retribution, that being punishing for "revenge" or "justice" or for the person to "get what they deserve," is something that must be abandoned with our understanding that there is no free will.

7 Necessary evil: Something that you do not like but which you know must exist or happen. (e.g. He considers taxes a necessary evil.) Evil is not meant in any religious context here.

8 When talking about causality, it's important to note that I'm using an umbrella sense of the word. Aristotle, for example, made attempts at defining different *types* of causes that he named as material cause, formal cause, efficient cause, and final cause. For the free will debate, any such types being defined become irrelevant as they all fall under this umbrella. Each type, no matter how defined, has a cause and an effect.

An exception might be the use of "essential" causality, also thought up by Aristotle. I address this later and clarify what this is and why it's not the correct usage of causality for understanding this topic.

It must also be noted that we don't even need to keep causality as a physical notion. A supernatural cause would hold the same logical problems as a natural cause. In no way do I bring up supernatural ideas to suggest they have any validity, but rather to make the point that the idea of causality and acausality addressed is not pigeon-holed in naturalism. Non-naturalistic thinkers who wish to be taken seriously will not be able to avoid the reasoning in this book. It's one thing to be someone that thinks outside of naturalism, it is quite another to deny our most consistent and reliable standards of knowledge in light of self-opposing or contradictory ideas.

9 The word "necessary" has various usages and semantic differences within philosophy.

One example is in regards to how such is used when addressing *knowledge* or *truth*. For such, there is a distinction between the words "necessary" and "contingent." Necessarily true propositions are those that are true in all possible worlds (e.g. all bachelors are unmarried is a necessary truth), while contingent propositions are those that are true in some possible worlds and false in others (e.g. that bachelor has two eyes). It must be understood that the distinction between these two things wouldn't change a thing in regards to them both being "essential" to the specifics (e.g. to the specific bachelor, it is true that he *is* unmarried and has two eyes, until such time he is no longer a bachelor or loses an eye).

I also find there is a problem with addressing "possible worlds" in the ontological sense (ontological meaning it addresses what "exists"), especially in the context of addressing if a universe is entirely causal (deterministic). In the epistemological sense (addressing knowledge), this is fine when talking about possible future worlds, but that would only be due to a lack of "knowing" all the variables in a deterministic world. In reality, there being a "possibility" of something being different is dependent on there being acausal events that could make such different.

Another common usage of "necessary" in philosophy has to do directly with causality. For such, there is an important distinction between a "necessary cause" and a "sufficient cause." If x is a *necessary cause* of y, then the presence of y necessarily implies the presence of x. The presence of x, however, does not imply that y will occur. If x is a *sufficient cause* of y, then the presence of x necessarily implies the presence of y. However, another cause z may alternatively cause y. Thus the presence of y does not imply the presence of x. In this case, I make a logical case against such "necessary causes" and the case that all causes need to be "sufficient causes." I don't, however, use these words.

I avoid these ambiguous philosophical usages of these words and opt for a more common usage of something simply being required for another thing. For it being "essential" to the other thing. Most people in the non-academic world understand what "It's a necessary consequence of..." means without ever needing to ask "Wait, did you mean it's contingent?" or "Did you mean to say sufficient?", to which I would answer, no, I mean "necessary" in its normal, everyday, common usage. Those other usages are only appropriate to a very specific (and much smaller) audience, and are *unnecessary* to the points and arguments within this book.

10 Note that I am addressing a specific "person" here, even though the line between that specific person and everything interacting with the person becomes blurred as explained in Chapter 15, "You and I". For all practical purposes, I'm compartmentalizing a person (willer) as the specific body and events occurring within that body. After all, that is what is being addressed with the claim that *"someone"* or *"I"* or *"you"* have free will.

11 When I say *"I don't think these definitions are what the majority of people feel they have,"* I'm in no way suggesting I know what people "feel." It's a claim based on my own intuition on the matter. Later in the book, I go further into this "intuition" when I address the thought experiment of a person who has a microchip inserted in their brain that a scientist is controlling. Within such, the scientist is able to control the chemistry and neurological sparkings in the brain in a way that the person thinks they are making the decision them-

self. I suggest that, intuitively, I don't think "most people" would think such decisions were freely willed.

The survey: *Surveying Freedom: Folk Intuitions about Free Will and Moral Responsibility by Eddy Nahmias, Stephen Morris, Thomas Nadelhoffer, and Jason Turner,* is an interesting study.
http://www2.gsu.edu/~phlean/papers/Surveying_Freedom.pdf

Per the study, given an example in which we are able to use a "Laplacian" type computer to predict a future outcome of a person robbing a bank and another of a person saving a child with 100% accuracy based on all of the variables, 76% of people in the survey said that the person robbed the bank of his own free will, and 68% said that the person saves the child of his own free will.

But here is the problem when asked about blameworthininess or praiseworthiness: *"83% judged he was blameworthy in the negative case and 88% judged he was praiseworthy in the positive case."* And when asked if the person "could have done otherwise," 67% responded that he *could have* chosen not to rob the bank, but on the other hand 62% answered that he *couldn't* have chosen not to save the child.

The study also uses an ethically neutral decision of "going jogging" in which 57% say he had to choose to jog given the deterministic computer's prediction.

The conflicting results of these studies show the prevalence of the average person's incapacity to think clearly about these situations. And the fact that the majority tied blameworthiness and praiseworthiness even knowing that, at least in the instance of the saving of the child, the person couldn't have done otherwise, is problematic at best. This main study suggests that most people don't find determinism to be incompatible with free will, even with the conflicting ideas surrounding what it means.

This, however, does not mean that most people hold to the free will definitions of the compatibilist. It simply is a concession that for many of them, if the universe was deterministic in this sense, they would *still* believe they have free will. It doesn't, for example, mean that they think people "could not have done otherwise" or "cannot choose between more than one viable option or action," regardless that in the scenario in which the computer is able to predict the outcome of the person saving the child, the majority of people think he could not have done otherwise. Also, the fact that the majority believed the robber could have chosen to not rob the bank, and that an even larger majority tie blameworthiness and praiseworthiness to the cases, is strong evidence that they intuitively (at a deeper level) think there was some "otherwise" possibility even if they are told there is not, given the "computer" scenario.

Some compatibilists think that such a survey makes the case that a majority of people intuitively think they can't do otherwise yet still think they have free will. It doesn't make this case at all. It only makes a case on what their free will position might be, given that they couldn't...not on what it actually is, which I think most likely ties into the confusions and cognitive dissonances we see when prompted with such a scenario.

The study gave another deterministic scenario in which identical twins make different decisions (regarding giving back money they found) based on their environment and genetics. The study gave similar results as the first study. This time, however, 76% of the participants said in both the negative case (of the person not giving back the money) and positive case (of the person giving back the money) that the person *could have* done otherwise. This is more evidence that my intuition is correct surrounding the "feeling" that most people think they possess. After all, even given the example of deterministic universe where they are directly told that variables outside of the person's control dictated their decision, the people *still* think they could have done otherwise. Even when the scenario strongly suggests that the person could not.

I'd suggest this has more to do with what they intuitively feel about the "free will" abilities they possess, and that such studies actually show something else: That such compatibilist ideas of free will allow people to hold on to the idea that they "could have done otherwise" even when they cannot based on most compatibilist definitions of free will. It allows for the confusion and conflation to happen between the free will they intuitively possess, and the free will that is compatible with determinism. One that does not allow for an "otherwise."

In regards to whether people's intuitions are compatibilist or incompatibilist, it's not as simple as some philosophers suggest. Another study of importance addresses the processes that generate someone's intuitions concerning ethical responsibility:

Nichols, S. and J. Knobe. 2007. Moral responsibility and determinism: the cognitive science of folk intuitions. Nouse 41:663-685. It can be found here: http://onlinelibrary.wiley.com/doi/10.1111/j.1468-0068.2007.00666.x/full

In this study, it shows how different kinds of psychological processes produce different folk intuitions (about incompatibilist intuitions and compatibilist intuitions):

"Philosophers who have discussed lay intuitions in this area tend to say either that folk intuitions conform to compatibilism or that they conform to incompatibilism. Our actual findings were considerably more complex and perhaps more interesting. It appears that people have both compatibilist and incompatibilist intuitions. Moreover, it appears that these different kinds of intuitions are generated by different kinds of psychological processes. To assess the importance of this finding for the debate over moral responsibility, one would have to know precisely what sort of psychological process produced each type of intuition and how much weight to accord to the output of each sort of process. We have begun the task of addressing these issues here, but clearly far more remains to be done."

So any study done needs to account for the fact that the process itself has an effect on whether someone will seem to hold one over the other. This, to me, says even more about how people simply have not given enough thought to this important topic.

12 When I use the term "authorities," I specifically mean popular philosophers or scientists. In regard to them defining free will in a way that does not align with the ability most people intuitively feel they have, I am addressing compatibilists. Compatibilists are those people who think free will is "compatible" with a deterministic (entirely causal) universe. An example of a popular compatibilist is Daniel Dennett.

13 Orion and Liberius are the main fictional characters in the dialogues about free will for this book. It's my hope that they are able to convey some of the information (in the chapters they are in) in a way that may not only be more entertaining, but easier to digest and understand. They are just another tool to help with the parsing of information.

14 Agnostic in this sense simply means that one doesn't have "knowledge" of the position. For example, they cannot know that an event is "acausal" simply because they don't see a cause for the event (yet).

15 If interested, here are some models of how the universe may have come into existence:
* Standard Big Bang model
* Ekpyrotic Universe theory
* Multiverse theories - Black Hole Cosmology

16 Carter himself has frequently regretted his own choice of the word "anthropic," because it conveys the misleading impression that the principle involves humans specifically, rather than intelligent observers in general. e.g. Carter (2004) op. cit.

17 Questions such as "Why did the universe happen" or "Why do events happen?" may not be relevant questions, as "why?" assumes a reason that is slightly different than the "how?" question. In this regard, the "how?" and the "why?" might become interchangeable. "Why?" seems to suggest a reason which implies a conscious decision. *Why did the chicken cross the road? To get to the other side.* Notice "To get to the other side" seems to be a conscious process for the chicken. It's the *reason* it decides to cross the road. The "how?" for the chicken is that it used its legs to walk across the road.

Notice if we try this with: *Why did the candy wrapper cross the road?*, we come up with a similar reason as the how: *It was blown across the road by the wind.* There is no real "why?" in the same sense as the chicken deciding, or something else deciding (e.g. the wind god wanted to blow it across). If there is no "conscious reason" for something, the "how" seems the more relevant question to ask. Of course, we can ponder if there is some "conscious reason" for things that appear to have none, but it would be incorrect to assume there was a "conscious reason" or to assume that such "why" question is in any way applicable when consciousness is not obvious.

More importantly, we need to be careful not to bypass the "how" answer in light of not having a sufficient (or possible) "why" answer. "But why?" is not a sufficient criticism of a how answer.

18 Notice that "something" doesn't necessarily imply something in the empirical or material sense. It also could be a quality within the same thing that the effect is happening in. For example, if the door has some weighted quality to it, that weighted quality, plus gravity, might cause the door to open. I also mentioned a "ghost" opening the door, not to give any credence to the existence of "ghosts" (I give none), but rather to show that we do not have to assume that the "something" is in the material world as we know it, but that the reasoning follows regardless.

19 The line between active events and inactive events isn't really an easy line. It has more to do with a perception of activity. For example, right now the earth is rotating on its axis at about 1,038 miles per hour if standing at the equator. This means that everything at the equator is moving that fast along with it. From our relativistic standpoint, however, a glass of water sitting at a table may appear inactive. Likewise, our Galaxy (The Milky Way) is approximately rotating at 168 miles per second. That is not a typo, it's per second. We are in that, yet that glass of water, technically moving at these speeds, to us appears "inactive" so long as it seems to be still and has nothing on earth interacting with it in a way to make it seem different. At the quantum scale, particles are constantly moving within the glass of water.

20 The *problem of induction*, simply put, is a problem with predicting or inferring. Deductive logic, for the most part, is demonstrably complete. The premises imply the argument's conclusion. This isn't the case with induction, where there are no consistent rules that lead to sound inductive inference. To quote from the Stanford Encyclopedia of Philosophy:

"The problem is how to support or justify them and it leads to a dilemma: the principle cannot be proved deductively, for it is contingent, and only necessary truths can be proved deductively. Nor can it be supported inductively—by arguing that it has always or usually been reliable in the past—for that would beg the question by assuming just what is to be proved." - Vickers, John, "The Problem of Induction", The Stanford Encyclopedia of Philosophy (Spring 2013 Edition), Edward N. Zalta (ed.), http://plato.stanford.edu/archives/spr2013/entries/induction-problem/

In other words, the application of induction itself is supported through the use of induction, meaning the use of "reliability of induction in the past" is an inductive response. Regardless of this, induction has proven itself time and time again within science. It's similar to the problem of logic itself, in which to prove that one should use logic, it already needs to be assumed if we are to make a "logical" case for it. And if we aren't making a logical case for it, what kind of case are we making? It all ties back to what is consistent, reliable, observable, intuitive, tautological, and so on. In other words, these methodologies stem back to what we *discover* about reality (or our perceptions of reality). From there the usefulness of logic, including inductive processes, is invaluable.

21 If all events were acausal, there would be no spatial or temporal determinacy for any of them. This means that there would be no consistency at all in the universe. Particles might appear randomly, disappear randomly, or never show and no particle would have an effect on another particle. There would be no atomic or molecular bonding, and no formation of matter and energy would be the same for each moment that occurred. The universe would be an absurd place in which no structure (including life or consciousness) could ever happen.

22 It's not the potential of the effect that we should consider as contradictory, but rather the state of the cause. We can fathom possible contradictory results (even though, if causal, only one is really possible), but to say that an unchanged cause can lead to either of those possibilities says something contradictory about the state of that cause, not the effect.

We could also say "(A) cannot both be the cause of (B) and also the cause of *not (B),*" and that would be true. But placing the focus of the effect by using "the cause of *not (B)*" allows us to make strange statements in regards to something being the *cause of "nots."* For example, the cause of you greeting your friend in the street could also be regarded as the cause of you not greeting millions of strangers (and everything else you did not do at that time). We don't need to go there, as the contradictory value is with the cause, not the effect.

The better way to say it is that (A) cannot both the cause and not the cause of (B). This places the focus on the cause (where it should be), rather than the effect. In essence, it would be the (A) that would hold contradictory values if it could be both the cause of (B) and not the cause of (B), for example, the cause of (C) instead.

Think of (A) as a *"thing"* made up of *"parts."* Suggesting the "parts" could force the next state to either (B) or (C) suggests that it is comprised of parts (A1) and not (A2), as well as parts (A2) and not (A1). It suggests a "thing" that hosts self contradictory "parts." It's not the (B) that would be contradictory with the *not (B)*, as they wouldn't ever happen at the same time. It is entirely the cause (A) that would hold such contradictory parts.

23 This idea that the causes that lead to a decision stem from prior to a person even coming into existence (being born) runs counterintuitive to most notions of who a person is. In an entirely causal universe, this, however, must be the case. In this way, who a person "is" is dictated not by them, but by events before a "them" even took place. Events before conscious entities even took place, in fact. And once in existence (as a conscious entity), the flow of that consciousness and all of our thoughts and decisions that arise within that consciousness are constantly pushed and pulled in the direction of every antecedent causal event prior. It's all part of the causal chains of events that stem from prior to our birth.

24 In set theory for determinism: a set of avoiding would, along with a set of unavoiding, be within the class (a set of sets) of the unavoidable. Unavoidable class (avoidable events set (X avoids brick, Y dodges arrow, etc.), unavoidable events set (P gets hit with brick, Q gets stuck with arrow, etc.).

25 The reason I say "if it could happen" has to do with the problems that arise in suggesting acausal events even "can" happen. There are a number of issues with the idea of acausality that are addressed more in depth in the book. It must be noted that I'm not a proponent of the idea of acausality/an indeterministic universe. I just give it enough credence to display what it would mean if it were the case, and more importantly how it could never help with free will. This is basically a rejection of the libertarian view on free will being grounded in indeterminism (that it can somehow assist with it being a possible).

26 The reason I decided to use the start of radioactive decay of an atom has to do with many people and physicists considering radioactive decay a "stochastic" or truly "random" (or, in our case, "acausal") event, in so far as it's impossible to predict when an individual atom will decay. At the same time, however, they understand that the chance that an atom will decay is constant over time. When given a collection of a large number of atoms, the decay rate for the collection is computable from the measured decay constants of the nuclides (or equivalently from the half-lifes). These sort of probabilistic calculations go against the very nature of acausal events that would have no spatial or temporal determinacy to them. Happening "inside" at the very location of an atom at the "time" the atom is in that location would be but a mere chance happening that wouldn't lead to a probability for a larger group of atoms.

Some also make such assumptions of the event being uncaused know-ing all well that for most atom types we cannot even determine the age of an individual atom itself, and since they are constantly created inside of stars, the age difference can be drastic between two atoms of the same type. So to suggest that, because we cannot predict when an individual atom will decay, that it's an uncaused event is not only the acceptance of a very specific (speculative, at best) quantum interpretation, but done for the wrong reason of not being able to know "when" without the information of a start point of the atom itself, or the possibility of some smaller config within the unstable atom itself.

Regardless of the example, however, the more important point is that even if it was acausal, the atom itself would have no say over the event happening. The event and the already existing atom would be independent until the event interacts with the atom in some way. The event not being the atom decaying itself shows the problematic nature of acausality.

27 "Spontaneous" is one of those words we need to be a little careful when using. Someone could say something that is caused was "spontaneous," as long as the cause was not apparent. I'm using it in a much stricter sense, since I am addressing an acausal event (therefore, obviously, it would have no cause). The sense I am referring to is something happening without the help of an external agent. If the person assists it happening, or some other agent assists it happening, there is a cause involved, and therefore, it wouldn't be spontaneous. Our lack of knowledge of causes may give something like the appearance of spontaneity, but that does not mean it is actually spontaneous.

The word runs into a similar problem as the word "random" addressed in Chapter 10. Unfortunately, describing an acausal event using other words has language limitations. All we can say is the event happens *without* something (a cause), and there are few words that sufficiently describe such "withouts" and what they imply.

28 Time "flying" isn't meant in a literal way. It addresses more of a perception of time than its actuality. This book contains an entire chapter on temporal possibilities and what they mean for free will. In short, none of them assist with making free will possible or compatible with determinism or indeterminism.

29 Not all cells get replaced. Neurons in the cerebral cortex, for example, are never replaced. No neurons are added after birth and any that die are not replaced. So be careful not to kill these ones off! That being said, most cells in the body are replaced, and that includes cells in the brain such as glial cells, which may make up approximately 90% of the cells in your brain.

Besides neurons, the other cells that get replaced vary on the length of time they die and replace.

30 The fact that almost all of the atoms in your body gets exchanged in about a year was pointed out by Dr. Paul C. Aebersold in 1953 in a landmark paper he presented to the Smithsonian Institute, "Radioisotopes - New keys to knowledge"
http://www.archive.org/stream/annualreportofbo1953smit/annualreportof
bo1953smit_djvu.txt
As a fun fact: thousands of other humans through history held some of the same atoms that you currently hold in your body.

31 Yes, I used the word "fart" in a philosophy book. I pondered on whether or not to take such a part out, but feel that is just part of Orion's character. It's something he would do, and wouldn't have the free will to do otherwise. Some might find it crude, distasteful, or out of place. If so, perhaps it's something memorable that could be latched on to. The juxtaposition of potty humor in a philosophy book. You'll find a few seemingly strange juxtapositions peppered throughout the book. The fact that you are reading this endnote means that even if you didn't like the word in the book, you were curious about why there might be an endnote about it.

32 In philosophical terms, it's an epistemological position rather than an ontological position.

33 Whether quantum entanglement counts as nonlocal (action-at-a-distance) depends on the nature of the wave function and decoherence, issues over which there is still considerable debate among scientists and philosophers.

Topics of interest if you care to research nonlocality further would be the EPR Paradox as well as Bell's inequality. From there, an assessment can be made between what each of the different quantum interpretations (as well as interpretations of the interpretations) mean for "locality." You will quickly recognize that it depends on which interpretation is being postulated as to whether or not "nonlocality" is being accepted.
* Einstein, A.; Podolsky, B.; Rosen, N. (1935). "Can Quantum-Mechanical Description of Physical Reality Be Considered Complete?". Physical Review 47 (10): 777–780.
* Bell, J.S. (1966). On the problem of hidden variables in quantum mechanics. Reviews of Modern Physics. 38(3). 447-452.

Another rejection of nonlocal hidden variables pertain to Legget's inequalities, though such does not pertain to some nonlocal hidden variable interpretations such as Bohmian Mechanics.
* An experimental test of nonlocal realism (2007) - Simon Groblacher, Tomasz Paterek, Rainer Kaltenbaek, Caslav Brukner, Marek Zukowski, Markus Aspelmeyer, and Anton Zeilinger
http://arxiv.org/pdf/0704.2529.pdf

Still others pertain to validating the Kochen Specker theorem, conflicting with *non-contextual* hidden variable interpretations.

* Experimental non-classicality of an indivisible quantum system (2011) - Radek Lapkiewicz, Peizhe Li, Christoph Schaeff, Nathan K. Langford, Sven Ramelow, Marcin Wiesniak, & Anton Zeilinger

http://vcq.quantum.at/fileadmin/Publications/Experimental%20non-classicality%20of%20an%20indivisible.pdf

34 *James Gleick in the prologue to Genius: The Life and Science of Richard Feynman (1992)*

35 "Observer effect" refers to changes in which the act of measuring or "observing" changes what is being observed. This is often the result of a measuring device or instrument rather than a person changing the state of what's being measured.

Many times this can be due to a measurement problem. For example, if we measure the temperature of a tub full of water with a thermometer, we could get a fairly accurate depiction of the temperature of the water even just before placing the thermometer into it. If, however, we have a small vile of water that is close to the size of the thermometer, the very act of placing the thermometer into the water will change the temperature of the water dramatically, preventing us from getting an accurate depiction.

Similarly, at the quantum scale, particles are so small that an act of "observing" through the use of an instrument must interact with the particle itself causing a different result than if the instrument didn't interact with it.

36 Examples of pseudo-scientific misunderstandings of the observer effect can be found in such movies as "What the Bleep do we Know?" and 'self help' books such as "The Secret." An interesting clip from "What the Bleep" can be found here. Within that clip there is a well done cartoon that does a great job explaining the double slit experiment using a character named Dr. Quantum. Great up until the end of the video where the quackery comes in: "The electron decided to act differently, as if it were aware it was being watched," and of course the device is this large "eye." He goes on to say, "The observer collapsed the wave function, simply by observing."

Of course, this is not what's happening at all. Instead, the measuring device needs to interact with the particle to measure it. It's not an eye or a camera, as electrons are too small to "see." In fact, they are so small that anything sent to interact with the particle to determine its location, interacts and changes the electron trajectory.

It may also be important to note that in 2012, scientists succeeded in correctly identifying the path each particle had taken without the collapse.

To do this, they used a setup such that particles coming to the screen were not from a point-like source, but from a source with two intensity maxima.

37 An excellent layperson article about virtual particles can be found written by Theoretical Physicist Matt Strassler here:
http://profmattstrassler.com/articles-and-posts/particle-physics-basics/virtual-particles-what-are-they/
My part in briefly discussing virtual particles has to do with the language used for them, making them seem like something magical almost, like a fairy *'POOF'* popping in to existence in front of your eyes with a strange look as if to say, "where did I come from" and then *'POOF'* vanishing again. It's nothing like that at all. Of course, it's important to mention that even if it was like that, they would still have all of the same problems as acausal events already discussed. Virtual particles acausally "popping" in to existence and back out could never help with free will, and if they were a part of conscious decision making, such would be detrimental to cohesive and rational willing.

38 Agnostic in this usage means not taking sides. If I am "agnostic" on whether the universe is deterministic or indeterministic, I'm saying I don't know which of the options really exists. I'm not claiming that one exists over the other. I'm placing the burden of proof directly on the person who is making the claim that one exists over the other.

39 The "von Neumann/Wigner interpretation" is one interpretation that postulates the consciousness causes the collapse. Niels Bohr, a main scientist associated with the Copenhagen interpretation, never had in mind the observer-induced collapse of the wave function. For him, Schrödinger's cat never really posed a problem. The cat would be either dead or alive before any conscious observer ever opened the box.

40 The Matrix (1999) - Writers/Directors: Andy Wachowski, Lana Wachowski - Movie starring Keanu Reeves about reality as we know it being generated in the minds of people placed in pods by conscious machines that have taken over most of Earth.

41 The Stanford Encyclopedia of Philosophy addresses various criticism of Bohmian mechanics. Here is an excerpt (bold by me): *"Bohmian mechanics has never been widely accepted in the mainstream of the physics community. Since it is not part of the standard physics curriculum, many physicists—probably the majority—are simply unfamiliar with the theory and how it works. Sometimes the theory is rejected without explicit discussion of reasons for rejection. One also finds objections that are based on simple* **misunderstandings***; among these are claims that some no-go theorem, such as* **von Neumann's theorem, the Kochen-Specker theorem, or Bell's**

theorem, *shows that the theory cannot work."* - Goldstein, Sheldon, "Bohmian Mechanics", The Stanford Encyclopedia of Philosophy (Spring 2013 Edition), Edward N. Zalta (ed.),
http://plato.stanford.edu/archives/spr2013/entries/qm-bohm/

42 For Bohmian mechanics, it's specifically considered contextual, nonlocal variables. Technically, the variables themselves are what the objects we see every day are "made of," and rather it's the wave function itself that is "hidden" (as it's not "visible").

43 Our limitation on knowledge is derived by the wave function in Bohmian mechanics. It's entirely in the epistemic sense, rather than the ontological sense that other interpretations place on it.

44 Einstein: Philosopher-Scientist, ed. P.A. Schilpp (Harper & Row, New York)

45 http://www.mat.univie.ac.at/~neum/physfaq/topics/mostConsistent

46 Taking something "with a grain of salt" is an idiom which means to view something with skepticism, lightly, or to not take it literally

47 People who contort quantum mechanics (and specifically, specific quantum interpretations) to conclude some extraordinary claim are otherwise known as "Quantum Crackpots." Examples of such contortions can be seen in movies such as "What the Bleep Do We Know!?" as well as written and spoken words of various *"New Age"* gurus such as Deepak Chopra. The popularity of such views and charlatans reflect an increasing unscientific attitude in society.

48 Daniel Wegner's book "The Illusion of Conscious Will" is not really a discussion about whether or not free will exists, or if it's compatible with determinism or not. Instead it's a discussion on the feeling of free will, when people feel it, and when they do not (within the confines of a mechanistic and deterministic universe). He understands that the debate between free will and determinism is based on how one defines or talks about "free will," and prefers not to take a side on such semantics.

That's fine; again, the implications are the more important thing. If the compatibilist defines free will in a less common way, and in a way not in conflict with determinism (or indeterminism, for that matter), the important part is that they be true in regards to the implications of their definition, and they make their definition so crystal clear that no person with a different (and more common) definition could confuse it.

For Wegner's reasons why he prefers not to take a side, you can read pg 318 of his book, the section titled "Free Will and Determinism."

49 Bell's theorem itself may, in some regard, rely on the notion of Free Will. Bell addresses this in "Speakable and Unspeakable in Quantum Mechanics," on page 100, Chapter 12 – Free Variables and Local Causality:

"It has been argued that quantum mechanics is not locally causal and cannot be embedded in a local causal theory. That conclusion depends on treating certain experimental parameters, typically the orientation of polarized filters, as free variables. Roughly speaking it is supposed that an experimenter is quite free to choose among the various possibilities offered by his equipment."

He goes on to explain the criticism by Clauser, Horne, and Shimony, and to defend it by explaining how a completely deterministic 'random' generator, given specific circumstances, would suffice for the theorem to still follow.

50 One example of entangled particles shown experimentally happened at the University of Science and Technology of China (USTC) in Shanghai where experimenters entangled four pairs of photons (eight photons), linking the polarizations of eight photons (Nature Photonics - Feb 12, 2012). You can read this article online:

http://www.nature.com/nphoton/journal/v6/n4/full/nphoton.2011.354.html

This extends the previous experiment of six entangled photons. (Nature Physics, 2007)

http://www.nature.com/nphys/journal/v3/n2/full/nphys507.html

51 Note that if the universe is entirely deterministic (entirely causal), the hard incompatibilist position falls to the hard determinist position. When it comes to a hard determinist position regarding the compatibility of free will in a deterministic universe, there is no distinction. The only distinction is that the hard incompatibilist also addresses free will's incompatibility with an indeterministic universe as well.

52 Modal logic allows us to assess multiple possible worlds. Such worlds, in epistemology, would be "contingent," which means it's not necessarily false that such a world exists, and it is not necessarily true that such a world exists. Either are possible, but only one is actual. We simply don't know which one is actual, so we assess both. And through those assessments we understand that, no matter which one of the possible worlds is "actual," that "actuality" is incompatible with the free will described in this book.

53 "Better" meaning more reliable, helpful, productive, and leading to less harm to conscious creatures. Betterment is a comparative measure of value states, which I'd argue ties into ethical decision making.

54 "Qualia" is one of those unfamiliar philosophical jargon words that sound impressive but really isn't. It's basically the way we experience. For example, seeing the redness of a rose, smelling the smell of lilacs, feeling the roughness of sandpaper as you glide your fingers over it, or feeling a sharp pain of a needle. Qualia, as most philosophers use it, are these internal features that seem to be inherent within conscious experience. Qualia and its properties, how it comes about, what mental states have qualia, whether its intrinsic, and various other ideas about it are discussed and debated within the realm of the topic of consciousness.

For this "free will" topic, the important thing to keep in mind is that qualia is part of a process that comes about causally, and though I'd suggest through entirely physical processes, that doesn't necessarily need to follow. And once experienced, our memory of that experience feeds back in to be a causal element of various other thoughts, feelings, and experiences. All conscious experience, including qualia, is part of the causal process.

This brings us back to the chapter called "Reductionism and Downward Causation," which explains that determinism isn't a reductive position. Rather, the whole of experience, including qualia, feeds back down and has an effect on the parts that initially emerged the experience.

55 Subliminal Advertising Leaves Its Mark On The Brain (2007) Dr Bahador Bahrami, Professor Nilli Lavie and Professor Geraint Rees of University College London http://www.sciencedaily.com/releases/2007/03/070308121938.htm http://www.ucl.ac.uk/media/library/notaware

56 Murder, She Wrote: Enhanced Sensitivity to Negative Word Valence (2009) Maha Nasrallah,David Carmel, and Nilli Lavie. http://www.ncbi.nlm.nih.gov/pmc/articles/PMC2759814/ http://news.bbc.co.uk/2/hi/health/8274773.stm

57 Innate versus learned odour processing in the mouse olfactory bulb (2007) Nature. Kobayakawa et al., Nature, Volume 450, p503-508 (2007) http://www.nature.com/nature/journal/v450/n7169/abs/nature06281.html http://www.s.u-tokyo.ac.jp/en/press/2007/24.html

58 The word "safely" is an important qualifier to the idea of equalization. There are a number of equalization strategies that are dangerous and harmful. Even if we accomplish equalization, if we equalize people down to

the lowest common denominator of wellbeing, it's not worth it. The idea is to hold on to the highest wellbeing possibility within the context of attempting to equalize.

59 Unconscious determinants of free decisions in the human brain (2008) Nature Neuroscience 11, 543 - 545 - Chun Siong Soon, Marcel Brass, Hans-Jochen Heinze, and John-Dylan Haynes.
http://www.nature.com/neuro/journal/v11/n5/abs/nn.2112.html
http://phys.org/news127395619.html

60 Free Will by Sam Harris: http://www.samharris.org/free-will

61 The law of identity states "each thing is the same with itself and different from something else" or "X is X and not ~X." It's a base rule of logic. To say that a soul can break logic is to say that a soul could also be "not a soul." This allowance of contradiction would break down every piece of knowledge a person thinks they've identified, including any knowledge of "free will."

62 Godzilla is a large, lizard-like monster that first appeared in Ishiro Honda's 1954 film *Godzilla*, and went on to become a worldwide pop culture icon starring in numerous other films, games, novels, comic books, and television series. The fictional monster is a recognizable symbol of Japanese culture. This endnote is here for some newer generations who may not have been exposed to such icon.

63 If we were to place such Omniscient God in syllogistic form, it may look something like this:

1. If God foreknows I will choose X, then I must choose X.
2. God foreknows I will choose X.
3. Therefore, I must choose X.

And then, if we are so inclined, we can go on (though it's not really needed)...

1. If I must choose X, I cannot choose Y instead of X.
2. I must choose X.
3. Therefore, I cannot choose Y instead of X.

1. If I cannot choose Y instead of X, I don't have the free will to choose Y instead of X
2. I cannot choose Y instead of X
3. I don't have the free will to choose Y instead of X

1. Y represents anything other than X
2. I don't have the free will to choose Y instead of X
3. I don't have the free will to choose anything other than X instead of X

1. If I don't have the free will to choose anything other than X instead of X, my choice of X is not a free choice
2. I don't have the free will to choose anything other than X instead of X
3. My choice of X is not a free choice

Some apologists incorrectly use the word "necessarily" in the philosophical usage of the term as it applies to truth claims. If God has foreknowledge, the word is "contingent" not "necessarily." In other words, the truth is contingent on God's foreknowledge.

1. If God foreknows I will choose X, then I must choose X -- is a contingent truth
2. God foreknows I will choose X.
3. Therefore, I must choose X -- is a contingent truth.

64 It would be problematic (since the accused is not responsible) to take a top down approach, that being taking the worst punishment at the expense of fairness of the person who commits the criminal act. A better approach is a bottom up approach. Any punishment used for deterrence must be at the most minimal expense of fairness to the criminal that allows for what is fair and functional for the entire society. A balance between the two.

The harm of parking in a no parking zone and the harm of raping a person are not equal, regardless of not being responsible. There is an order of magnitude difference between these two actions, and it would be silly to suggest that determinism or no free will removes this. A dog that rips up a flower bed is an order of magnitude different than a dog that tries to bite the face off of any person it sees.

Responsibility is not a requirement to be able to address these levels of harm, and both would be addressed differently depending on the circumstances.

Also keep in mind that it's incorrect to conflate retribution with deterrence. The two are entirely unrelated. A retributionist system would punish the criminal regardless of deterrence. So if it did not deter, but was punishment for the sake of revenge only, that would have to be okay in the retributionist system.   Otherwise retribution would only apply to those accounts that deter, which renders retribution pointless.

We are weighing factors such as: A) The criminal may need rehabilitation. B) We cannot allow the criminal to further harm others, so incarceration may apply. C) We need to be proactive in reducing the amount of same types of problems. D) We need to be conscious about degrees of harm an act causes, and balance our steps with what is acceptable to allow (but that we just need to reduce) with those acts that are unacceptable entirely. E) We need to do so in the fairest way possible to all concerned, not just the offender.

Given that free will does not exist, we need to rebalance the priorities of our current criminal system.

65 This type of system is called FAD which stands for Free Will and Determinism. This system has been expounded upon by Delroy > Paulhus and Jasmine M. Carey in "The FAD-Plus: Measuring Lay Beliefs Regarding Free Will and Related Constructs" in which they say "We describe the development of FAD–Plus, a 27-item measure of lay beliefs in free will and 3 closely related constructs: scientific determinism, fatalistic determinism, and unpredictability. Previously published measures included only a subset of these variables and tended to assume an a
priori pattern of relations among these 4 beliefs".

Though there are still problems with the indirect questions of the FAD system, the recognition, at the very least, needs to be made for the split out of these three categories. If, for example, you see a study that is using FAD, and if the comparison is made between those who believe in free will and those who don't, rather than those who believe in free will compared to scientific determinism compared to fatalistic determinism and compared to unpredictability, then the study is problematic.
http://www.researchgate.net/publication/49707972_The_FAD-
Plus_measuring_lay_beliefs_regarding_free_will_and_related_constructs/fil
e/b23ad407579ed50086d1a5fa31513ee3.pdf

66 An example of someone who appears less than impartial on the free will topic is Roy Baumeister, a Professor of Psychology at Florida State University. He and others have run many of the problematic studies I have suggested. Roy has written articles such as "Do You Really Have Free Will? Of course. Here's how it evolved" in which he takes a compatibilist position.
http://www.slate.com/articles/health_and_science/science/2013/09/free_
will_debate_what_does_free_will_mean_and_how_did_it_evolve.2.html

Needless to say, he is invested in the idea of free will just as much as I'm invested in the understanding that we lack free will. Such investment doesn't necessarily mean the person *would be* impartial, but when you look at the studies and the way the participants are "induced" to disbelieve in free will, and for others how their supposed "lack of belief" is (mis-categorically) assessed as well as the incorrect conclusions of these participants as "chronically disbelieving in free will," either there is some partiality happening or there simply is a misunderstanding on how stringent the requirements need to be as well as what they are concluding. For example, the study below says "current results suggest that disbelief in free will reduces helping and increases aggression" when in reality it suggests no such thing. Rather it suggests "an induced disbelief of free will on a person who has a psychology built on free will reduces helping and increases aggression (for studies 1 and 3), and a category error of certain types of thinking that do not necessarily represent a lack of belief in free will (e.g. there was no direct asking of such a question) or a rational lack of belief in free will (in study 2), may reduce helping." Sure, that's long winded, but at least it's honest.

Prosocial Benefits of Feeling Free: Disbelief in Free Will Increases Aggression and Reduces Helpfulness (2011) Roy F. Baumeister, E. J. Masicampo, C. Nathan DeWall

67 Dawkins, Richard (1976). The Selfish Gene. New York City: Oxford University Press. ISBN 0-19-286092-5.

Dawkins, Richard (2006). The Selfish Gene (30th Anniversary edition). New York City: Oxford University Press. ISBN 0-19-929115-2.

Index

91939097R00197

Made in the USA
Middletown, DE
04 October 2018